# THE NEW NASDAQ MARKETPLACE

## Zicklin School of Business Financial Markets Series

**Robert A. Schwartz, Editor**
Baruch College/CUNY
Zicklin School of Business
New York, NY, USA

## Other books in the series:

Schwartz, Robert A., Byrne, John A., Colaninno, Antoinette:
*Electronic vs. Floor Based Trading*
Schwartz, Robert A., Byrne, John A., Colaninno, Antoinette:
*Coping with Institutional Order Flow*
Schwartz, Robert A., Byrne, John A., Colaninno, Antoinette:
*A Trading Desk View of Market Quality*
Schwartz, Robert A., Byrne, John A., Colaninno, Antoinette:
*Call Auction Trading: New Answers to Old Questions*
Schwartz, Robert A., Byrne, John A., Colaninno, Antoinette:
*Regulation of U.S. Equity Markets*

# THE NEW NASDAQ MARKETPLACE

edited by

Robert A. Schwartz, John Aidan Byrne
and Antoinette Colaninno

Springer

Robert A. Schwartz
Zicklin School of Business
Baruch College
CUNY

John Aidan Byrne

Antoinette Colaninno
Zicklin School of Business
Baruch College
CUNY

Library of Congress Control Number: 2007921683

ISBN-10: 0-387-48600-3
ISBN-13: 978-0-387-48600-0
e-ISBN-10: 0-387-48601-1
e-ISBN-13: 978-0-387-48601-7

Printed on acid-free paper.



9 8 7 6 5 4 3 2 1

springer.com

# Contents

# List of Participants

Paul Arlman*

*At the time of the conference, Mr. Arlman was Secretary General of the Federation of European Securities Exchanges.

| | | |
|---|---|---|
| Kim Bang | Bloomberg Tradebook | CEO |
| Andrew Brooks | T. Rowe Price Associates | VP & Head of Equity Trading |
| Jeffrey Brown | Charles Schwab & Co., Inc. | Senior Vice President |
| William Christie | Vanderbilt University | Professor of Finance |
| Chris Church | Radianz, Inc. | Executive Vice President |
| Christopher Concannon | The NASDAQ Stock Market, Inc. | Executive Vice President |

Paul Davis*

*At the time of the conference, Mr. Davis was Managing Director at TIAA-CREF Investment Management.

| | | |
|---|---|---|
| Robert Felvinci | Alliance Capital Management | Senior Vice President |
| Anthony Fortunato* | Instinet, LLC | |

*At the time of the conference, Mr. Fortunato was Director, US Equity Sales & Trading at Nomura Securities International.

| | | |
|---|---|---|
| Reto Francioni* | Deutsche Börse | CEO |

*At the time of the conference, Dr. Francioni was Chairman of SWX Swiss Exchange.

| | | |
|---|---|---|
| Roger Freeman | Lehman Brothers | Analyst |
| Adena Friedman | The NASDAQ Stock Market, Inc. | Executive Vice President |
| Robert Greifeld | The NASDAQ Stock Market, Inc. | President & CEO |
| Allan Grody | Financial Intergroup Advisors | President |
| William Harts | Banc of America Securities | |

| | | |
|---|---|---|
| Frank Hatheway | The NASDAQ Stock Market, Inc. | Chief Economist |
| Robert Hegarty | TowerGroup Securities & Investments Group | Managing Director |
| Peter Jenkins | New York Stock Exchange | Senior Vice President |
| Nari Jote | Baruch College, CUNY | Professor |
| Andrew Kagan | Lava Trading Inc. | VP, Product Management |
| David Krell | International Securities Exchange | President & CEO |
| Matthew Lavicka | Goldman Sachs | Managing Director |
| Mark Madoff | Bernard L. Madoff Investment Securities | Director of Listed Trading |
| Miranda Mizen | American Stock Exchange | Vice President |
| Michael Murphy* | Piney Run Capital LLC | Founder and President |

*At the time of the conference, Mike Murphy was Institutional Client Relationship Manager at Wachovia Securities.

| | | |
|---|---|---|
| Terry O'Connor | Cedar Creek Management | Investment Manager |
| Michael Pagano | Villanova University | Assoc. Professor of Finance |
| Gerald Putnam* | NYSE Group, Inc. | President and Co-COO |

*At the time of the conference, Mr. Putnam was CEO of ArcaEx. In March 2006, ArcaEx merged with the New York Stock Exchange to form the NYSE Group.

| | | |
|---|---|---|
| Brett Redfearn | Bear, Stearns & Co., Inc. | Senior Managing Director |
| Richard Repetto | Sandler O'Neill & Partners | Principal |
| C. Thomas Richardson | Citigroup | Managing Director |
| Howard Ross | Baruch College, CUNY | Professor |
| Dan Royal | Janus Capital Group | Co-Head of Equity Trading |
| Stephen Sax | Floor Brokers Network | Vice President |
| Justin Schack | Institutional Investor Magazine | Reporter |
| Jamie Selway | White Cap Trading | Managing Director |
| Jeffrey W. Smith | The NASDAQ Stock Market, Inc. | NASDAQ Economic Research |
| Benn Steil | Council on Foreign Relations | Senior Fellow and Director of International Economics |
| Bruce Turner | CIBC World Markets Corp. | Managing Director |
| Lisa Utasi* | Legg Mason | |

*At the time of the conference, Ms. Utasi was Senior Equity Trader at Citigroup Asset Management.

| | | |
|---|---|---|
| Wayne Wagner* | ITG, Inc. | Consultant |

*At the time of the conference, Mr. Wagner was Chairman of Plexus Group. On January 3, 2006, Plexus Group was acquired by ITG, with whom Mr. Wagner is now a consultant.

| | | |
|---|---|---|
| Don Weeden | Weeden & Co. L.P. | Executive Vice President |
| Henry Yegerman | ITG, Inc. | Director |
| Ken Zimmer | Frontier Capital Management | Senior Trader |

# Conference Sponsors

ArcaEx
Bloomberg Tradebook LLC
INET
ITG, Inc.
Liquidnet, Inc.
The NASDAQ Stock Market, Inc.
New York Stock Exchange
Pipeline Trading Systems LLC
Plexus Group
Putnam Lovell NBF Securities Inc.
Security Traders Association
SWX Swiss Exchange

# Preface

This book is based on the proceedings of *The New NASDAQ Marketplace*, a conference hosted by the Zicklin School of Business at Baruch College on May 3, 2005. The text contains the edited transcript of the panel discussions and two major presentations, one by Gerald Putnam, President and Co-Chief Operating Officer of the NYSE Group; the other by Robert Greifeld, Chief Executive Officer of the NASDAQ Stock Market. Putnam was CEO of Archipelago at the time of the conference.

As with the other books in this popular series, this book is more than an historical record. The manuscript has been heavily edited for clarity and unity of ideas. New material is included from interviews after the conference with many of the speakers. The intention has been to round out the discussions while being careful not to sacrifice the essential nature of the original dialogue. A paper is included by Pagano and Schwartz[1], and a separate paper by Jeffery Smith on the NASDAQ crosses is also provided.[2] The former paper is the basis of Michael Pagano's remarks on the first panel, "Reengineering a Marketplace."

All through the editing process, we worked closely with the panelists so that we did not to put words in their mouths. They have all approved the final draft and we thank them here for their assistance. We also gratefully

[1] Reprinted, with permission, from Pagano, M. and Schwartz, R., "NASDAQ's Closing Cross: Has its new call auction given NASDAQ better closing prices? Early Findings," Journal of Portfolio Management, Volume 31, Number 4, Summer 2005, pp. 100-111.

[2] This article is reprinted with permission from Institutional Investor, Inc. It originally appeared in the Summer 2006 issue of the Journal of Trading. It is illegal to make unauthorized copies of this article. For more information please visit www.iijournals.com. All Rights Reserved.

appreciate our sponsors who made this conference possible (see page ix). Their funding and endorsement of our mission are deeply appreciated.

In her greetings to the audience at the opening of the conference, Kathleen Waldron, President of Baruch College, put the event into context. "In many ways, today closes a loop that began eight years ago when Baruch College held a conference on the changes in equity trading being considered by NASDAQ. Those changes have created a new NASDAQ marketplace that relies heavily on electronic trading, which has a hybrid order driven and quote driven structure, and which has experienced significant growth and development. The purpose of today's conference is to put that transformation in perspective, to discuss the opportunities and challenges that NASDAQ has created, and to reflect on NASDAQ's future directions."

I remember the old days. I remember a time when small companies going public would start trading on the OTC. Then, after they got bigger, they would go to the AMEX. Finally, after they got large enough, they would list on the NYSE. It was sort of like a young faculty colleague compiling a great vita and, in so doing, progressing from Assistant Professor, to Associate Professor, to Full Professor. Then along came NASDAQ, and NASDAQ itself grew and grew until, some while ago, it itself has achieved the full status of a premier marketplace.

In the U.S., we have two distinct marketplaces – OTC/NASDAQ and the NYSE/AMEX. We are fortunate to have two because this gives us choice, good alternatives, and meaningful competition. Countries on the other side of the Atlantic have not been so blessed. In Europe each country pretty much has just one major exchange market.

There was a lot of excitement in 1975 with the Securities Act Amendments. Then came the SEC's new Order Handling Rules, the removal of NYSE Rule 390, decimalization, etc., etc. In the face of new regulation and new technology, the scene has been changing rapidly. Just before the start of this May 3 conference, there were two major announcements – NASDAQ's acquisition of Instinet's INET, and the New York Stock Exchange's acquisition of Archipelago. Overall, our two premier market centers were undergoing seismic change at the same time. I felt like going over to the guys in the Statistics Department and asking them to calculate the probabilities of these two major acquisitions being announced within just one, single week.

Of course, these were not random events. We are all being affected by various factors, technology and regulation chief among them. Competition is a third big driver of change. All of this is certainly providing much terrific material for our conferences.

This is my eighth year at Baruch. I arrived in 1997 and will always remember that year. It was the same year that the Order Handling Rules went into effect. I moved into my office in August and ran a conference in

October titled *Rethinking Equity Trading at NASDAQ*. This is the conference that President Waldron was referring to in her opening remarks. Now, in 2005, we are focusing on NASDAQ again. There have been a lot of changes in this market. Since that first conference, NASDAQ has indeed reengineered itself. I have been hearing a lot of positive comments about the New NASDAQ Marketplace from its users. But nice things do not necessarily result in an interesting conference. At the 2005 conference, we had a good deal of lively debate, along with a reasonable amount of conflict.

As you might expect, we had a lot to talk about on May 3, 2005.

*Robert A. Schwartz*

# CHAPTER 1: REENGINEERING A MARKETPLACE

Moderator: Paul Arlman[3],
Reto Francioni, *CEO, Deutsche Börse*[4]
David Krell, *President & CEO, International Securities Exchange*
Michael Pagano, *Associate Professor of Finance, Villanova University*

PAUL ARLMAN: Before I introduce my very distinguished panel, let me make a few remarks about how we see things in Europe. When it comes to restructuring exchanges, Europe is a very different place. One difference has to do with jurisdictions. If you do not take account of the fact that this is a multi-jurisdictional region, you have lost before you have started. The second big difference is that we have so many languages. Reto Francioni's Switzerland has four within that single country.

In 1990, when I joined the Amsterdam Stock Exchange, the main Dutch newspaper had an item under the heading, "Requiem for the Stock Exchange." In 1990, competition did not exist in Europe. You had the jurisdictions, you had the exchanges, everybody had a nice monopoly, and nobody was complaining. And all of the exchanges were mutual organizations.

Then competition hit. The exchanges de-mutualized and became companies. The major ones became listed companies, they all became electronic, and some included the call mechanisms that Bob Schwartz has been advising about. Many of them integrated clearing, settlement, data, funding, the derivative markets, and so on and so forth.

I am proud to say that in Amsterdam we introduced remote membership in 1993 before it was approved by all the regulators. Everybody else in Europe did it when it was legal in 1996. I read in The *Wall Street Journal*

[3] At the time of the conference, Mr. Arlman was Secretary General of the Federation of European Securities Exchanges.

[4] At the time of the conference, Dr. Francioni was Chairman of SWX Swiss Exchange.

that one of the exchanges here in America has recently introduced remote market membership – this was an extremely proud and excessively important decision. But it dates back to 1993 in Amsterdam.

All of these changes had a major effect on European markets. Bob Schwartz has asked me to explain how we did it. I will give a very Dutch answer. The larger members bribed the smaller members. The larger members had the strategic view to see that an international market like Amsterdam could survive only as a full-service exchange if it was a company run for the benefit of the market, and not for the benefit of the owners. And that is exactly what we did. Bob also asked me if these changes in Europe were successful. Yes, they were quite successful.

The regulatory scene in Europe changed as dramatically as any changes that you are now contemplating here in the U.S. We had a total change in the legislation and regulation for securities markets in Europe. Now this is all being done at the EU level, and no longer at the national level. We also had a major change in terms of supervision. The European regulators got together and started a major debate about what, 20 years down the road, would become a European SEC-type organization.

Other areas are currently being intensely debated in Europe. Competition between exchanges, takeovers among exchanges, consolidation, and so on and so forth. Direct access for investors is an issue that will not go away. Internalization, clearing and settlement, data storage and vending, are obviously big issues that are being discussed. Then there is the issue of placing our trading screens in the United States.

If you do not know it yet, ladies and gentlemen, the SEC is a highly protectionist body. When we started to talk with the commission about having our electronic trading screens in the U.S. market, the SEC said, "Well, we are very busy with Y2K coming down the road." My suggestion was to postpone Y2K and do this first, but that did not work (laughter). Then they said that they were dealing with the national market structure, and could not be bothered. Then they were too busy discussing self-regulation.

Three weeks ago, I thought this issue must be settled by now, so I sent an e-mail to SEC Chairman William Donaldson, saying, "You have not got terribly much to do anymore, so how about discussing trading screens?" But then you had your two big merger announcements, and now they tell us they have to discuss major consolidation issues. Once again, trading screens are on the back burner.

Now I would like to introduce my panel. Firstly, Reto Francioni has already been mentioned. He was the co-CEO of Consors Discount Broker. Before that he played a very crucial role in the modernization of the Deutsche Börse AG, a powerhouse in its own right. He is currently the chairman of the board of SWX Group. And he wrote the book *Equity Markets in Action* together with Bob Schwartz. Reto, you have the floor.[5]

RETO FRANCIONI: Thank you Paul. Bob, congratulations on how you timed this conference.

On the topic of reengineering a marketplace, the key issue involves optimizing the value chain. Every issue concerning market architecture must involve optimizing this value chain. The big reasons for making changes in the marketplace include strengthening investor protection, enhancing price discovery, and lowering costs. These are the goals that every change in market structure must advance.

I was lucky to start my career at a time when SOFEX, the first options and futures exchange, was being built. SOFEX was the basis for Eurex, which is now one of the bigger derivative trading platforms. I also have had the opportunity to build up from scratch the Swiss electronic trading platform. This was basically a transformation from floor trading to electronic trading. Then, in Frankfurt, I had the opportunity to convert the floor into an electronic platform. We improved transparency in terms of open order books, so that you could track almost every move within the trading platform.

I will focus in a few minutes on the German market, but first I want to say something about IT. IT is a tool. It is a necessity. But it is not sufficient by itself to implement market changes and get an overall advantage. For instance, in 1992, London had about 30 percent of the German market. Then the German market introduced IBIS.[6] IBIS was an overly complicated and inefficient system. You had to press a lot of buttons just to get the match. But the effect of IBIS was crucial. The German market got back most of the 30 percent even though they were using a clumsy system. On the other hand, you could have a brilliant system and still not be able to conquer or acquire another market in terms of getting the order flow.

For instance, with the Xetra system in Europe, we wanted to attack one rather famous security, Nokia. By just using IT, we could have spoken directly to Nokia and offered a deal, such as a fee-free period of half a year in exchange for its listing. But it does not work that way. More components than just IT are necessary. With IT, you have a lot of advantages. You can go international. You can develop an international strategy because you do not depend on a physical location for trading. You can achieve greater

[5] See Francioni, R. and Schwartz, R., "Equity Markets In Action: The Fundamentals of Liquidity, Market Structure and Trading," John Wiley & Sons, 2004, 468 pages.

[6] Germany's IBIS was introduced in 1991. It was replaced in 1997 by the Xetra (Exchange Electronic Trading) system.

economies of scale. With IT, you can easily add additional functionality to a system as the need arises. But if IT becomes too complex, it becomes very difficult to handle. It becomes very, very costly, and this can happen very, very fast. Accordingly, one major task is to control the complexity of the IT.

I have some remarks about implementing change in the marketplace itself. We have several constituents including participants and inter-mediaries. As a market architect, you have to come in with a tailor-made, customized solution that is feasible and which fits the needs of the different constituents. If a solution is not feasible, a lot of difficulties will be encountered during implementation. For the exchange as a market, the solution must be functionally feasible. For the exchange as a business, the solution must generate acceptable returns on investment. Will a solution have political implications? If so, what is the power structure in the market? What are the legal ramifications? What are the technical requirements? These are very heavy feasibility issues.

In Germany, as mentioned, we had floor trading on the one hand, and the electronic platform, IBIS, on the other. The question was, "What are we going to do with the specialists"? It was very difficult to find a solution for this because the issue involved repackaging risk and return in a new structure. The Xetra system was designed as a fully-fledged, integrated electronic platform. It is an order-driven, open-order book facility. The money was made, and is made, by realizing economies of scale.

For most of the liquid stocks, the order-driven is the better system. With the blue chips, you will never have a problem getting tight spreads. It is a liquid market. You see depth and breadth. As a big institutional investor, you can calculate exactly what your price will be. Therefore, you can define your trading strategy, and so on. However, for the less liquid side, you need market makers, or market maker functionality.

In every country in the world, the markets grow from the bottom to the top, not vice versa. You have small companies, and you have big companies that have a very small free float. You need a market that is comprised of not just one type of trading or another, but that is a hybrid, which comprises more than one type of trading mechanism. This is very important. Do not exclude one type of trading outright. Instead, consider what would be an optimum solution. To find the optimum, there is an absolute need to talk to all of the involved and committed parties in the market.

We succeeded in Frankfurt. We came up with a platform that seemed to work. This is the case for the liquid stocks. But it proved not to be the best platform for the less liquid or illiquid stocks. For those stocks, we have market makers. To find the optimum solution for a market, never forget the supra-ordinate goals – investor protection, quality of trading, enhanced price discovery and lower costs.

ARLMAN: Reto, thanks very much. We will move right on to David Krell who, as you all know, is founder, President, and CEO of ISE. David has been with the New York Stock Exchange, he has been with the Chicago Board Options Exchange, and he has served with a number of financial firms. I am very pleased that he is here, and very interested to hear what he is going to say. David.

DAVID KRELL: Thank you very much Paul. I would like to frame the discussion for today by talking about change. Starting this summer, I will have been on Wall Street for 35 years. In those 35 years, the one thing that has been constant is resistance to change. Let me tell you about some of my experiences with Wall Street's resistance to change.

I entered the options business in 1973.[7] The CBOE opened its doors, and every market maker opposed it. They did not think that it was going to succeed. Within less than two years, 90 percent of those market makers were out of business. In 1983, index options started to trade. These options were very much opposed by the market makers on the CBOE floor. I was at the CBOE at the time, and I launched trading and index options. The market makers did not like cash settlement of index options and they threatened not to trade options on indexes.

Despite their opposition, the CBOE 100 was launched, and within six months it became the most popular, most active options product in the world. It then changed its name to the S&P 100 Index. In 1990, the SEC proposed an options linkage. The linkage was opposed by all the largest options marketplaces. In 2002, Chairman Pitt invited the five CEOs of the options markets to his office and basically read us the riot act. Pitt said, "You will create a linkage," and that was that. Within 18 months, an option linkage between the markets was created.

In 1998, I announced, together with three other founders, the formation of the ISE. Nobody believed that it would succeed. Why? Because the generally accepted view was that the option market in the U.S. was different.

[7] Until 1973, the U.S. options industry was relatively parochial, small and it was concentrated in New York. That came to an end with the launch in April 1973 of the Chicago Board Options Exchange (CBOE). Trading began in humble circumstances, a former smoking lounge at the Chicago Board of Trade. Soon, however, market volume exploded, encouraged by the popular application of an options pricing model by finance economists, Fischer Black and Myron Scholes. This provided investors a better understanding of risk and reward. Later, another landmark event had even more profound consequences when the all-electronic International Securities Exchange (ISE) was launched in 1997. It was followed by some copycat activity, including the introduction of more technology at the CBOE. As of early 2006, there were six U.S. options exchanges. Despite garnering a huge portion of the options volume in a short period, ISE's advance may have leveled off. As of this writing, the ISE and CBOE each control about 30 percent of all options volume in the U.SA.

Everyone thought that face-to-face trading was the only way it could occur in a large market like the U.S. We started to trade in May of 2000, and within three years we became the largest equity options market in the United States. So, why is there so much resistance to change?

I postulate that there is much resistance, not because people do not like new products or because they do not like new systems, or because they are fearful of new strategies. Rather, Wall Street carries a lot of baggage. That baggage is mostly anachronistic thinking. It must be jettisoned. Change is with us. We have to adapt to change. Whether we like it or not, things will continue to change. The last couple of months are just another indicator of the change that is occurring.

We have reengineered the options markets in the United States. We introduced electronic trading. We introduced tighter quotes, greater efficiency, and lower costs. But I submit to you that the ISE did not become successful simply because we introduced electronic trading. There was a lot more to it than that. We created a new market structure in the United States. We took the best features of electronic trading, and melded them into an agency auction market, and the specialist system of trading. We wanted to introduce the benefits of both the electronic and the agency auction facilities. We wanted the speed, transparency, anonymity, and accessibility of electronic trading together with the customer priority, continuous quoting, and accountability that the agency auction market provides.

For the first time in the U.S. options market, we also introduced firm quotes, quotes that you could actually interact with. We displayed accessible size. We introduced WYSIWYG, "what you see is what you get." ISE was revolutionary when we launched in 2002. But it was very important to grow this market. We also brought in new liquidity providers – groups that were not in the options market at the time. We went to the existing large market makers, Timber Hill and Hull Trading. We also went to new liquidity providers – Morgan Stanley, Deutsche Bank, Knight, Merrill Lynch, Lehman, CSFB, and the newest one, Citadel, which is now one of the largest options market makers in the world.

Our philosophy was to go after the liquidity providers that had the expertise, that had the technology, and that had the capital to grow this market. This was key in our thinking. We wanted to grow the options market, not just take market share from one market or the other. We also wanted to reduce cost. All of this led to a tighter, more efficient, and far lower-cost market. The result? Trading volumes have soared.

So, what is happening now? Paul, you talked about remote market making taking place. The CBOE hybrid system is rolling out remote market makers. They also rolled out eDPMs, electronic designated primary market makers, some time ago. AMEX is introducing ANTE[8], Philadelphia, the PHLX-XL[9], and the Pacific PCX Plus. Now they all believe in electronic trading. The Boston Options Exchange, BOX, started trading in February of last year. We now have six options markets moving towards electronic trading. What is the result? There is more competition. Also, public investors are now getting the best deal ever in the options business.

What has happened to volume? In 2003, as an industry, the equity options business totaled 830 million contracts. Last year, it totaled over one billion contracts, a new record for this industry. So far, in 2005, we are tracking an even higher level than in the comparable period in 2004. Competition is good for the business, it is good for volume, and it is good for the investor. That is what we stand for. We welcome more electronic trading in the U.S. options markets.

ARLMAN: David, thanks very much. That was a clear message if I ever heard one. Our third speaker is Michael Pagano. Mike is one of those rare academicians who combine very thorough academic research with real experience in the markets. Michael, you have the floor.

MICHAEL PAGANO: Thank you very much, Paul. I have the opportunity to speak with you today about some of the research that I have been working on principally with Bob Schwartz. Given all the changes that we are hearing about, I am excited because we have only scratched the surface as far as research projects go. There is a whole bunch of things going on here that will be quite interesting to look at.

I would like to review some exhibits that are related to papers that Bob and I have worked on. How does all of this structural change affect market quality? We have answered this important question from both an academic and a practitioner point of view. We focused on Euronext Paris in 1996 and 1998, and on NASDAQ in 2004, years when both markets introduced electronic, closing call trading systems. How did these systems affect trading? How did they affect the quality of the market? The short answer is, "They clearly had a positive impact." But these impacts can be difficult to detect. You have to set controls and tease out exactly what happened.

What brought these changes about in the first place? The closing calls were introduced because of pressure from institutional investors who were trying to get better closing prices for rebalancing their portfolios. Dealers also wanted to close out or square up their positions at the end of the day, and for this they needed better closing prices. There was also a need in the derivatives market. If you have an option that is based on an equity market price, and that market

[8] Amex New Trading Environment (ANTE).

[9] Philadelphia Stock Exchange Extreme Liquidity Platform (PHLX XL).

price is not so reliable at the close, the market for your derivatives positions will be affected.

We looked at the effect of a market structure change – the introduction of a closing call – on market quality. How did we define market quality? We focused on what we call the accuracy of price discovery.[10] We define that accuracy with respect to the co-movement of prices across stocks. For example, how does a stock move relative to a broad market index? Many of you are familiar with the idea of a market model. In brief, you take the return on the stock and regress it on the return on the market index. One can use this basic model and see what is going on with prices at the end of the day. Are they more informative? Are they getting more reliable? Is volatility being reduced at the end of the day?[11]

We conducted two tests of the effects of introducing a closing call in Paris – one in 1996 for small caps, and the other in 1998 for large caps.[12] Then, in 2004, NASDAQ phased in a closing call, which enabled us to run a third test. Here are the data for Paris in 1996 and 1998 (see Exhibit 1).

| **Interval** | **Small Cap** | **Large Cap** |
|---|---|---|
| **1-day** | **140.0*** | **18.8** |
| **2-day** | **77.8** | **72.8*** |
| **10-day** | **52.6** | **72.9*** |
| **20-day** | **88.0** | **55.4** |
| **Average** | **101.7*** | **59.9*** |

*** Significant at the 99% confidence level.**

Exhibit 1. Empirical Results for Euronext Paris, Percent Change of $R^2$ Market Model

[10] Price discovery is the process of determining the price level for a commodity based on supply and demand conditions. Price discovery may occur in a futures market or cash market.

[11] A market model is used by academicians and market practitioners in portfolio management and empirical analysis.

[12] See Pagano, M., and Schwartz, R., "A Closing Call's Impact on Market Quality at Euronext Paris," Journal of Financial Economics, 68, 2003, pp. 439-484.

The small cap data are in the first column, and the data for the large caps are in the second. This data reflect the informativeness of the prices at the closing call. We examined how much explanatory power the market model regression equation has, as reflected in its $R^2$ statistic. What the exhibit shows is the percentage increases in $R^2$, whether you use one-day returns or 20-day returns to estimate the market model.[13] At the bottom of Exhibit 1 we list the average percent change in the informativeness of prices. For the small caps, the informativeness of prices doubled.

In 1998, the experiment was replicated with large caps. Again, we found a very large and statistically significant increase in the reliability of closing prices. Accordingly, we conclude that market structure really does have an impact, that it really can improve market quality.

In 2004, Bob and I worked on another paper that focused on NASDAQ's closing call, which was introduced in Spring 2004.[14] A complementary way of assessing the informativeness of prices is to measure the impact of the closing call on pricing errors. To do this, we applied a relative return dispersion (RRD) measure to one of the most stressful trading times for NASDAQ, the Russell 2000 rebalancing which occurs every June. We compared the seven days before and the seven days after that rebalancing in 2003 and 2004. In 2003, NASDAQ had no electronic call at the end of the day. In 2004, NASDAQ did. If this market structure change was beneficial to the market, we would expect to see that the pricing errors were reduced. As you can see in Exhibit 2, the dotted lines that represent 2004 are significantly lower.

[13] The market model says that the return on a security depends on the return on the market portfolio and the extent of the security's responsiveness as measured by beta. The return also depends on conditions that are unique to the firm. The market model can be graphed as a line fitted to a plot of asset returns against returns on the market portfolio. The slope of this line is the beta. This relationship is sometimes called the single-index model. Source: The New York Times Dictionary of Money and Investing. Gretchen Morgenson and Campbell R. Harvey, Times Books, 2002

[14] See Chapter 9 in this book or Pagano, M. and Schwartz, R., "NASDAQ's Closing Cross: Has its new call auction given NASDAQ better closing prices? Early Findings," Journal of Portfolio Management, Volume 31, Number 4, Summer 2005, pp. 100-111.

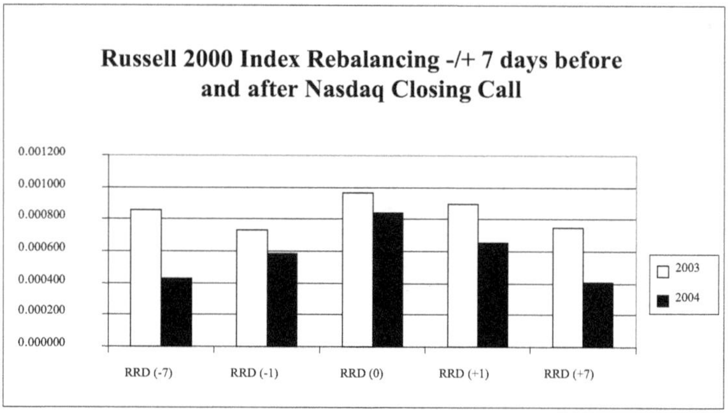


Exhibit 2. Empirical Results for NASDAQ's Closing Call, Change in Relative Return Dispersion (RRD)

We see a reduction of between 10 and 35 percent, depending on which quintile you look at. What does this mean? It means that, if you respond to customer demands and change the market structure in the right way, your prices will become more informative. I cannot show you all the data from these two papers, but I will note that short t term price volatility was also reduced as a result of these changes.

ARLMAN: Reto, is it easy to steal somebody else's liquidity?

FRANCIONI: It depends. First of all, there has to be an appropriate analysis of the situation. We had very fragmented markets in Europe. Empirically, we saw that liquidity was very difficult to move away from the home market. When Daimler Chrysler was dual listed in Frankfurt and on the NYSE, everybody asked, "What is going to happen now?" How will the poor guys managing the stock exchange in Frankfurt compete with the New York Stock Exchange?

What happened is the following. Due to a very good marketing job by Daimler Chrysler, as well as shareholder option plans, etc., the overall liquidity was increased. But the executions took place in Frankfurt, because that is where the spreads were narrowest and costs were lowest, not only in trading, but also for settlement. Another example of an attempt to get liquidity from another home market in the blue-chip area is provided by virt-x/SWX in London.[15] SWX Swiss Exchange had a marvelous idea. The exchange went back to the roots where the flows are. They went back to the biggies, Deutsche Bank, Merrill Lynch, Morgan, etc., and said, "We have an idea. We do a contract with you. You get a share of the stock exchange, and you get, essentially, a waiver of trading fees." This consortium had two incentives. They owned 40 percent of the stock exchange (now that is called leverage!), and they had fee reductions or waivers resulting in a large savings in trading costs. What happened? It did not work out at all. No meaningful additional liquidity was gained, neither due to the guaranteed fee releases nor to the stake in the stock exchange. In this, and only in this respect, the strategy did not work out. Nevertheless, the virt-x strategy for a cost effective pan-European blue-chip exchange is still, in any case, a necessary strategy for Switzerland, a strategy that requires a market presence in London. That is without question.

ARLMAN: Thank you Reto, and the rest of a panel for a lively discussion.

[15] vir *t* x Exchange Ltd. (virt-x) was founded in 2001 in an arrangement among Tradepoint Financial Networks plc., TP Group LDC and SWX Swiss Exchange. virt-x is now wholly-owned within the SWX Group. virt-x Exchange Limited is a London-based Recognized Investment Exchange with a single rulebook, supervised by the Financial Services Authority (FSA). It is a regulated market under the Investment Services Directive.

# CHAPTER 2: KEYNOTE ADDRESS, GERALD PUTNAM

Gerald Putnam, *President and Co-Chief Operating, Officer, NYSE Group, Inc.*[16]

GERALD PUTNAM: Good morning everyone. I would like to start by thanking Bob Schwartz for having me this year. I had to skip last year because we were in the middle of the IPO, but I am excited to be here today.

As I was preparing for today's presentation and was thinking about the new NASDAQ marketplace, I decided to look back at the old NASDAQ marketplace, and at the exponential rate of change that we have been experiencing over the last few years. As everyone knows, the most sweeping change in the OTC marketplace occurred in the mid '90's when, with the implementation of the order handling rules, the SEC took a bold step in the direction of competition. The SEC's far sightedness in 1997 was a catalyst for reinventing the OTC marketplace. Coupled with technology innovations of the last decade, competitive barriers were lowered. This produced an explosion of innovation, efficiency and choice for investors.

A major development that resulted from these rules was the emergence of the ECNs. Looking back at some of the presentations and speeches that I have given over the past six or seven years, I noticed that every presentation that I looked at started with a slide that read, "What is an ECN?" I am happy to report that I no longer need to address that question with an audience like this one. But now the question I am asked is, "What happened to the ECNs?" Strike and Brut merged, as did Archipelago and Redibook. Then Island and Instinet merged, and Archipelago evolved into ArcaEx, the

[16] At the time of the conference, Mr. Putnam was CEO of ArcaEx. In March 2006, ArcaEx merged with the New York Stock Exchange to form the NYSE Group.

exchange. Arca then acquired GlobeNet. NASDAQ acquired Brut and now finally we have NASDAQ's announced acquisition of INET ECN.

I believe that all the change and consolidation in the last five years has led to an OTC marketplace that has never been more vibrant, competitive, cost effective and responsive to the needs of traders, investors and corporate issuers. It would be difficult to argue that the ECNs were not key contributors in the shaping of the current OTC marketplace. In addition, the ECNs have been major drivers of much of the innovation and progress that we have seen. While remaining responsive to the changing needs of the trading community, the innovation and competition that has occurred will continue to thrive, even with the recently announced consolidations. This has led us to an OTC marketplace where every major liquidity pool uses a best execution model. Order types come in multiple flavors, and execution speeds are measured in milliseconds. The ultimate beneficiaries of these technological advances have been investors. The users have enjoyed tighter spreads, and greater efficiencies when trading OTC stocks.

In addition to its advances in trading automation, the OTC marketplace has been at the forefront of change in market data and information. There is more breadth and depth of real time market data for trading OTC stocks. The need for reliable, fast, and robust information is more crucial to the trading community and to corporate issuers than ever. As the number of quotes has multiplied, exceeding everyone's wildest expectations, there have been some growing pains. Innovative marketplaces and data vendors have worked diligently to alleviate these pains.

At ArcaEx we are constantly looking at new ways to provide data more quickly and efficiently. In an effort to channel some of this information and to make it easier to digest, Archipelago introduced ArcaVision; a database of current and historical data that market participants can use to analyze trading information and trends. We have continued to improve and upgrade our proprietary data feed, ArcaBook, to meet the growing demands of a more computerized and changing market. We firmly believe that investors' needs are best served when innovative marketplaces create and reinvent the way in which information is served.

As we look to the future of the NASDAQ marketplace, we see some critical changes looming that will reshape the future of NASDAQ trading. The first is the implementation of Reg. NMS, which is scheduled for early 2006. More specifically with regard to Reg. NMS, is the application of the trade-through rule to the NASDAQ marketplace. As many of you know, our opinion at ArcaEx has been that no additional regulatory intervention is necessary in this area of OTC trading. Though that was not the final outcome at the SEC, resolution of this long-debated topic is welcome. ArcaEx is a fully electronic market that uses a best execution model and does not trade-through better prices on competing systems and we, like our electronic competitors, are already connected to other marketplaces. Consequently, the trade-through rule will require few changes. All of that is in place in our system today.

At the open meeting held in April by the Securities and Exchange Commission (that ultimately led to the approval of Reg. NMS), Chairman Donaldson presented a statistic in support of the trade-through rule – one in 30 internalized trades is executed at a price that is worse than the current best bid or offer. Donaldson further concluded that, since broker/dealers frequently internalize trades for retail customers, small investors in particular would benefit from a rule that guarantees them the best price on every execution in the post trade-through rule environment.

The ability for internalized trades to receive price protection in a non-exchange environment may pose challenges for market makers. Simply using NASDAQ as a print facility would not offer the protection required to adhere to this rule. Like in the past, technology can supply solutions and options that will better insure compliance. For example, just last week, ArcaEx filed a market making rule with the Securities and Exchange Commission. Upon approval, the rule will provide one avenue of compliance. AraEx's new rule for market makers will not only encourage additional price improvement and supplemental liquidity for stocks traded on ArcaEx – it will also be linked to our electronic best execution model, which will insure that better price orders on the ArcaEx book and in the national market are not overlooked.

Displayed limit orders will retain standing in the ArcaEx book on a price and time priority basis. By protecting best prices on all markets, ArcaEx's program will do more than enable clients to achieve enhanced execution quality – it will also insure compliance with the trade-through protections approved by the SEC and Reg NMS. Proposed changes to existing market making capabilities include enhancements to ArcaEx's current directed order process, and the addition of lead market makers for stocks with a primary listing on ArcaEx. Market makers will have the ability to provide price improvement by using our existing order types, and they will receive automated protection of trade-throughs against the ArcaEx display limit order book, and against orders that are held in other markets. If approved, these enhancements to our existing market making capabilities will provide more liquidity, to the benefit of both corporate issuers and investors.

I would also like to address the recently announced consolidation in the U.S. marketplace. In just a moment, I will focus more specifically on our announced merger with the NYSE. Regarding NASDAQ's acquisition of Instinet, I will start by saying that we had a choice of which partner we wanted to pursue. It was a great position for us to be in, and we simply picked the transaction that we thought was a superior transaction for us. We picked the one where we got the best synergies, and where we could diversify our product offering. We felt that the best was a transaction with the NYSE.

One concern that I have heard revolves around whether or not the NASDAQ acquisition will have an impact on Arca's large liquidity pool. I do not think that this is a situation where the market share of NASDAQ plus INET will actually add up to the total market shares of both marketplaces today. One plus one in this case does not necessarily equal two. As a potential buyer of Instinet, when making projections concerning market share for a combined ArcaEx – INET entity, we took into account that there would be some loss of market share to NASDAQ. It is an important assumption to make. It was part of the formula for determining the value of Instinet to our business. Additionally, contrary to some of the anxiety about decreased competition as a result of this merger, I believe that the consolidation of three OTC liquidity pools into two will actually benefit market participants. And it will do nothing to lessen competition. We have fought a tough war over the years, and it is not over yet. You will no doubt continue to see two very aggressive and focused competitors fighting for market share each and every day.

Archipelago has helped shape the NASDAQ marketplace for over eight years. We expect that our recently announced merger with the New York Stock Exchange will help redefine and strengthen not only the listed marketplaces, but the new OTC marketplace as well. Through this combination, ArcaEx is better positioned to retain its leading position in the trading of OTC stocks. If approved by the regulators, NYSE members, and Arca shareholders, as part of the NYSE Group ArcaEx will continue to operate like it does today, as a totally open, fully electronic, order driven exchange. We will continue to be at the forefront of trading innovation. We are committed to expand and improve upon the services that we provide.

We strongly believe that another key beneficiary of this merger will be the corporate issuer. Over the last year we have been working diligently to grow our listings business. We have had some recent successes with, for instance, the listings of Metropolitan Health, Networx, American Dairy and Options Express. The opportunity to build a listings business alongside the NYSE, and to have a solid and viable alternative for those issuers that aspire for a listing on the big board but do not currently qualify, will position ArcaEx as a more viable and reasonable alternative to NASDAQ. Additionally, a combined ArcaEx – NYSE will provide corporate issuers more meaningful information and substantive trading data.

In summary, we believe that combining the NYSE and ArcaEx will create new opportunities for investors, traders and issuers. By uniting the strengths of the New York Stock Exchange and the speed and entrepreneurial spirit of Archipelago, the NYSE Group will be positioned to be the preeminent global marketplace, not only for all U.S. cash equities, but for options and other derivatives as well. As I look ahead, I see a future where U.S. markets will be better positioned against global competitors, where investors will continue to be the beneficiary of the advances in trading technology, and where competition remains a driver in the progression of markets. Thank you. I am happy to take questions.

DON WEEDEN (Weeden & Co. L.P.) [From the Floor]: I want to turn the question away from NASDAQ for a moment and ask you about the relationship with New York going forward. I have two questions. At the NOIP and STA meetings, no one talked about the reduction of competition in the listed market. Can you speak to the fact that the largest market and the most aggressive and sophisticated market coming together would essentially eliminate all other competition in the making of listed markets? The second question would depend on the answer to the first.

PUTNAM: Concerning competition, the Justice Department will look at this deal. They will also look at the NASDAQ-Instinet deal. Then, with the help of the Securities and Exchange Commission, a decision will be made. The way that this deal is structured is that investors will continue to have a choice about how they want to trade listed stocks, on the NYSE Floor or electronically on ArcaEx. Some might have suggested, "Why not shut ArcaEx down and just trade listed stocks on the New York Stock Exchange?" Well, that is not going to happen. We will give traders a choice.

There will be improved integration between the two systems. There will be a private linkage between them. We will open at 4 AM, and close at 8 PM. We have solved the extended hours issue for the NYSE. They were losing market share to us in the hour before they opened, because the special situation stocks would heat up. We are the only market that provided a real quote at that time. We paid SIAC17 to get an early quote for this reason. And we started to take market share from them. But, going forward, the two systems will trade side by side. New York will open the way it opens, with its new Hybrid system, and ArcaEx will open at 4 AM. If you want to trade a stock on our system, you are free to do so and, if there is a great benefit available through the Hybrid system, you are free to trade it there. So, at the end of the day, everyone has a choice. This choice will eventually lead to an outcome that is best for the marketplace. We are not being shut off, so there still is a choice. Then there is also the NASDAQ system, which competes for trading NYSE's list of stocks as well.

[17] SIAC is the Securities Industry Automation Corporation, the Securities Information Processor for the NYSE and Amex.

WEEDEN [From the Floor]: Here is my follow-up question. People from the NYSE at both of those conferences said that there would be a complete separation of the two markets for some time in the future. Remembering your testimony about the hundreds and hundreds of trade-throughs that occurred when a better price appeared on Arca, and another transaction took place on New York at a worse price, can you give me some idea of how this will be resolved?

PUTNAM: It was a great opportunity to hear John Thain talk at the testimony about the importance of trade-through protection. Then I got to go next. I simply said, if it is so important, why do you guys do it 2,500 times a day on our system? Or, is it just important as it relates to New York, but not to other markets? John heard that. I do not know this as a fact, but it seems he went back and started putting pressure on the floor about the trade-throughs. I think this because the result has been – we have seen it – that they are stopping. We get inadvertent trade-throughs today in hyperactive ETFs, and that would happen regardless of the trade-through rule. Because the quoting is quick, and a print goes up as the quote is moving into it, it appears to be a trade-through. But, for the most part, the trade-throughs that we had been experiencing in listed stocks have disappeared.

There was a conversation before we even started the merger discussion, about better linkage between New York and Arca. I think New York realized that they needed something outside of the ITS system to answer the demands from their customers for better execution. The NYSE was looking to build that private linkage. We became a member of New York about a year and a half ago. We actually use a private linkage to connect to them. So, we were looking to build that anyway and, obviously, this transaction is going to help facilitate an even better coordination between our two markets.

JUSTIN SCHACK (Institutional Investor Magazine) [From the Floor]: Given that you have been so critical of the New York in the past, and that not long ago you looked at Arca as an eventual winner against the NYSE competitively, is this a bittersweet deal for you at all?

PUTNAM: No, it is not at all. This is a great outcome. Over the years, the NYSE was the great competitor to compare ourselves to – in the beginning, they had 80 percent market share, and we had none. Then with some really good marketing work, we got our point across, and we have built a pretty good listed business. We had a 4.5 percent market share in NYSE listed stocks yesterday. The fact is, there was a need for some reform and change in that marketplace. Investors are demanding more electronic, seamless access to the market, and the NYSE is responding.

When our board made the decision that we would pursue this deal with the NYSE, it was with a vision of a much better outcome for our shareholders. The opportunity for us to jumpstart the listings business – something that we have invested two years of time and money into – is really enhanced by this deal with the NYSE. The eventual outcome is that you will see more stocks start to trade on a pure electronic system, like ours, with this new market making capability that we are adding to it. That is going to lower cost and improve the execution quality of trading really active stocks.

The other several thousand stocks that are not as liquid will benefit from the human intervention that the NYSE's new Hybrid will bring. But eventually, as long as the two sit side by side, if the market wants to take it in the direction of ArcaEx, it is free to do so and, if the outcome is that Hybrid is the best, we will go in that direction.

ANDREW KAGAN (Lava Trading) [From the Floor]: For those liquid stocks that you envision trading mostly electronically, do you see the opening shifting over to the electronic opening that you use today on ArcaEx? Would that allow the stocks that are less liquid to be the ones that the specialists open on the NYSE floor?

PUTNAM: Yes, some of that is happening now, anyway. The list of stocks that we have a greater than 10-percent market share in is growing. We put out a couple of emails a day to highlight those names for our customers, and we used to have three or four issues on the list. Currently, on any given day, the list of firms that we have a greater than 10-percent market share in is on the order of 70 to100 stocks. It is because of our opening early. For some of these special situation stocks, there really is no other place to see a quote and trade on except for ArcaEx. More and more people started trading there and, as this happened, others who did not have connectivity had to come in. We have built a critical mass of connectivity on our system for trading listed stocks. If the market wants to take it in that direction, they will be able to do so with this arrangement.

ANDY BROOKS (T. Rowe Price Associates) [From the Floor]: How long and how complicated would it be for either New York and Arca or NASDAQ and Instinet to trade fixed income securities? What would that involve?

PUTNAM: That is absolutely part of the plan. Fixed income securities will be traded on our system. We have been responding to some demand for trading fixed income securities, in particular corporate bonds and some agencies. We explored that and had a plan in place to build our functionality to trade bonds. At the same time, the New York Stock Exchange has been working with the SEC for the last two years to get some rules changed that would allow them to trade the corporate bonds of NYSE listed companies, even if the bonds are not specifically listed with the New York Stock Exchange. The rule that they currently have only allows trading in corporate bonds that are actually listed there. To the extent that GM bonds exist but are not listed with the New York Stock Exchange, they could not trade them if the rule is approved. The plan going forward is that New York gets the rule revised, and then we start adding bonds on ArcaEx.

DAVID KRELL (International Securities Exchange, Inc.) [From the Floor]: You mentioned before, Jerry, that the NYSE's market share is about 80 percent, and that it has stayed stable. Your market share has grown from zero to about 4.5 percent.

PUTNAM: That may be a high. It has been averaging 3.5 lately.

MICHAEL PAGANO (Villanova University) [From the Floor]: This is a follow-up to Andy Brooks' question about fixed income. Do options play a role in this with the Pacific Coast Exchange?

PUTNAM: We have been negotiating with the SEC for some time over the structure needed for us to acquire the PCX. The Commission's concern basically surrounds the self-regulatory organization. They have some requirements that they have asked of us, and a rule filing should come out relatively soon. We have been drafting it, and as we negotiate some of the final pieces of it, you will eventually see a rule filed. It will go out for comment, and there is some extra time required after that before we get an approval order. There is also a proxy that needs to go out to PCX shareholders. When all of that is done (we still think that it will be completed this summer), we will have closed the PCX transaction, and at that point we will be in the options business.[18]

PAGANO [From the Floor]: Do you envision that integrating with options trading?

PUTNAM: Any integration that can be done will differentiate our offering. It is potentially good for our business and good for the industry as a whole. We have seen tremendous growth in options trading, in particular. Our attempts to make that integration more seamless will further lower the risk of trading. New demand for trading derivative products will result, and then we will see another explosion in derivatives trading. There is an awful lot of upside for all of us as an industry from combining equities and options trading.

SCHWARTZ: Jerry, had I known that we would have had this big development; we would have structured the program to devote more time to your session. I thank you.

PUTNAM: Thanks, everyone.

[18] Archipelago Holdings acquired the Pacific Exchange in September 2005.

# CHAPTER 3: RECENT DEVELOPMENTS AT NASDAQ

William Christie, *Professor of Finance, Owen Graduate School, Vanderbilt University*
Christopher Concannon, *Executive Vice President, The NASDAQ Stock Market, Inc.*
Adena Friedman, *Executive Vice President, The NASDAQ Stock Market, Inc.*
Frank Hatheway, *Chief Economist, The NASDAQ Stock Market, Inc.*

WILLIAM CHRISTIE: It is an honor to be here. We have a tremendous panel today. As you know, there have been remarkable developments recently at NASDAQ, so we are excited to have several key NASDAQ players on the panel. We have Adena Friedman, executive vice president of corporate strategy and data products; Chris Concannon, executive vice president of transaction services, and Frank Hatheway, NASDAQ's Chief Economist. I have known Frank for many years. I just met Chris today. Adena was a student of mine in 1993 at Vanderbilt, where she got her MBA. So, I would like to take some credit for Adena's incredible success. I will give each of the panelists a few minutes to share their thoughts on these recent NASDAQ developments, and then will open it up for questions. Adena, take it away.

ADENA FRIEDMAN: One of the great things about being at NASDAQ is that the world moves very fast. It is never dull. It is always an enjoyable experience. In the last year, for instance, we have been focused on a lot of innovative products and new initiatives. And then there is the large transaction that we just completed.

As the head of corporate strategy, I work with all the business units, and with Chris in particular. We are looking for new opportunities for NASDAQ to grow, to integrate, and to continue to serve investors. Over the past year I have been focused on the opening and closing crosses, the transaction with

BRUT and, most recently, the signing of the deal with INET. I will be happy to answer any questions about these and other transactions.

CHRISTOPHER CONCANNON: I run transaction services at NASDAQ. A lot is happening. There is Reg NMS, and the two transactions that have certainly caught everyone's attention in the industry. Aside from these items, we have been putting our heads down and executing a plan that we laid out about two years ago. Number one, we have already completed the transaction with BRUT, which was an ECN. BRUT is now integrated into NASDAQ as NASDAQ Transaction Services. That transaction closed September 7th of 2004. We have already executed on that integration plan to have what we call a virtual book. We will use a very similar integration plan with INET. What is attractive about INET, among other things, is that it has had its own experience with integration when it migrated Instinet onto the Island platform. So, you have two parties coming together who have already done this type of integration work, both on the legal side and on the business side. That is very valuable when you are talking about the execution risks of a major transaction like this.

What we have done with BRUT has been very exciting for us. NASDAQ was a somewhat closed system, with SuperMontage only routing to participants who chose to be in SuperMontage. With the BRUT transaction, we are opening the system up and, effective this month, we will have routing through SuperMontage using the BRUT router, reaching all destinations. That is an important historical event for SuperMontage. It will matter a lot to the overall market structure, to fill rates, and to the user's experience. We were also able to accomplish the virtual book, bringing BRUT's entire liquidity pool into the SuperMontage[19] depth of book, to avoid any trade-throughs at any price level. It certainly has increased the value of the total product, the full depth of book data feed that NASDAQ currently sells.

The closing cross is something that we focused on in '04, and the opening cross is a product that we rolled out at the end of '04. We have seen great liquidity in the opening cross. The two crosses have changed the market structure on NASDAQ at the two most important points of the day – the open and the close. We have also instituted the early open, or what we call the pre-market trading session. This session involves much more than just opening the market earlier, changing the official opening time. We chose to deliver our electronic platform at an earlier time. The institutions have been proponents of this strategy. People were concerned about the not auto-exable quotes that were published in the morning hours.

[19] SuperMontage was later known as the NASDAQ Market Center, which was eventually integrated with BRUT into the INET platform. The NASDAQ Market Center was retained as the name for this integrated platform.

By turning the system on for dealers and market makers, we have everyone whose quotes are subject to instantaneous execution. That is a transparency event that NASDAQ needed in the pre-market. We were able to accomplish this with the help of a lot of vendors, along with others in the trading community. In the past, people used ECNs in the pre-market. We created a pre-market product that has been well received by the dealer community. Now a dealer can actually use its name, attribution is live and accessible, and if a dealer is on the quote or has size to do, that dealer will put it in its own name.

The other product that we announced, using the assets that we obtained in the BRUT transaction, is our "free DOT" product. We became a member of the New York Stock Exchange (more accurately stated, BRUT became a member).[20] We leased a seat, which was an exciting process for me. We now have a DOT product that enables people to access our fully automated liquidity pool prior to going down to the DOT system. This has been very well received by the community. A lot of people have asked about it, and we are currently rolling it out to a number of large firms. That is NASDAQ in a nutshell. I will turn it over to Frank.

FRANK HATHEWAY: I would like to talk for a few minutes about the introduction of the opening and closing crosses. With them, NASDAQ has expanded its functionality to meet the needs of issuers and investors, and to respond to competitive pressures. I also want to relate my comments to remarks made by David Krell in the first panel about resistance to change in our industry, and by Reto Francioni on the importance of looking beyond the IT. We very much agree with Reto about the importance of looking at the humans who are going to use the system and looking at the environment that the IT will be operating in, to create something that accomplishes the goals that we set out to achieve.

We set out to create a closing auction in 2003. The first thing you do when you are building an auction is to call Bob Schwartz (laughter). We called Bob Schwartz, and got Bob on board, along with a number of people from the industry who helped with the design process. We then went about creating an auction in what is essentially a decentralized dealer market. Whether we are now a limit order book market, a dealer market, or a hybrid of the two, is debatable. But we are not centralized. The challenge with an auction is that auction orders do not necessarily pair off at prices that, ex-post, people would like to trade at. You need a mechanism for people to respond to the auction and to establish a price that, ex-post, everyone considers fair. We did a couple of things to accomplish that. First, we differentiated participants by their urgency to trade. People who only wanted to trade at the close were handled one way. Other participants in the

[20] BRUT had membership in the NYSE that pre-existed its acquisition by NASDAQ.

auction were handled differently. We gave that second group another set of tools to work with so that they could react to the folks who indicated that they wanted to trade at the close. We set up a competitive, transparent process that we thought would create a closing auction, which would be a reliable benchmark for anyone looking to use closing prices for NASDAQ listed securities.

We created the closing cross first because it is an easier auction to institute. There are a lot of reasons for this, and I will not go into all of them. But here is one simple one. For the most part, the participants who want to trade on the close are institutions looking to get an execution at the price setting the net asset value for them for the day. It is used by a relatively small group of rather sophisticated people. The open is a much more complicated process because it could be used by everyone. There are dealers who had never used an auction, and we felt that it would be better to keep the system simple and to involve as few people as we could. Thus we started with the closing cross.

We rolled out the closing cross in March and the opening cross in November. How are they working? In terms of volume, we did roughly ten million shares a day in March on the open and on the close. On the quadruple witch in March, we did 140 million shares on the open and 104 on the close. Of course, a big event, as Mike Pagano showed us earlier, was the Russell rebalancing. Last June, over 300 million shares were executed in a process that was only about two months old. The full rollout was what, three weeks old? Two weeks old at that point?

It worked. In five seconds it handled a tremendous amount of order flow. That is the IT piece. We did not need ten minutes, or 20 minutes, or 30 minutes to do all of these stocks. We got the Russell done in ten seconds. On a typical day it is five seconds. What about price discovery? I indicated a moment ago that part of the challenge is that without dealers you have orders for the auction that are going to pair off at a price that is not necessarily a reasonable price in the market. We have this tool for people, the dealers, who are not necessarily submitting auction orders, but who want to react to it – the tool is called an *imbalance only order*. That is what we use to try and make sure that the price in the auction and the price that has been on the continuous market are roughly the same.

Think about the close. Institutions are trading to try to do portfolio transactions at the end of the day. There is no information there. There should not be a significant amount of price dislocation. We want to make sure that the prices are as close on the auction as they have been in the continuous markets. How do we do that? Well, generally speaking, we release information anywhere from five to ten minutes ahead of the auction, whether it is the open or the close.

The first look that we give the market about where the auction may execute is usually 50 cents away from where the continuous market was trading at that point in time. In a minute or two, the two prices have moved together, and it is usually the auction price that does most of the moving. The continuous market, in the words of a former associate, is the battle-tested market. The auction market has expected new information about order balances, but not about the stock. The auction price is the one that should adjust and it does.

The last measure that I have for how well these processes work, along with volume and the accuracy of the price, is the extent to which they are drawing liquidity to the market that was not there prior to the start of the auction process. *Latent liquidity* is what, as an academic, I would call it. Most of the volume that offsets the imbalances at the auction comes from reactive orders. It is from the *Imbalance Only* orders that dealers put in, in response to the transparent process that we have created. Some of the liquidity comes from other auction orders, and some comes in from the continuous market, but it mostly comes from these reactive orders. In addition to these orders that are coming in to meet the demands of the auction, there is typically an extra three million shares or so of trading interest at the closing auction that is near the auction price. These shares are there to offset an imbalance and to provide a surplus to what we actually needed. This is for auctions that are doing about ten million shares a day; this additional available liquidity is a third more than we needed. At the open it is about two million shares – another 20 percent beyond what we need to provide liquidity. Overall, I think the process has worked well.

We created a process that took advantage of what technology can do, recognizing the institutional and human constraints that we had to deal with, and responding to the benefits to investors and issuers in the NASDAQ marketplace. We are looking to extend this process to the opening of IPOs, and to the resumption of trading following trading halts. We think that the two NASDAQ crosses have set a standard in the United States for electronic trading on an auction basis, as opposed to a continuous limit order book. That is something that we are very interested in seeing developed over time. Bill, back to you.

CHRISTIE: Terrific. Thanks, Frank. Let's go ahead and open it up for questions from the audience.

ROBERT SCHWARTZ [From the Floor]: I do not know how many years I have been talking with you guys about a call auction. One afternoon, I received a call from Frank Hatheway. It was approximately ten minutes to five. He said, "Bob, we are going to put in an auction." Just then the fire alarm went off. It was very loud, and the bell is right outside my office. The security guard gets on the PA system and says, "This is not a test. You must vacate the building." I shouted back, "but they are putting in a call!" The announcement to evacuate immediately continued, and I had no choice but to tell Frank that we would have to continue the discussion tomorrow. It turned out to be a false alarm. It went off because some professor on the tenth floor had suddenly overheated (laughter).

The call is very different than dealer intermediation. You always worry about your vested interest and your business model. That is one reason why we put together this panel to begin with, to explore the concerns about setting up a call, and the problems of reengineering the market in general. But then, all of a sudden, you guys went ahead and instituted a call. You were able to do it so well. Is there anybody who is part of your constituency who is upset about it? I am not aware of anyone. Could you speak about how you were able to pull it together so quickly?

HATHEWAY: There is a trend that we have seen over the years that has led to our ability to put in a cross. You can trace that trend back to the Christie-Shultz study. It is noteworthy that Bill Christie is moderating this panel. That study led to the beginning of market structure change at NASDAQ. It all goes back to Bill Christie. Some people like that, and some do not. In terms of restructuring, the change in the order handling rules led to ECNs coming into the market. This in turn led to order books being very accessible and prominent in the NASDAQ market. This in turn led to NASDAQ going from a dealer model to an agency model. It is that agency model that allowed people to embrace the closing cross first, which has now been followed by the opening call.

Before the cross was introduced, the NASDAQ close was not an efficient way to price stocks. We had this race to 4:00 p.m. that simply was not price discovery. The closing price is so important to so many people, and we definitely needed a far more efficient way to achieve it. The AMEX was able to launch a pilot with S&P that shook the industry, and that clearly accelerated the pace of change.

People questioned how the close should work. We had planned to do the opening cross first, followed by the closing call. The SEC clearly wanted the opening cross-instituted quickly. The Commission was a big proponent of opening the market with an auction-type process. But we did the closing cross first. In hindsight, this was a good decision from a technology standpoint. We had a group of constituents who had a lot of IT expertise. We were able to test the opening cross technology and could see how it interacted with the continuous market. A really unique part of our cross is that we have a call auction that is interacting with the liquidity of the continuous market. This is an important feature that we had to build in. In brief, the most compelling reason to embrace the NASDAQ closing cross was our having changed to an agency model within the dealer community.

CHRISTIE: A question from the audience.

UNIDENTIFIED SPEAKER [From the Floor]: Given that there is occasionally gaming in the cross, is there anything that can be done to prevent it?

HATHEWAY: Could you explain what you mean by gaming first? Could you do this without revealing any profit opportunities that you might have (laughter)?

UNIDENTIFIED SPEAKER [From the Floor]: Maybe gaming is the wrong word. The one incident that comes to mind is the Russell Rebalance where there were stocks that were substantially off of where they were closing. That probably was a one-time occurrence, but it could happen again. Is there any thought about what can be done to prevent it?

CONCANNON: We have found statistically (and have experienced in general since Russell) that the closing crosses have gotten extremely efficient, and we do not see those breaks any more. That is basically how collars in the closing cross avoid trades that go excessively outside of what we think the market was at the time. Those collars were triggered on seven stocks in Russell. It was a new product going into Russell, which was the biggest trade of the year for that time. We did not yet have all of the participants in the cross. In fact, we had a number of participants who admitted to us after Russell that their management held back the amount of capital that they could commit. I am talking about firms that are committing billions of dollars (not just millions but billions) in capital in those trades. There was a lot of holdback because, if you got trapped in a system that went down because it was not truly tested and that did not work right, and you had all that capital exposure, you were in big trouble. A lot of people held back. That capital holdback represented a lot of liquidity that could have absorbed some of those moves. We actually saw that capital come in after Russell.

When we rolled out the open – and the Triple Qs were traded out of range in a single opening cross – we found something very similar. There were participants who were not even looking at the Triple Qs. It was not a trade for them on that day. It was a quad-witch and there was no trade on the Triple Qs related to the index. A lot of people were caught off guard. A lot of liquidity providers just did not have it in their basket. We have not seen that kind of thing happening since. There is a learning process that occurs with these crosses as people come to understand the opportunities. The academics call it market efficiency; I call it selling a product a little bit better.

HATHEWAY: The implementation or simulation issues that Chris referred to not withstanding, there is a lot of money at stake at the open and at the close. This creates incentives for people to try and affect prices. However, we have in place a strong regulatory program administered by the NASD. I will not go into the details of what they do in terms of monitoring behavior around the open and close. One of the questions implicit in what you said was, is it better to create a process that ex-ante is 100 percent impervious to any type of gaming, or to rely on ex-post regulation? We think that the cross is designed with a transparency that is resistant to ex-ante manipulation. But I would never claim it to be totally immune. We have an effective blend of both processes now. If there is anything particular that you have seen that you would like to tell me about afterwards, I will be happy to pass it along to the NASD (laughter).

UNIDENTIFIED SPEAKER [From the Floor]: I have a two-part question. First, we have heard Jerry Putnam and others say that when you combine two technologies like INET and NASDAQ, one plus one does not necessarily equal two. I would be curious to hear your thoughts regarding his comments about potential market share losses. Second, other than market share losses, what do you view as the two or three most significant competitive threats to NASDAQ resulting from the Arca and NYSE merger?

FRIEDMAN: With regard to the first question, we looked at INET from several different angles, the first being technology. We think that INET provides a platform for growth and innovation efficiency. It is extremely efficient, extremely fast. It is probably the fastest platform on the market today. And it is very low cost. Why did we do the transaction with INET? What we are hoping to accomplish with the transaction has a lot to do with providing a platform for growth.

In terms of the market share question, we have very successfully used the BRUT platform to attract clients who we were not able to attract with SuperMontage. The speed, efficiency, and low-cost of INET will allow us to continue down the path of being a low-cost provider. We looked at the transaction in terms of how it would enable us to compete with New York, to compete internationally, and to innovate in new product classes.

Regarding the Arca - NYSE merger, I want to point out that we were as surprised by the news as everyone else. We were hunkered down doing the INET transaction and were in the final strokes when the announcement came out. It provides a new competitive playing field. We are very pleased with the fact that we have such strong relations with our issuers. We spent years and years building our relations with our issuers, all 3,000 of them. To the extent that our competitor in New York makes a play for a different set of issuers, we think that we are well positioned to compete actively there.

Changes to the playing field have more to do with Reg NMS, and to the fact that regional exchanges will have an equal seat at the table at the best price. We have very powerful clients. We know and respect that. We will continue to provide exactly what they are looking for: superior service, pricing, and functionality. But to the extent that a regional wants to participate, it will have a much easier time and a lower barrier to entry to participate in our marketplace.

NARI JOTE (Baruch College) [From the Floor]: In this fast paced changing world, with the globalization of processes, trading volume has increased from ten million to 300 million. Is this increase due to technology or to human initiative? If it is due to both and they are driving each other, on a scale of one to ten, how much is technology and how much is human behavior?

HATHEWAY: I do not know if I can give you a scale. Historically, when you lower transaction costs in any market, you get increased transaction volume. Look back as early as the 1970s when fixed commissions were eliminated. That is when firms like Charles Schwab come into being. As you lower transaction costs, whether it is commissions, whether it is back office transaction costs, or whether it is just trading costs in general, you accelerate volume.

Technology certainly plays a big part in lowering transaction costs. By converting from a manual, floor-based exchange to an electronic exchange, you are lowering transaction costs and transaction friction (which is a cost of trading). That also leads to increased volume. With New York converting to an electronic trading platform, we hear a lot of predictions that volume will accelerate. Overall, volume could grow as far as NYSE listings are concerned.

JOTE [From the Floor]: Basically, the customer, client, or anyone else who wants to invest looks at three factors: the cost or price, quality, and time. Do you think that human behavior will be affected because of the faster technology?

HATHEWAY: There is another factor that customers look at – information. That is what you see in a normal algorithm, an algorithm that is thirsty for information. That is how one decides to trade. Rather than the traditional trader who had to review all different types of information, the algorithms now are reviewing that information in real time. The trader is the parameter setter of the algorithms, so the human element still exists. It is the tools they are using that are changing. The change is rapid. The tools are changing as the destinations are changing. In a traditional listed trade, you typically use last sale to trade listed stocks because of the issues of transparency on the floor. You are either using a floor broker, or you are using last sale information. That will change dramatically. On NASDAQ, people do not pay as much attention to last sale. They still look at it, but it is the quotes that drive a lot of decisions. As technology allows these destinations to change, you have increased volumes and new tools that the ultimate trader uses.

PAUL DAVIS[21] [From the Floor]: Are you thinking about products that will compete head on with Pipeline and Liquidnet, and firms like that?

FRIEDMAN: We definitely see Pipeline and Liquidnet as providing a very valuable service to the buy-side. We actually have an investment in Pipeline from a while ago. In general, these firms serve the buy-side very well, and our client base is the sell-side broker-dealers.[22] We want to make sure that we provide the best possible service to our customers so that they can provide the best possible service to theirs. We are not in the business of competing with our customers. It is important to recognize that. After buying Instinet, we immediately sold off their broker operation because it is not a business that we believe we should be in. Our sales type clients provide a very valuable service to them, and we hope that they continue to do that in a way that best meets their needs. But our job is to make sure that they have an efficient marketplace to come to, as the ultimate destination to serve the client.

HATHEWAY: It is important to study our market structure to see if we are doing something wrong, something that requires the buy-side to look for alternatives in the primary market. We are constantly doing that. The area that we have to focus on is in the illiquid securities. That is where the buy-side is having the most difficulty finding capital and liquidity. It is a constant struggle. As you deliver market efficiencies, the willingness to provide upstairs capital dissipates. That is just a struggle that we have as a primary market. We do not just ignore the buy-side. We want the buy-side to have an alternative in how to trade.

JEFFREY BROWN (Charles Schwab & Co., Inc.) [From the Floor]: What do you see as the future of internalization by your market makers? Is it a viable business? I ask this in light of your move towards an agency market, the shrinking margins for market makers, Reg NMS, as well as your eventual exchange status if it ever comes about.[23]

CONCANNON: A lot of people have predicted that Reg NMS would effect internalization, but that is not how the rule works. With regard to retail internalization (internalization that typically occurs at the inside), Reg NMS should have no impact. With respect to institutional internalization, a block trade done outside the inside Reg NMS has an impact. There is a lot of debate about that one feature of Reg NMS. There is a potential block trade exception, which is referred to as a stop-order type. There is another potential block trade exception called a VWAP exception. There may be opportunities to commit capital outside the inside for institutions, and not

[21] At the time of the conference, Mr. Davis was Managing Director at TIAA-CREF Investment Management.

[22] Pipeline also has sell-side clients.

[23] In January 2006, the SEC approved NASDAQ's application to become a registered securities exchange.

have a dramatic impact upon internalization. The stat that most people miss (as Reg NMS applies to NASDAQ) is the stat of trade-throughs on NASDAQ. That is where the debate has centralized. If you believe the SEC stats or our stats, you are still talking about less than two percent of the NASDAQ market being non-compliant with Reg NMS. There are exemptions built into Reg NMS. There certainly will not be 100 percent compliance with elimination of trade-throughs. But it is a small number that has to wrestle with the Reg NMS trade-through rule. And we have to see how big the exemptions are for internalization.

The compression of profit opportunities in internalization has occurred over the past three years. You have seen a move to an agency market. Fewer and fewer firms will internalize and take the position risks. They will just push the orders into the central market. I do not know if there is a straight trend-line that suggests that, at some point, internalization dissipates. But, historically, there has been a negative trend-line.

BILL HARTS (Banc of America Securities) [From the Floor]: This question is for Adena or Frank. It is about market data revenues. Under Reg NMS there is this complex new formula that will be adopted. Many people comment that it is too soon to tell what this is all going to mean. Does NASDAQ know, or have an idea, given current trading behavior, who the winners and losers will be in terms of market data revenues? Who will be the winners among trading participants and among markets?

FREIDMAN: We certainly did take a look at it. Complex is an understatement. It is a very very complex formula. We met with the SEC to understand it better, and to understand their motivation behind it. The Commission wants to make sure that the market that produces the quote then receives the execution, at least receives data credit for it.[24] To clarify, the

[24] As of early 2006, 50 cents of each dollar allotted for market data, under the Reg NMS plan, is to be credited for each trade report while the remaining 50 cents is credited for the best price quoted. At the outset, the SEC's objective under Reg NMS, was to reward market centers that drive the quote as well as where trading occurs. Indeed, some analysts noted that Reg NMS encouraged brokerage firms to establish ATS facilities, partly for the market data revenue they would generate for themselves. Ultimately, the agency was looking to reward price discovery. But at the same time, it was attempting to discourage a practice known as tape shredding in which participants enter multiple, typically small orders, simply to generate market data revenue. Many observers described the initial market data formula proposed by the SEC as overly complex. It allocated revenues for market data among the SROs, "based on measures of the utility of their trades and quotes in the security." Each SRO would qualify for an annual payment equivalent to the sum of the SRO's trading shares, quoting shares and NBBO improvement shares in each network security for the year. However, to ascertain how much revenue each network was entitled to relative to the trading of each security in the network, the formula involved taking, "the square root of the dollar volume of trading in each security." There are three main networks that distribute and collect fees for market data for securities listed on the NYSE,

way the market data works in our space is that there is a gross revenue pool that is generated by user revenues. Each month we charge our market data out to the end user and we collect a general pool of revenue. That pool is then split among the market centers, based on their relative market shares. The way the NASDAQ's pool works is that it is split evenly[25] by share volume and trade volume. So, your relative portion of share and trade buying determines how much of the gross pool you receive. The SEC is proposing a far more complex formula that introduces quoting behavior as well as trading behavior. Also, it creates individual buckets of money for each security within the market. But it does not necessarily address anything related to the size or type.[26]

The logic is that if the formula rewards quoting behavior, then the firms that quote most actively will find themselves with more money. But we have concerns about that because you do not actually have to exchange money to quote in the market. We believe that it will give rise to some concerns related to capacity, gaming and the quoting space. How that revenue is then given out to market participants will depend on trends in the marketplace. There are some markets that do share. We share some of our data revenue with our market participants. Whether market participants will see any benefit from that data pool depends on whether markets have a sharing program.

We expect that there will be a lot of concern about adding the quote formula into the market data formula because of gaming possibilities and capacity. The SEC is moving forward with a quote formula. Who the winner or loser is today, really has no bearing on how it will end up playing out.

UNIDENTIFIED SPEAKER [From the Floor]: Which regulatory agency will we have to work with if something is listed on both NASDAQ and New York?

CONCANNON: It depends on where the trade occurred. If it is a technical trade-through, you report the trade to the SRO that is responsible

---

AMEX, regional exchanges and NASDAQ. In 2004, data revenue generated by NASDAQ, NYSE and the other market centers, accounted for $434 million, according to the SEC. NASDAQ and the NYSE, for instance, collected data fees from broker-dealers, buy-side firms and market data vendors. After deducting for expenses, net income is distributed to the individual market participants in each network.

[25] The "distributable revenue per trade" for a network, such as the network in NASDAQ securities, according to the SEC, is calculated by dividing the total distributable net income of the network by the total number of reported trades for the network's securities. Under the plan for NASDAQ referred to by the speaker, revenues are allocated to NASDAQ based on the average number of trades and the share volume of trades reported.

[26] The speaker is referring in part to the dollar volume of a trade. The SEC argued that a formula based only on dollar volume "would not adequately allocate revenue to the source of quotations relied on in pricing block trades."

for insuring that you complied with the trade-through rule. For example, consider a block trade of a listed security that you trade reported to NASDAQ. If it trades through the NBBO, we are obligated to have the NASD research why you traded through and to check your compliance. The cost of compliance will fall on us to ensure that you are complying with trade-throughs that come through our marketplace.

UNIDENTIFIED SPEAKER [From the Floor]: I am sorry. I was talking about an electronic order. If we send an electronic order and sweep NASDAQ and sweep New York, it effectively traded on both.

CONCANNON: If it is an electronic order, and it is a sweep order (which is a specific exemption), once you give NASDAQ the flag that you are doing the sweep order, you have transferred the obligation back to yourself. It becomes a membership obligation, ironically, and Reg NMS will be responsible for insuring your compliance with the trade-through. There is a membership component as well as a market component to it.

ANDREW BROOKS (T. Rowe Price Associates) [From the Floor]: I am thinking that you have done a lot of good things in terms of market structure, specifically, in your opening and closing process. You should be congratulated. It is terrific. But I am also wondering about something else. In some respects, our markets are like Sarbanes-Oxley. Perhaps we have overshot some things. With respect to Bill Christie, would you consider doing a five-cent minimum price variation pilot program to see if it might reduce inter-day volatility in some of your stocks?

CONCANNON: That would have to be done at the national level.

BROOKS [From the Floor]: Absolutely. You would have to be with everybody.

CONCANNON: But we would have to approach Congress because they have…

BROOKS [From the Floor]: I do not think so.

CONCANNON: Well, they were very much involved. I am not saying that we would need legislation, but Congress was very much involved in the decimal program that the SEC ran. Someone like Chairman Oxley was personally involved in decimalization. I have read some of the Christie study. There are compelling arguments in the study. However, the question is, at what level do you affect the increment of trading? The SEC, in Reg NMS, made a decision to affect the price increment based on the level of a stock's price. Sub-pennies are permissible for under a dollar stock. They basically said that the stock price should affect the increments, because you know how sub-pennies are permissible for sub-dollar.

This is a very difficult issue because as you create certain inefficiencies in the market, you also reduce volatility and maybe you get a little more liquidity on the inside as a result. So, are you taking benefits from the retail investor who trades in pennies? As you know, those dollars matter.[27] It is a balancing act that we have to wrestle with. I think, politically, that it will be very difficult to go to nickels in any stock that is publicly traded right now.

ROGER FREEMAN (Lehman Brothers) [From the Floor]: You have talked about some of the technology benefits BRUT brought you. I am wondering, as you integrate INET from a technology standpoint, what do you anticipate keeping from it, and what from BRUT?

FREIDMAN: INET is the fastest system in the marketplace. We obviously examined it as we did our due diligence. It is also very low cost. For those two reasons, we anticipate integrating onto the INET platform as the ultimate platform for all three of the liquidity boards. That is something that Bob Greifeld could talk a bit more about this afternoon in his session with Professor Schwartz. We look at that as something that we can do about a year out from when we close. That is our plan. As a standalone organization, we currently have plans to migrate to a new platform ourselves. We have the BRUT platform, we have the NASDAQ legacy SuperMontage platform, we intend to migrate BRUT onto NASDAQ, and then migrate NASDAQ onto a new platform altogether. In our roadmap that we described to the Street and to investors, we have an end date of about mid-2007. With the INET acquisition, we are saying, okay, we are into it a little bit differently. We are going to migrate BRUT onto NASDAQ, and migrate NASDAQ onto INET, that being about a 12-month integration. This way of doing it shaves some time off of moving to a new platform and getting a lower cost infrastructure.

CONCANNON: We took our time on the transaction. We studied the integration carefully. When we announced the deal, we wanted to come out front and tell the entire industry, "Yes, we have an integration plan." Migrating the entire NASDAQ trading onto the INET platform is full of details. It is a pretty compelling development. We thought that was the most important point. I personally know the INET platform, having worked for Island years ago. There is a guy by the name of John Ross who has changed that platform quite materially. It is far more scalable, much more transportable. That is what we found so attractive about it. It is an important acquisition for us from a technology standpoint.

FREIDMAN: We also considered how easy it would be to migrate new functionality onto the INET platform because NASDAQ has functionality

[27] At issue for the speaker are the unintended consequences of introducing a pilot five-cent minimum price increment program. That is because there are now potential benefits for retail investors who trade in pennies. Even though penny pricing has created certain inefficiencies, the gains from switching to a nickel price variation could be overshadowed by negative outcomes such as a reduction in liquidity. For this reason, the speaker says weighing up the pros and cons of nickel increments is like a balancing act. Switching to nickels would also be politically difficult.

that INET does not have, most notably, the open and the close. We want to be sure that we continue to bring the best of all our products into the new environment. We spent a lot of time understanding how easily we could add new functionality into the platform so that we could continue to innovate. This also involved looking at whether we will want to trade securities other than equities, and whether we will want to be able to transport that technology to other spaces. In our opinion, it is a very, very flexible platform for us to build on.

CHRISTIE: I know how these conferences work. There is always a hard open and a hard close for lunch. We will leave it at that. I thank our panelists very much for their most informative participation.

# CHAPTER 4: THE NASDAQ MARKETPLACE

Moderator: Wayne Wagner, *Consultant, ITG, Inc.*[28]
Kim Bang, *CEO, Bloomberg Tradebook*
Robert Hegarty, *Managing Director, TowerGroup Securities & Investment Group*
Richard Repetto, *Principal, Sandler O'Neill & Partners*
Jamie Selway, *Managing Director, White Cap Trading*
Henry Yegerman, *Director, ITG, Inc.*

ROBERT SCHWARTZ: Like many of you, I remember the days when we had NASDAQ and Instinet, and everyone viewed these two entities as standalone competitors. But I always believed that Instinet, even back then, was part of the broader NASDAQ marketplace. Look at it from the perspective of the issuing companies. The issuers care about the market where their stocks are traded. The fact that Instinet benefited customers in trading NASDAQ stocks added value to the broader marketplace. That same sense of contributing to the broader marketplace persists today in new areas.

After the order-handling rules were introduced in 1997, Instinet discovered for the first time that it was, in fact, an ECN. Fast forward a little. Now Instinet finds out that it is not an ECN anymore, but instead is part of NASDAQ. Yet the broader NASDAQ marketplace continues to exist with a variety of new alternatives, including Pipeline, Liquidnet, and others. This is the new NASDAQ marketplace that we will focus on in today's conference. So, let's keep our vision of the NASDAQ marketplace broad. And who better to lead the charge to the broader marketplace than Wayne Wagner!

WAYNE WAGNER: We are going to do this a little differently than the previous two panels. We will open this up to the audience as soon as I get my own two cents in. I was flying over here in the new American Airlines pretzel class. To ward off thoughts of starvation, I was thinking about what

[28] At the time of the conference, Mr. Wagner was Chairman of Plexus Group. On January 3, 2006, Plexus Group was acquired by ITG, with whom Mr. Wagner is now a consultant.

is going on in this industry. What are the underlying motives behind this consolidation?

I came up with three hypotheses. First, what we have is a gathering of allies in preparation for the clash of the titans – New York and NASDAQ – to determine who will be the dominant market in the future. Second, on a more clandestine note, what we are seeing is the establishment swatting down the flies who have made their lives so miserable for the past 15 to 25 years. Basically, the major market centers are trying to put out of business the ones who have been sapping lifeblood from the major exchanges. Third, we are witnessing a re-gathering of the strength of a central market. This is in contrast to what has happened in the past 15 years, a time when the buy-side dominated the debate about what is needed, and about which way it is going to go; something that I am quite familiar with and highly support.

When you think about the needs of the big institutional traders – I am including hedge funds – there are two things that an exchange must do. First, it must gather and enhance liquidity. Reto Francioni spoke about that. Second, it needs to preserve confidentiality and trust. You cannot have an institutional-sized trading market unless your orders are kept confidential and anonymous. You also must have the ability to create liquidity when the ebb and flow of the buy and sell streams are not producing it. Now I would like to congratulate myself. This is my first speech in about ten years that did not include the word 'iceberg' (laughter).

Let me introduce my panel. We have Kim Bang from Bloomberg, Rob Hegarty from TowerGroup, Rich Repetto from Sandler O'Neill, ITG's Henry Yegerman and White Cap Trading's Jamie Selway. All of these professionals are extensive users as well as tremendous thinkers on markets and market operations. Let me bounce one question down the line. Who will be the 800-pound gorilla?

KIM BANG: The only 800-pound gorilla in our space is Bloomberg. We sit on top and are fully integrated with that 800-pound gorilla. But in terms of transactional space, we are quite modest. Our focus is very much on servicing the Bloomberg client, the institutional client if you like. Actually, there is a fair amount of speculation now that Bloomberg Tradebook is one of the few independents left holding an ECN medallion. The question is, does that now create a business opportunity for us? My response is, the economics of operating an ECN have diminished significantly. When you look at some of the ECN business models (some of them are public), you can see that the revenues and profits associated with that endeavor are minimal at best. To have a valuable business proposition in that space, you probably have to morph into an exchange, charge for market data, membership fees, and compete for company listings. We do not see ourselves in the exchange business. We are going to stay focused on servicing our institutional Bloomberg Tradebook clients as a global agency broker. That means building our trading technology, order tools, strategies, transaction cost analysis, etc., on the client's desktop. We will remain agnostic in terms of the liquidity venues that we integrate with and provide our clients access to.

WAGNER: Rob?

ROBERT HEGARTY: I believe that the question you asked is, who will be the 800-pound gorilla? If you could take a gorilla and split it up into two 400-pound gorillas, I think it is pretty clear now who they will be (laugher). But in the future, you have to place your bets on innovation. I agree totally with Kim's point that this is a highly commoditized marketplace now. The economics of that model are not what they were when the markets were first formed back in the late 90s. It strikes me as strange, but the ECN marketplace and the U.S. equity marketplace are starting to look a lot like the auto industry. We will wind up with the Big Three. If you play that out a little, it opens us up to lots of things. In other words, when you look at the auto industry today and what happened with the Big Three, we see serious consolidation that opened the way for foreign competitors. Consolidation in our equity markets today makes them ripe for foreign competition.

So, when looking at who is the 800-pound gorilla here in the U.S., it is only going to be a matter of time before the one that innovates fastest becomes the big gorilla. Clearly, the race is on between our two markets.

RICHARD REPETTO: First, I am a sell-side analyst, and I have to mention my research restriction on NASDAQ. I cannot speak specifically about the company. I have permission from the lawyers to talk about the marketplace. What I find interesting is that we have come full circle. Previously, it was the battle of two 800-pound gorillas, the NYSE and NASDAQ. Now, through technology, innovation, and the entrepreneurial efforts of a guy like Jerry Putnam, you are seeing a lot of competition. Liquidity is definitely fragmented in the NASDAQ market.

In the space that I cover–which is trading companies, whether it is the online brokers, or the Knights, or the exchanges – you are starting to see the first major consolidations that can offer significant synergies. The NYSE and Arca (which I can talk about) are unique because they are not really integrating their trading platforms. The potential here is to bring together liquidity and to reduce costs. I think that is what we are going to see in the future. I agree with Rob, we are getting closer to models were we see multiple products and diversification, like you see on Euronext and on Eurex overseas.

HENRY YEGERMAN: I agree with much of what has been said so far. Obviously, the conventional wisdom is that NASDAQ and the NYSE are going to fight it out and that, at some point in time, one of them will win.

Then there will be a battle with some of the big European exchanges as people go after the global marketplace. But, if we look at all of this as a kind of evolution, we know that sudden shocks brought about by regulation or technology innovation sometimes move markets in unforeseen directions. When they do, they can create exotic organisms. I want to point this out because Wayne asked us something that was a little controversial just to start some conversation…

WAGNER: I asked you to start a fight (laughter).

YEGERMAN: If we accept that the buy-side and other participants in the market want competition, where might that competition come from? I would like to throw out one possibility: perhaps a new wave of competition might come from the Order Management Systems (the OMS vendors) somewhere down the line. But it is not going to happen tomorrow. This is how it might play out. You will see consolidation in the OMS marketplace. You will end up with a couple of OMS vendors that have hundreds of large institutional clients. At that point in time, they might seek to internally match the buys and sells among their clients. The OMSs are moving away from a subscription model to more of a revenue capture model. They have tremendous stickiness on their client's desktop. They are hooked into the client's back office systems. As they seek to grow, they will respond to what the ultimate clients want. I want to throw that out, not in terms of who the 800-pound gorilla might be, but who in the future could tender to that gorilla.

JAMIE SELWAY: Can I throw the first right cross (laughter)? Sounds like Henry is describing Liquidnet to me (laughter). To answer Wayne's question, the 800- pound gorilla is the client. It is the guy with the order, particularly the buy-side trader. What you have seen over the past month is the old-line exchanges going out and acquiring businesses that were built around servicing customer needs, servicing the people with the orders. This is a radical transformation. Exchanges will no longer be protectors of vested interests for people who are out running businesses, people who are trying to grab orders. Ultimately, the exchanges will be into investor fulfillment for the first time. That is a real sea change.

YEGERMAN: Just to follow up. The way I just put it is, whoever controls the order flow, will use it to their own advantage.

WAGNER: Let's open this up to the audience.. I have a series of fiendish questions to ask my panel, but I would rather get questions from the audience. Jim.

JAMES ANGEL (Georgetown University) [From the Floor]: The restructuring of the U.S. equities business brings up many questions about how the markets have been regulated. I am interested in the panelists' views about what kind of regulatory structure makes sense in the new environment.

HEGARTY: I will take a stab at that. My sense is that surveillance is a function that requires some intimate knowledge of the trading process, and that it probably should be organized by the marketplace. Member regulation is somewhat redundant today, as we have multiple regulators overseeing multiple markets. We would be having member related interactions, books and records, registrations, with three different entities, the NASD, the NYSE, and the SEC. That could potentially be normalized into a single regulator. Actually, the SEC, with that concept release,[29] is now in the process of looking at these very questions.

WAGNER: I would add the CFTC to the list.

BANG: As we talk about products broadening out and having a wider set of options, the regulatory oversight could be multiple entities. The question is, should we be looking for a single regulator across multiple products and exchanges? The other interesting point is that the regulatory obligation is shifting from exchanges to market participants. The buy-side traders invariably incur more fiduciary regulatory responsibility as the marketplace becomes more electronic, and as they gain more ability to facilitate their own executions and to make decisions as to where and how they execute a trade, how and where they route an order, and the various strategies and tools they employ.

REPETTO: Jamie says the market looks to be more customer focused. The only reason it has moved in this direction is regulatory change. If the NYSE was not getting automated, if Reg NMS was not being implemented, or if you step back even further, if it was not for the order-handling rules, we wouldn't have had the ECN development. We are definitely moving to customer-centric models now, but regulation has got to be right beside it. I do not know what is the best regulatory structure, whether it is a single regulator or not, but the regulator will have to be separated from the markets, especially in light of today's scrutiny of bias and objectivity. Regulation should be easier with more electronics. Currently, systems are being gamed. We have seen a lot of problems. I cover LaBranche; you have specialists, or human [intermediaries], with a role where they can take advantage of the system.[30]

YEGERMAN: I believe the question was about what type of regulation would make sense. Regulations make sense if they are commensurate with the technology that is feasible to implement them. If we have regulations that go beyond the scope of the firms that need to comply with them, we will end up in a situation that will ultimately blow up on somebody. Much more

[29] SEC Concept Release Concerning Self Regulation, Nov. 18, 2004. See, http://www.sec.gov/rules/concept/34-50700.htm

[30] At issue were regulatory investigations into specialist activity at the NYSE.

data will need to be captured. That translates into a very practical problem of handling databases, being able to maintain clean data, and a lot of other issues that take place on a nuts and bolts level. If we try to regulate beyond what firms can actually do, we will end up with another Sarbanes-Oxley situation. People will be spending millions and millions of dollars. They will be diverting their resources trying to comply with these regulations. Ultimately, they will perhaps be trying in vain.

WAGNER: I have to hand it to the SEC on their remarkable restraint in setting up some directions in which they want to head, and letting the market sort it out.

TERRY O'CONNOR (Cedar Creek Management) [From the Floor]: Could one of you tell us whether you think the current clearing and settlement systems are appropriate for the market that you think will develop in the next several years? Is there a better model? How do you think clearing and settlement will change in the next few years?

HEGARTY: We just looked at the different clearing and settlement systems across the globe. As it turns out, the U.S. clearing and settlement system is pretty efficient when you compare it to the rest of the world. In Europe, for instance, it is very fractured. The various systems are not in sync with each other. From a model perspective, our current clearance and settlement system, with DTCC at the center, is pretty efficient. In many ways, it did a lot to bring the markets back together when the marketplace was fragmented. There was still a single place to go to in the clearing and settlement process.

The biggest challenge is dealing with the volumes that we will experience. We heard on the previous panel that we have not seen anything yet in terms of volumes. I completely subscribe to that. Also, in terms of quote volumes, which is independent of the clearance and settlement issue. But there is no question that we will see an even greater increase in trade and share volumes. A lot of people do not realize that share volumes have been flat for so long while, in the meantime, over the last three and a half years, trade volumes have quadrupled on both exchanges. What happens when share volumes also take off? Those trade volumes will go through the roof. It will be exponential growth.

WAGNER: Yes but, Rob, compare the securities clearance with say MasterCard or Visa. Within minutes of your signing the restaurant check, it is possible to get a record of the debits and credits in the transaction. From that standpoint, it does not look so efficient to me.

HEGARTY: I would have to agree with you that, on the timing side, it is not very efficient. Let's drag out the old argument. We should be going from T 3 to T 1, right? There is room for improvement there, but the model itself works. The timing could certainly use some improvement.

SELWAY: If I could ask a question, how does the DTCC process compare to the clearance and settlement process for the Chicago Mercantile Exchange, the CME? Because one of the thrusts of the question could be that, as we watch this consolidation, some people are declaring an end to the equity trading business in terms of growth. They wonder about these new companies, this new NYSE group, the new NASDAQ with INET. They wonder what they will do. Will they trade options? Will they trade fixed income? Is there something they can do that looks Merc-like, or Deutsche Börse-like, in terms of building the vertical silo that does trading, clearance, and settlements under the same roof? In your study Rob, how does our clearance and settlement on the equity side compare to the other markets?

HEGARTY: The biggest difference, again, is the timing. On the Merc, it is possible, desirable and, in fact, necessary to have real-time trading, clearance, and settlement. It is necessary to have them all at the same time due to the volatility in those markets. I do not agree that we are looking at the end of growth in the equity markets. There is no question that some of the other asset classes will grow faster. But that has less to do with market structure, and a lot more to do with the types of investments involved. Frankly, the buy-side, whether you are talking hedge funds or traditional funds, are more interested now in trading things like derivatives because, number one, they can. They can because these instruments are more transparent and, number two, they are becoming more comfortable with those instruments over time.

The name of the game is trying to achieve alpha. Over the last three or four years, the buy-side has recognized that achieving alpha in the equity markets is next to impossible. When you combine equities with options, derivatives and commodities, it becomes much more feasible.

BANG: I would add that clearance and settlement are quite efficient in the States. Outside the U.S., they can be very complex. We are seeing trends in the U.S. where clients are asking us to provide a wide array of services. Clients do not just want access to execution venues. They also want, for instance, algorithmic strategies, direct market access strategies, special tools, and ways to trade across multiple liquidity venues. With regard to trading across multiple liquidity venues, our clients want one, single, average price ticket at the end of the day, with one central settlement party.

In Europe, there is fragmentation across multiple liquidity venues. For instance, take a stock like Nokia. Not all clients are able to settle a stock like Nokia in the market of their choice with one average price ticket, having access to liquidity across multiple exchanges. That sort of best execution service has been invaluable to our clients.

WAGNER: Jamie, we had a conversation about how the distinctions between markets, participants in the markets, and users of the markets are blurring to the point where you are not sure exactly who you are looking at. Would you share some of your thoughts?

SELWAY: Sure. It is a trend to watch. My sense is not to say that the equity markets will stop growing, because I do, in fact, think they will grow. But these companies casting about for things to do raises some interesting questions. You can be metaphysical about what is an order type, and about what is a trading strategy.

Exchanges provide pegged orders. ECNs provide pegged orders. Is that an algorithm or is it an order type? Is pegging a function that should belong to an exchange, or to the user of an exchange? The NYSE has CAP orders.[31] The best I can tell is that CAP orders are a poor man's VWAP engine. It is conceivable that the exchanges themselves could start to provide some algorithmic functionality. It makes you think back to the days of early ECN-hood, in the 90s, when the ECNs were competing with the market makers. You had this tension between the market participants and the marketplaces. This is something that will increase, not decrease.

WAGNER: Well, that is particularity true in the hedge fund world where you really cannot tell if somebody is consuming liquidity or is providing liquidity.

BANG: I would add something. NASDAQ said earlier that it had zero intention of providing their particular order types and functionality directly to the buy-side. They are looking to provide these indirectly via their members. Part of the problem with a particular exchange or liquidity venue providing these various liquidity tools and functionality is, as we discussed earlier, the opening and closing crosses that NASDAQ has. The crosses are off to a good start, but they do not include all of the ECN participants' liquidity in the continuous market. Think about how large the ECNs' market share is, and how aggressive price setters, the ECN price setters, tend to be around the open and the close. All of that liquidity does not participate in the opening and closing spin. To facilitate an auction cross, exchanges will have to be all-inclusive, to integrate ECNs and other exchanges' liquidity.

[31] The NYSE, in a filing with the Securities and Exchange Commission, defines CAP, or Convert at Parity Orders, as orders as "orders in which the specialist may convert all or part of an unelected portion of a percentage order, and may trade on parity with the elected or converted portions of the order, as long as the specialist is not holding orders at the same price that do not grant parity." Bloomberg Tradebook's Kim Bang, in a public comment letter to the SEC dated Jan. 6, 2003, raised objections on several grounds to NASDAQ's proposal to establish a Closing Cross where trading interest is subject to automatic execution. The letter contended, for example, that because the Closing Cross would exclude trades, and therefore liquidity, in NASDAQ securities from ECNs that use "order delivery" rather than "auto-execution," the closing price would likely be imperfect. The letter also contended that the proposed rule change would mean a denial of access to ECNs, amounting to an inappropriate burden on competition.

Exchanges have gone a long way to establishing bilateral linkages, smart routing and so forth among themselves, but opening and closing crosses that are focused on just one liquidity venue will have limited upside potential.

REPETTO: When anyone would ask John Thain about a potential IPO, prior to the NYSE and Arca merger announcement, he would always allude to the need for growth at the NYSE. To be a public company, he wanted to show that the NYSE had a growth vehicle. I know for a fact that the NYSE has looked at all of the revenue that is tied to the exchanges, and it is in the billions of dollars. But, unfortunately, a lot of those dollars are tied to membership. As the NYSE completes the merger, if it goes as planned, the members will get equity in the company, and Thain will not have the same conflicts. I can easily see him reaching out to grab more revenue that is generated from the exchange.

WAGNER: What an interesting concept. There is a question back there.

UNIDENTIFIED SPEAKER [From the Floor]: I would like to ask about NASDAQ's closing cross, and then maybe expand across other trading initiatives that have been introduced recently. The way the closing auction is designed, the disclosure of trading imbalances prior to the close should encourage the participation of contra-side liquidity from dealers who are providing capital. It is well known that dealers will not provide capital on the close unless they feel that there is an opportunity to extract a profit from that type of trading pattern. So the NASDAQ cross, through its design, raises issues including pre-trade market impact. Post trade, the question is whether the trading price is somewhat exaggerated to benefit the interests of the capital provider over those of the fiduciaries.

If we consider the effect of new systems on transaction costs and on transaction cost analysis for fiduciaries, should we think of the regulators as having a role to promote disclosure of information about transaction costs? For example, should they know the basis point cost of using this close versus other trading methods? Or, should we think that the fiduciaries themselves are responsible for conducting their own research, and for understanding whether they are getting a fair shake with these trading systems? I use the closing cross here as an example. I would like to ask the question more generally in terms of the broader issues that have come up.

WAGNER: Jamie, you are an active user of those crosses. Do you have any comment on that?

SELWAY: I would say that that they have been a great success. We heard earlier today from Professor Pagano about some of his academic research with Bob, and we heard Frank Hatheway explain it. I won't go through that again. But, to the institutional broker – which is what we are – the crosses allow you to participate in liquidity events at the open and the close.

The liquidity events are particularity interesting for small-cap names. Before this, they just were not possible.

Before the cross, if you used a Market On-Close or Limit On-Close order, or if you were an indexer, you called a dealer and got a guarantee. The dealer priced the order, sometimes based on a 100-share print. Progressing from that non-transparent environment, to an environment where the imbalance is displayed for the final ten minutes, has been very helpful. You can now bid for the imbalance. You can compete for it. Have you been to an art auction and bid against dealers? If you want the item you are bidding on, you probably can beat them because of the dealer's cost consideration. The dealer needs to take the item into inventory and then re-sell it. But if you really want the stock because you are working for a client who wants to own it, you can be more aggressive.

Maybe you can answer further, Wayne. The SEC has a concept release out there about the disclosure of institutional trading costs.[32] It turns out that it is a really hard question, and maybe one best left to the marketplace. If you do a bad job for someone in Pipeline, Liquidnet or the NASDAQ closing cross, the client is probably going to know it before the SEC disclosure report that comes out next month tells them that they did a bad job.

WAGNER: I am in agreement here. You do not want to go very slowly on this. Particularly, you do not want to mislead. The easiest things to report are commissions, but commissions are only part of the big, I am not going to say it… (laughter).

YEGERMAN: I want to add to that. I personally do a lot of transaction cost analysis, and a lot of clients on the buy-side are doing precisely the kind of thing that you are talking about. They are measuring the costs relative to different destinations. They are measuring the costs by different strategies, by different order types. They are tying it into 10-minute, 15-minute or half-hour time windows. They are doing comparisons, to see what works and what does not work for the next kind of innovation. This is something for people on the buy-side who actually have that information available to them, and can capture it in their systems. They get into a virtual feedback loop in terms of measuring and improving their own trading strategies while reducing their costs. What you are talking about is the present, not just the future.

WAGNER: I put that into the category of research. Research into your own process and how it contributes, is part of the edge that an investment manager has. It should not, to my mind, become public property. It should

[32] See, SEC Release No. 34-48966, Dec. 19, 2003. Re. "Measures to Improve Disclosure of Mutual Fund Transaction Costs." http://www.sec.gov/rules/concept/33-8349.htm.

be exercised in the interests of the clients of the investment management organizations.

BANG: Our clients are looking for the ability to do real-time transaction cost analysis. They want to do pre-trade analysis, monitor trade impact in real-time, and undertake pos t trade analytics. They want to do it not only on the NASDAQ closing cross. They want to do it across strategies, liquidity venues, and brokers. They want to compare. They want to be able to design their own benchmarks, and they want to see how those various venues, brokers, algorithms, and crosses compare. They want to know how they stack up relative to the benchmarks they are being assessed and evaluated against. Traders are actively searching for superior results. They are learning to use real-time TCA, or Transaction Cost Analysis.

WAGNER: Paul.

PAUL ARLMAN (Federation of European Securities Exchanges) [From the Floor]: Two members of this panel, and one or two of the previous panel, mentioned competition with European exchanges. However, when I see that the SEC stops trading screens in the U.S. from European, Canadian and Australian stock exchanges, when I see that the futures community did not exactly welcome Eurex when it applied (hail to the CFTC as they were consistently open), when I see that Americans may own European Exchanges (IPE, the International Petroleum Exchange in London, is one case in point), and finally, when you talk to American politicians they say that ownership of an American exchange by foreigners is basically a "no-no," I have to wonder what kind of a tilted playing field we have here. I would be very happy to hear comments about this from the members of this panel.

WAGNER: Sounds like a rhetorical question to me (laughter). Does anybody want to comment?

REPETTO: I know a little bit about the CME. Certainly Chicago was not welcoming Eurex, but there were also significant barriers to entry. This goes back to the original question about the clearing advantage. If you are going to trade Euro dollar futures, you have one place to clear that, and that is with the CME because they are vertically integrated. So there are some impediments that did not allow the Eurex to gain traction here. You mentioned the IPE. That is owned by an Atlanta-based company, and it is doing very well. It is going all-electronic, and is one to watch. It is a U.S.-owned exchange that has already penetrated in Europe.

HEGARTY: I am one of those who believe that the changes have opened up the market to, I do not want to say more foreign competition, but to more global competition. There is a big difference between the two. The difference is that we will have global firms owning the markets. It will be less relevant where the parent company is based. You even saw that in the

NYSE and Arca deal. It is hard to know who bought whom there. What we will see is a merging and a globalization of these markets. The fact is that an Atlanta firm owns the IPE (a lot of people do not know that). But we are going to see a more global marketplace. It will not matter where the markets are based. The New York Mercantile Exchange, NYMEX, is going to be the competitor to the IPE, and its floor-based energy exchange will be run out of Dublin, Ireland. So we are seeing a crossing of the borders at least with the commodities and futures exchanges.

WAGNER: Question in the back there?

UNIDENTIFIED SPEAKER [From the Floor]: I do not want to pick on the CME, but do any of the panelists have an opinion about whether or not they will open up and allow their products to be traded on other platforms, for instance NASDAQ or the NYSE?

REPETTO: Here is a sell-side analyst's opinion. I say absolutely not. They have no incentive to see any liquidity pulled off their platforms. They own the futures exchanges, the Euro dollar contract, and these equity-emitting contracts. When Jerry gets up and talks about diversification, he is going to have to build liquidity. He has bought an auctions exchange so he has some small measure of liquidity there. But to grow in the future, I do not think that the CME will ever let him license liquidity over to the NYSE.

WAGNER: That is a standard response. It is always perfect just the way it is right now. We do not want any competition, and we cannot have it. Every time that happens, every time you get that competition, what happens to trading volumes?

SELWAY: But part of it is a regulatory hurdle, right? The CFTC allows exchanges to mint monopolies, and the SEC does not. The SEC has a concept of UTP, or unlisted trading privileges. If Jerry Putnam convinces some small company to come to list on NYSE junior (ArcaEx), NASDAQ can file its own papers so that this same company can trade its listing simultaneously on NASDAQ under these UTP arrangements. On the equity side, that has hit ahead on the exchange traded fund product. An ETF is sort of a hybrid. It needs to be structured using an index, or using a piece of intellectual property. But it is an equity and so it can trade everywhere. We won't bore you with the details of the lawsuits that have been sorting that out over the past year, but the same thing is happening with index options now. Essentially, it just comes down to a regulatory question. The CFTC allows something that the SEC does not.

REPETTO: That is the difference. I do not know if everybody gets that. If you look at David Krell on the ISE, there is one clearing corporation, the Options Clearing Corp. You can trade an option on any one of the five or six exchanges, and you can buy it on one exchange and sell it on another. On the CME, you cannot do that.

HEGARTY: I will add one thing to that. The key word there was "allow." "The CFTC allows something that the SEC does not." I am not sure if they are going to have a choice eventually. I know that it is a regulatory environment, but we keep asking the question, "Will this one allow that one to trade?" It does not matter whether they allow it or not because, if it is a regulatory issue, regulations can be changed. We have seen that happen twice in a huge way in the last eight years, with the order-handling rules in 1997, and just recently with Reg NMS. If the regulators determine that it is good for the market to allow instruments to be traded elsewhere, they are going to regulate it in. It is this balance between competition and regulation that we are looking at now, and it is difficult to tell the difference between what is being regulated and what is the result of competition.

NARI JOTE (Baruch College) [From the Floor]: With this global market, a lot of European companies are not very happy with this regulatory compliance. At one conference last year, I was told by the leader of the German delegation that they do not like it, and many other companies want to de-list from the stock markets here. Is it good for us here in the U.S. or not? Is it going to create more competition or not? What is your opinion?

HEGARTY: Are you talking about Sarbanes-Oxley specifically? There are burdens placed on companies that are trying to get into the U.S. market. But you do not have to go outside our borders to find those burdens. I personally know people who own companies who have decided to de-list because of the burdens that things like Sarbanes-Oxley places on them. I have a friend who owns a 12 million dollar company, and it was going to cost him almost a million dollars to comply with Sarbanes-Oxley. He de-listed. Do the regulations hinder our ability to grow and to garner business? No doubt about it. There is no question about it.

JOTE [From thc Floor]: It is good for us hcrc?

HEGARTY: I do not think it is good for us here. I do not think it is good for global expansion. I do no think it is good for the markets.

JOTE [From the Floor]: OK, thank you.

YEGERMAN: If I could take a little different view on that. I generally agree. However, you have to view regulation as a form of insurance. You keep paying out insurance, and you keep paying out insurance, and you never see any benefits from it, it is just a cost. Until, that is, a disaster or a catastrophe strikes. Then, all of a sudden, the insurance is valuable. I agree that it eats away at business here. I have heard a lot of talk about people de-listing, especially European companies. But if there is some sort of crisis or scandal at some point of time on a European exchange that can be attributed to a lack of regulation, then the pendulum can swing back. Then people will see the value of the regulation. Then investors in turn will consider it a more necessary requirement. We do not have a crystal ball, but I see regulation as a form of insurance and I think that it should be understood that way. Whatever we think about insurance (laughter).

WAGNER: Not reinsurance, right (laughter)? Any comments that anyone would like to make on another topic here?

YEGERMAN: Yes, Bob Schwartz mentioned NASDAQ at the start, so I have to give you these numbers. Right now, there are 2,768 companies listed on the NYSE with an overall market cap of 20 trillion. There are 3,271 companies listed on the NASDAQ (about 500 more than the NYSE) with a market cap of 3.7 trillion, one fifth of the NYSE. Regarding volumes on the exchanges, the margin is starting to narrow. Yesterday's volume was about the same. But, on average, you see volumes on the NASDAQ that are 1.8 or 1.9 billion, but there is a lower volume on the NYSE. Now this is an informal study. If you are saying that there is only one fifth of the market cap on the NASDAQ, how much volume can really trade on the NYSE when it gets automated? I would look at other things like the float of these companies. I would look at the volatility, I would look at what sectors they are in. But, however you cut it, there will be a volume increase. It is just a matter of trying to get your arms around how big the increase will be.

BANG: I would like to comment on that. I think, Henry, that you are spot on. Reg NMS's impact is clearly on NYSE listed securities. It is interesting that the NYSE has a trade-through rule. But there is a lot to think about – the way Reg NMS pans out with respect to differentiating between slow, manual quotations and fast executable quotations, and with the exception for the sweep function, and so forth, and with New York's Hybrid proposal, and with the Open Book proposal being out there. Reg NMS will take the NYSE into the 21st Century. There will be greater transparency in the marketplace. There will be more electronic access to quotations on the NYSE. The fiduciaries will demand connectivity to all of the regionals, to all of the ECNs. They will contemplate alternative execution decisions. I am referring not only to how they route and sweep, but also to which venues they choose to post their orders.

In the intermediate term, we are going to see fragmentation in the NYSE listed stocks, and much more automated electronic trading. W expect that trade volume will increase significantly. Anecdotally, I have heard statistics from Ameritrade and E*Trade that 70 percent 80 percent of their clients trade NASDAQ listed stocks. Basically they trade NASDAQ listed stock because of better price transparency and electronic direct market access. Retail and institutional investors will begin to trade more effectively in NYSE listed stocks once Reg NMS is fully instituted.

WAGNER: Kim, your comments make me think about the dealers here. How will they be affected by that? Their services are dearly needed in any marketplace I have ever seen. Are we discouraging dealers? Are we encouraging, are we opening up new opportunities? What is going on?

SELWAY: I would say that we are transforming them. The NYSE will look a bit like NASDAQ. On NASDAQ, the old-fashioned dealers making block bids are still there, just a lot less involved than they used to be. There is a new type of dealer though, the high-end, high-frequency, statistical arbitrage firm, that is doing 80 to100 million shares a day. Their idea of a profitable trade is making 3/10 of a cent. That is not possible for listed securities today because the cost of trading on New York – both the informational costs of leakage and the opportunity costs of not getting a cancel – are too high. But when those strategies are brought to bear on the listed side, they will be the liquidity provision drivers of the volume that other people have talked about. But it is more a transformation of dealers. Proprietary trading will always be there. Risk taking and liquidity provision for profit is intimately important for the markets. It is not going away, it is just being transformed.

WAGNER: Professor Schwartz.

SCHWARTZ [From the Floor]: All these changes afoot have implications for the existence of the floor at the New York. Will the floor endure? If the floor does not endure, where would you see all of those orders going that today are being handled by the floor brokers, not the specialists, but specifically the other floor brokers? Electronic? Internalized upstairs? Maybe both, but predominantly which?

BANG: The inherent problem is that, if you hand an order to the floor, it is a single destination exposure, and you will not have representation. You will not have representation because the quote or the order is not going to be sitting on a specialist's order book. It will be with the floor broker. That means, by definition, that they can be readily traded through, and I believe they will be. There are some similarities when you look back at the evolution of the NASDAQ marketplace. The dealers used to be the source of the manual quotations, SelectNet used to be the order delivery protocol, and if a dealer received a request to trade against the quote, he or she had a certain amount of time to respond to that order. The dealer would have 10 seconds, sometimes 20 or 40, and sometimes they did not even respond. As a result, the electronic venues in NASDAQ picked up market share over a period of time. As they did, clients readily traded through the market makers' quotations. I think that you will see something similar at the New York, with respect to the floor brokers. Certainly, this will happen in the top 100, most liquid stocks. When it comes to the less liquid stocks, there is value to having a floor broker negotiate and go through the auction process of trying to attract the other side.

WAGNER: David?

DAVID KRELL (International Securities Exchange) [From the Floor]: You all spoke about the titans and gorillas clashing here, but you have not said one word about the regional exchanges. What happens to them?

HEGARTY: I will take a shot at that one. First of all, some of the regionals are ripe for acquisition. Look at what happened with the Pacific. If they do not have a value proposition for their members, if they cannot demonstrate how they are adding value to the process, they can go in only one of two directions: either they get acquired or they go out of business. We have seen some of these regional exchanges get fairly innovative, and start to do product expansions. You have the electronic options being done on the Boston Stock Exchange, with some amount of success. Look at the Philadelphia and what it is trying to do in terms of building liquidity. If the regionals do not have a game plan other than trading off of New York's listed equities, their time will be limited. They have to become more electronic, and shutter a lot of the posts on their floors.

ALLAN GRODY (Financial Intergroup Advisors) [From the Floor]: We have heard about the futures markets acquiring each other across borders. Do any of you in your strategies think about the electronic futures exchanges, as more equities markets move away from floor-based to electronic trading? Has anyone building these electronic equity platforms looked deeply into these electronic futures platforms to understand how they were built out? Has anyone thought about how they may incorporate some of the unique features of the futures markets into these new electronic equity markets? The futures markets have evolved their electronic trading systems independently of the equities markets. These futures markets can do things in unique, different and spectacular ways.

BANG: We have seen a lot of interest from our clients, not just in futures, but also in options and foreign exchange. We are not a market center. We are an agency broker that provides access to those liquidity venues. I can definitely confirm that there is a lot of interest in derivatives trading. That business is up by 50 percent in just the last couple of months at Bloomberg Tradebook. We started trading financial futures about a year ago, so we already have pretty good traction. Futures are a very rapidly growing space, and demand for the direct market access and electronic trading in energy and metals should be next.

WAGNER: Think of what you could do if, in one venue, you could trade futures, single stock futures, options, ETFs, bonds, you name it. Oh, yeah, and also stocks (laughter). What kinds of strategies could you come up with, with those things being easily arbitraged and worked against?

HOWARD ROSS (Baruch College) [From the Floor]: Do you people have any thing against honest income statements (laughter)? I would like to know, because the value of Sarbanes-Oxley is above some of these steep compliance laws. I know how the small firms suffer, but I think you ought to take into account the value that this kind of protection has for the investor.

BANG: The value is clearly there. The problem is that there is regulatory arbitrage going on. In the transactional space and listings, the risk is competition from overseas, or even within our own exchanges. Locally, in the regional exchanges, there are different rules regarding short selling and things like that. This creates a regulatory_fractured marketplace, and opens the door for competitive arbitrage. That is problematic. I am not suggesting that we should go out and adopt the regulatory oversight that the European regulators demand. But, certainly within our own marketplace, we should try to harmonize the way in which stocks are being transacted across multiple liquidity venues. The SEC is attempting to do this with Reg NMS. It makes sense from a regulatory perspective. There should not be different ways of short selling in one exchange versus another exchange.

HEGARTY: I want to respond because I was the one who said it. I think it is bad for everybody all over. Clearly, there is value in honest balance sheets and accounting. I agree with Kim entirely, the value is there. The real question becomes the cost of implementing Sarbanes-Oxley. Its premise is absolutely on target – restore honesty, trust and confidence in markets. It did a lot of that. The real question is, at what cost to different firms?

REPETTO: I do not know the answer to that. I can tell you, though, that the optimal cost is not one million dollars for a 12 million dollar company (laughter). At some point there has got to be a balance.

WAGNER: We have had a great time. But we promised to get the babysitter home, so we have to end. Please join me in thanking out panel (applause).

# CHAPTER 5: REFLECTIONS FROM THE SELL-SIDE

Moderator: Brett Redfearn, *Senior Managing Director, Bear, Stearns & Co., Inc.*
Jeffrey Brown, *Senior Vice President, Charles Schwab & Co., Inc.*
Matthew Lavicka, *Managing Director, Goldman Sachs*
Mark Madoff, *Director of Listed Trading, Bernard L. Madoff Investment Securities*
Michael Murphy, *Founder & President, Piney Run Capital LLC*[33]
C. Thomas Richardson, *Managing Director, Citigroup*
Bruce Turner, *Managing Director, CIBC World Markets Corp.*

BRETT REDFEARN: In the NASDAQ space, we have seen the seven-plus ECNs effectively combined into one market. On the New York Stock Exchange side, there has been active competition from Archipelago, and now the NYSE and ARCA are being combined into one market. There are pros and cons here. Some of the pros are more consolidation and potentially more market efficiency. The con, of course, is this fundamental concern about a lack of competition in a world with two superpowers where each has significant dominance in their particular marketplaces.

If NASDAQ jumps to 80 percent market share post consolidation, it will further increase its significance in the NASDAQ market. What does that mean? Is that good or bad for competition? What are the pros and cons? Mark?

MARK MADOFF: Both of the deals will be very positive for competition in the marketplace. They will result in a far more efficient market. You will see NASDAQ with better technology. You will see the New York with better technology on the auto-ex, or automatic execution side. If all goes well, looking a couple of years down the road, with the New York Stock Exchange offering auto-ex and the NASDAQ offering auto-ex, there will be more competition. We are setting the table for more competition, not less.

[33] At the time of the conference, Mike Murphy was Institutional Client Relationship Manager at Wachovia Securities.

The most difficult hurdle that a market participant faces is a fragmented market. A fragmented market is inefficient. It can also result in a single participant gaining dominance and control.[34] As you add technology to the mix, all of a sudden everybody has access to a quote rather than only the select few who are standing on the floor of the New York Stock Exchange. Both of these mergers will be dramatic positives for all market participants. Market makers in particular will have a far bigger role going forward than they ever had in the past.

The market may look different. I do not know what we will find. It might be characterized by the same desk of 300 people, each making markets in 25 names. But more and more firms will be making markets off the floor of the New York Stock Exchange. They will do so because they can. It may not necessarily be a person standing there in the crowd. It may be an algorithm that is saying when to buy, or when to sell. Once the doors are open and there is electronic access because of these mergers, the barriers will all be gone. It seems like a fairly rosy picture going forward.

REDFEARN: You are talking mostly in terms of the listed market becoming more electronic, and you anticipate more upstairs market making in listed securities. Does anybody have a comment on that?

THOMAS RICHARDSON: I have heard a lot about the pro-competitive results of these mergers. It is the kind of competition that would be applauded by the likes of John Rockefeller and Bill Gates. It is all about swallowing your competitors. It reduces a number of those entities that have caused the positive competitive changes that we have seen over the last five or six years. That is a troubling thought. Who will now be driving competition going forward? Think back a mere ten years. We had two markets, NASDAQ and New York. Did they fiercely compete with one another? I suggest that they did not. I believe that competition will be severely hampered if that is the environment we end up with.

MICHAEL MURPHY: One of the reasons why there were two markets back then was that NASDAQ traded stocks in a different kind of market structure from today. Since then we have gone through this period of technology growth, the new frontier if you will. Ten years ago, you would come to conferences like this and there would be only a handful of people in the audience who really understood what a few people were trying to do.

[34] As an example, Madoff cited, in a subsequent interview for this book, the New York Stock Exchange. He explained that trading in NYSE stocks was effectively fragmented by the exchange, because it was able to dominate the market with the support of its membership. He is referring here to the exchange's ability to curb competition for better-priced executions away from the exchange. However, under the SEC's Reg NMS, competition in the trading of listed stocks is opened up with "trade-through" reform, which permits executions at better prices on other market centers.

Now we have a new generation of people coming into the business who grew up on technology and understand how to use it. Today you can build a business and make money-using technology efficiently. That is one reason why we had so many ECNs and so many different sources of liquidity at the time.

Some people had the ability to go out and take advantage of other people who knew how to use it. Now that we have more people with a better understanding of the field, we have been able to have not nine or 10 ECNs but two: the NASDAQ and the New York Stock Exchange formats. There will be some competition, but not as much as one might think there should be. This is because the world is more efficient, and people understand it better.

RICHARDSON: Pricing is a dictating factor here. As NASDAQ integrates Instinet, they will have about a 50 percent market share of the ECNs on the Montage platform. And with the New York Stock Exchange taking over Archipelago, Archipelago is clearly going to keep a watchful eye on NASDAQ's pricing. Not to mention the regionals that, by virtue of Reg NMS, are considered the chosen ones. They will have top of the book protection. If any of the regionals hook up with a new ECN, or an old ECN platform, or Lava-like technology, they will be able to keep prices low and competition will continue to exist.

REDFEARN: So you think that New York's acquisition of Archipelago is going to mean that Arca will able to compete more aggressively for NASDAQ's flow? There is also the issue of Arca potentially being able to compete on the company listings side as well…

RICHARDSON: If they choose, they will definitely be able to compete on price. That will keep NASDAQ in check.

On the listing side, Archipelago is stating that when it merges with the New York Stock Exchange, it will offer an NYSE-lite type of listing. In my opinion that would potentially cannibalize the New York Stock Exchange' brand. Right now you have a pretty wide spread between what NASDAQ gets for listings versus what the New York gets. If Archipelago aggressively gets into it, that spread will narrow. This would not be a good thing for the NYSE in terms of its revenue model.

BRUCE TURNER: In terms of running a business on the trading floor, it is clearly easier to deal with two entities rather than the multitude of entities that were out there before. The aggregators were able to combine everything, but they charged a fee for their services. It would be more efficient if there were only a couple that were linked and easier to access. The problem is that you have to balance inefficiency with pricing power.

The last thing you want to hear is a sell-side panel whine about costs. However, the reality is, if these two entities, for example, get pricing power, and raise their fees, I cannot pass along the additional costs to my institutional customers, since I do not have any pricing power. And our e-costs, are something that we look at very closely. I would echo Tom Richardson's point. There is an opportunity here for some of the regionals to offer a low-cost alternative to get your bids protected in a Reg NMS world, certainly by top of the book. But even if they have bids below best execution, the execution quality statistics should drive participants to take those bids out anyway. One or two of these electronic regionals could potentially provide low-cost competition to the big two. That will keep prices down somewhat. But I am not optimistic that prices will continue to decline. There has been a pretty dramatic transaction cost price war over the past three or four years. This has obviously been benefiting everyone. But there is a risk of turning course in the not too distant future.

REDFEARN: Do you think that exchange transaction prices will be going up?

TURNER: I am afraid they will, yes.

MATTHEW LAVICKA: We have been talking about two 400-pound gorillas. But the 800-pound gorilla in all of this is (and has been) the SEC. There will be competition as long as the regulations provide a level playing field. All you need is a quote somewhere in the Montage, whether from a regional exchange, or from the NASD's Alternative Display Facility (ADF). You may see it as a kind of consolidation and the pricings may get a little higher, as was suggested. But I do not think it is far-fetched to suggest that competition will pop up to drive prices back down.

REDFEARN: Let's move past the issue of competition in the equities markets. New York has announced that they will be trading options, that they are looking to trade fixed income products, and have mentioned possibly getting into other businesses. It sounds like NASDAQ is thinking similarly. Do you folks feel that NASDAQ now has to diversify its business offering to stay competitive? Is diversification the key to their ability to compete in the future?

JEFFREY BROWN: It always makes sense to have a one-stop shop where you can find whatever financial product you want to access. The problem is this: As an equities market begins to diversify and add derivatives to its flow, and you are an electronic market, it raises the issue of side-by-side trading, something the SEC has never approved. Yet, that issue may be removed now. As electronic, automated markets are developing for the equity and derivative products, you can, in your workstation, set up nearly the same environment that you would have if the SRO offered all those products itself. I am not certain that it really benefits markets to diversify. They should focus on what their strengths are, and make that the most competitive, the most attractive product for their customers.

REDFEARN: So, you think the front ends will be able to integrate different securities markets, so that the markets themselves do not have to do it?

BROWN: We have seen them do it with regard to fragmentation in the equities market. There has been a market solution to that problem. We have seen the market itself subsume those efforts.

REDFEARN: Does anybody think that there is a benefit to the market having the equities and the options products all trading in one spot? Is this compelling for the sell-side?

MURPHY: It is a perception problem. The New York Stock Exchange has always had the perception that they would be the bigger of the two. NASDAQ has come a long way trying to grab part of that territory. But think worldwide. There is a world out there that is bigger than the New York. It is a big coup for the New York Stock Exchange. I think that NASDAQ should and probably will respond.

BROWN: But New York has tried derivative products in the past, and they did not do very well. New York ended up selling them off. We will see how well they do this time.

LAVICKA: There are clear advantages to the market makers and specialists who are providing liquidity and trying to manage their risk. If they can do that, in a combined fashion, across the equities and options, it makes a lot of sense. Does NASDAQ need to do that now? I do not know. They are probably not going to have to focus on it. But there are some advantages to the marketplace if they are able to do it.

RICHARDSON: I see consolidation among exchanges continuing. But I think that combining derivatives with futures markets makes much more sense than combining derivatives with single stocks. You do not necessarily need a platform to trade both single stocks and derivatives.

Jeff Brown's point is well taken. The New York has been in this business before. They got out of it. It is funny, now they are back in it. But that is not why they bought Archipelago.

MURPHY: Much has changed since New York was in the business. There is a much better understanding of it out there. Better technology is one of them.

TURNER: I want to go back to the first question: Does NASDAQ need an option or a derivatives platform? NASDAQ right now needs to get its act together in terms of Instinet being integrated. I give them a lot of credit for what they have been doing with Brut. That is going very well from my perspective.

NASDAQ has the advantage of getting Instinet, versus the Arca-New York combination. NASDAQ has done Brut already, and they are a more electronic market. That gives Instinet NASDAQ a big leg up.

NASDAQ can add derivatives at some point. But I would like to comment from the trading desk point of view. There would have to be more demand for these derivatives products-from the upstairs trading desks. We are in the facilitation business. But I am not seeing any incredible demand for derivatives trading even if there are some trading participants who approach the market saying 'Oh, I am long on stock, I will go sell a derivative.'

If I could hedge my business, trust me, I would have been doing it a long time ago. There are times when you can get away with a slight hedge. But the markets are now much more efficient and transparent, so this does not have the same importance as before. Because the markets are all electronic (courtesy of the ISE and others), a lot of information is more widely accessible. So NASDAQ does Instinet, they get tremendous market share, they put a lot of product through their plant, and it would be significant improvement from our point of view.

MADOFF: The difference between today and years ago, when the New York Stock Exchange had difficulty trading derivative products, is that the table has now been set for the derivative products, effectively, to be traded on the New York Stock Exchange. The technology is there – Arca, of course, comes to mind – so there is no reason why you should not have side-by-side trading of equities and options, or other derivative products.

So there is a difference. Today, you can go to the upstairs market where the competition is not coming from one specialist versus another. It is coming from every major firm on the Street who can now effectively become a market maker in the equity, in the option, and in the future. We are in an entirely different world compared to what it was in the past. Technology allows everything to come together. On one floor of Tom's office they can make a market in the equity, on another floor they can have technology that is making a market in the option, and on yet another floor they are making a market in the future. In addition, you have an algorithmic approach that is tying it all together.

It all gets pumped out looking like a single quote. Both NASDAQ-INET and New York-Arca will now provide the perfect platform for all of this to take place. It is very likely that you will see success where there had never before been an opportunity.

TURNER: You are arguing the technology efficiency case that we did not have in the past. I would suggest that, at the end of the day, it is much better to have all the various trading platforms consolidated.

There are stat arbitrage guys out there doing this all day long. They have built these machines that are wildly fast. The ECNs will tell you how important it is to have their order flow. That is why the ECNs worry about hundreds of milliseconds of trading speed to get their executions done.[35] They have actually built systems to support this sort of thing.

The initial question was, should NASDAQ accommodate it? At some point yes, they should. But I do not think the benefit to NASDAQ right now is getting that flow. The reality right now is that NASDAQ needs to get Instinet done.

REDFEARN: It used to be at brokerage firms that the NASDAQ desk would be completely separate from the listed desk. But there has been a convergence there, those desks have merged. Does anybody think that, two years down the road, the equities business and the derivatives business will come together upstairs to take advantage of some of this convergence and the opportunities out there?

TURNER: In some cases, they already have.

LAVICKA: Yeah, and it is not two years – it is now.

REDFEARN: This may be true in some cases, but certainly not at the majority of firms. Let me ask another question with respect to that. Electronic trading is basically changing not only the nature in which commissions are being charged by firms. We are also seeing other trends happening at the same time. There is an increased use of direct market access by our customers, and increased pressure to un-bundle stock trading and research.

We can see what the FSA is doing in London. The broader issue of unbundling is indirectly linked to other changes in the marketplace. This raises new questions about the implications for the sell-side, and about what it means for the prospects of our business.

Would anybody be willing to comment about how this will affect the way that the sell-side is operating, and our profit opportunities in the future?

TURNER: I will give it a try. Most trading desks have the ability to cross between NASDAQ and New York. I suppose that a few dinosaurs are out there that are single-exchange focused. But, for the most part, everyone has already done that morph. We talk about algorithms. Clearly, having an automated market in New York will help. It is all about efficiency. Algorithms are a fancy way of saying efficiency, of using machines to do mundane, routine orders that used to be 20 percent of your volume. Now you put your order in a VWAP, or a TWAP machine. You pick your algorithm and you put it in there. It is all about our needing to get more efficient on the sell-side.

[35] Turner is referring to stat arb firms and hedge funds that use ultra high-speed trading systems to send trades to the NYSE, practically at the speed of light. These firms install computer applications within close proximity of the NYSE to reduce the latency, or the length of time it takes to receive and process market data and to send orders to the exchange for execution.

The sell-side probably is still over-brokered. I know I am talking about cost a lot, but we are fighting a cost battle both on the regulatory front and on the infrastructure front that we need to get ahead of. The only way to do it is to bring technology to bear. That is what is happening on the upstairs trading floors.

LAVICKA: Flexibility will be the key. It is not just a matter of unbundling. How do you set your various price points for all the different services that you are offering? Some firms play in just the algorithmic space; they will have just one price point. Some firms will play with DMA all the way up to capital commitment; they will have all kinds of levels within there. I do not view it as simply unbundling. And you have two products; there will be a range of prices for an array of services.

REDFEARN: Do you think that this will be driven by regulators, or by the increased downward pressure on commissions along with institutional customers who are increasingly demanding?

TURNER: It is already there. We already have a tiered structure. We have not officially said what the value of research is, and perhaps we do not want to discuss this here. But we have that…

REDFEARN: What is that formula?

TURNER: You have a tiered rate for customer executions that goes all the way from three mills to five cents a share, or maybe six cents in some cases. These sophisticated guys on the sell-side have gone out and run buy-side client profitability models. From these models, they get a sense of the value of what they are providing. They find out what their customers are getting from their services. It is very hard to quantify the value of research, but they are attempting to do it. The reality is that every major institution today is transacting on multiple price points.

RICHARDSON: I was going to piggyback on what Bruce said. I agree with him. The FSA has pushed the envelope very, very hard on soft dollars and on bundling. But, in the end, they backed off. I think they got the intended consequence of what they wanted, in the form of a back door on bundling[36] and brokers coming up with these profitability analyses, as well as fund companies pushing for transaction cost analysis. They are saying "Hey, what are you really paying for, what are you really getting?" I do not

[36] The UK's Financial Services Authority (FSA) in late 2005 published regulations on "Bundled Brokerage and Soft Commission Arrangements." The regulations require U.K. investment managers, "to disclose to their customers details of how commission payments have been spent and what services have been acquired with them." The regulations do not call for the unbundling of research and executions. However, some analysts expected the FSA's policy to encourage this in the U.K. and across the globe, especially in U.S. markets.

think the regulators will push hard. They will get what they want from market forces.

MURPHY: It is difficult to put a price on research. Its price is always changing, depending on market conditions. In the late 90's the cost of research was very high, and money managers' performance was very strong. Now we have been in a flat to down market for a few years, and it is very difficult to make money. Most of us managers will tell the brokers that research is not so important right now because we are not making a lot of money.

It is interesting to go through periods like this. It is very difficult for a broker to build a business when he does not know, until the market turns one way or the other, what his services are worth. Execution is an important part of the process but, just as important or maybe more important, is the idea portion of the equation. We must be careful. If you squeeze all of the juice out of the orange, there will be no one there to provide the ideas. What happens is that the process falls down, and the investor loses in a major way. For me, it is very difficult to put a price on research.

REDFEARN: I have one more question, and then we will open the discussion up to the audience. My question has to do with regulation. The consolidation and convergence occurring in the marketplace leads me to question whether or not we need two regulators. I know this was mentioned earlier, but I want to hear your thoughts about it. Do we or do we not need two regulators coming in to inspect brokerage firms when they often ask a lot of the same questions?

BROWN: I will start off, Brett. As we consolidate the markets, we need to consider consolidating the regulatory structure that we have today. There is no greater cost, both from an administrative viewpoint and from a compliance viewpoint, than regulatory oversight. With two prominent SROs – the New York Stock Exchange and the NASD – we have duplication and divergence. We have duplication in the sense that, for the same rule, you have to provide both entities with the same information on exams, audits, and inquiries. We also have divergence when, for the same set of facts, we have different sets of rules.

We must have different sets of procedures in place, we must monitor those procedures, and we must have the CCO and the CEO sign off, confirming that we have done all these things properly.

The regulatory structure must be reconsidered and made cost effective. Regulation is of paramount importance to any broker. I do not think that anyone in this room would say that we need to cut regulation. What we need is to make regulation cost effective. To do this, the first step would be to form a single SRO that would provide the necessary oversight in a more cost effective manner.

RICHARDSON: A couple of things have to happen first. As a part of its deal to buy Archipelago, the NYSE will have to spin out the regulator. And NASDAQ has to get their exchange license, which they do not have yet.[37] That should enable them to get away from the NASD. We could then move in the direction of, hopefully, one SRO. That would be a great wish list for me, or for our firm.

REDFEARN: With that, let's take some questions from the audience. No softballs, just bring on the good ones. Back there on the left?

UNIDENTIFIED SPEAKER [From the Floor]: Under the new Reg NMS rules, broker-dealers will be allowed to sell their own market data. This is something that some of the broker-dealers have been arguing for. They believe that it is their market data, and that they should be the ones to get the revenue. But a lot of work is involved in becoming data providers. What are your thoughts about whether the broker-dealers will get into the market data provider business?

TURNER: All right, I will admit it. I did not know that we could sell our market data.

BROWN: It is proprietary data. It is likely that you will be allowed to sell your own proprietary data. That is defined as data that are not included in the National Best Bid or Offer. It is really the property of the plan that governs securities – whether it is the New York Stock Exchange (which is the Consolidated Tape Association) or the NASDAQ role (which is called the NASDAQ UTP Group). They will be allowed to sell their proprietary data.

TURNER: The exchanges or the broker-dealers?

BROWN: The exchanges. You raise a good point. We at Schwab would take exception to the very fundamental premise that the SROs own the data. We do not believe they do. By law we are required to give that data to our SRO, and then we have to buy it back from them. It seems to be an insane way to set up a structure. But that is the way it is. You are correct. They will be selling their own data soon.

REDFEARN: A clarification is needed there. I do not think we are saying that broker-dealers can sell the bid, ask and last sale market data. I believe that the rule makes a distinction between what data coming from exchanges must be part of the overall Securities Information Processor, or SIP data, and other proprietary data products that individual markets and exchanges can sell separately. We have a situation here where there is a new potential cost for broker-dealers and a revenue opportunity area for exchanges. For example, the markets are offering a new array of data

[37] NASDAQ became a national securities exchange in NASDAQ-listed securities on August 1, 2006.

products, most notably depth-of-book data, which is becoming increasingly important for market participants who want to see deeper liquidity. We have got NASDAQ selling their TotalView product and other proprietary data products as well, such as OrderView, OpenView and ModelView.

On the listed side, we have the New York Stock Exchange selling its OpenBook, another proprietary market depth product. This SIP only has to include the best bid and offer at each market as part of consolidated quote. On the NASDAQ side, with Level II data, a lot of this data have, to date, been consolidated; going forward less of this has to be part of the consolidated tape or the NASDAQ UTP plan. Whereas before a lot of this was consolidated, less of it is now part of the consolidated tape or the NASDAQ plan. More of it is being sold separately. With transaction costs potentially getting squeezed lower, this is an alternative revenue source for the marketplaces. And it could be a real cost concern for some of us in the brokerage community. Is that what you were getting at?

UNIDENTIFIED SPEAKER [From the Floor]: My reading of Reg NMS was that broker-dealers would be allowed to sell their proprietary data, as Jeff Brown was saying. But the broker-dealers would be able to sell it directly, not through the exchanges. Is that your reading of Reg NMS and, if it is, do you think the sell-side will start selling that data?

LAVICKA: If the broker-dealers have a public quotation, they are obligated to provide it to an SRO. The quotation then becomes part of the public quotation system, and there is a separate fee structure for it. Beyond that, I think that if the broker-dealers have some kind of unique data that they think they have an ability to sell, I do not think there are any restrictions on that.

TURNER: At the risk of being direct, if there were money involved, then we would sell it (laughter). But I do not know the details of how I would do it.

BROWN: Yeah, but that is going on right now. The ECNs have published their books on the Internet for free for years. So that data have been available. That is all they really have to offer. But it has been offered for free.

LAVICKA: You have to be careful. If it is pricing information that is the best quote and you start selectively giving it out, you are going to run afoul. Someone could say, we think that is a quote from your firm, and you must do that through an SRO. That is one of the problems. The SEC mandates that this quotation be provided to the SRO, but they do not necessarily mandate how much people can charge for disseminating it.

REDFEARN: Any other questions? Yes, sir?

NARI JOTE (Baruch College) [From the Floor]: I was reading Securities Industry News, and mention was made of "data czars." How is this handled in each company? Who is responsible for the data, the information technology department or the business alliance that supports it? Any stock, or any information about buying or selling, depends on reference data, contemporary data, pricing data and so on. There is no one person who knows everything about that. What are your views?

TURNER: I think they are addressing the fact that we all – I will speak for our firm – have disparate systems. We are in the process of going through all this regulatory change. AML[38] regulation and Sarbanes-Oxley are ones that come to mind. As part of the requirements, we are trying to get all this data together. Part of it is how you deal with the customer. It also ties to client profitability, and transactions, and what sectors you are in. People want to get a sense of running the trading business far more efficiently and effectively, and they are trying to get the data together.

We are in a data quagmire that we are trying to get out of. We have these very disparate systems. People are approaching us saying, "We will figure out a way to get it in all together." Frankly, the Fed does not care that we have disparate systems. They want to make sure that your AML data are right. That is what we are facing. It does not tie into market data, the quote and transaction data that you have to publish.

REDFEARN: The Securities Industry News article is talking about market data being utilized all over the place within firms. Several different people have different levels of responsibility for it. We need to centralize it more efficiently with all of the issues that are at play here.

BROWN: Brett, you and I served on one of the committees that oversee the market data world. Something that we face at Schwab, and that we have been pressing for, is more unification of the administrative process. We have four plans that govern all of the market data generated by the financial industry in the United States, for equities and derivatives on equities, and each of them has its own contracts that we have to sign. Each of them has its own audit. Each requires its own procedures that we have to put in place, monitor, and provide information on.

The system is woefully inefficient and costly to broker-dealer firms. We see consolidation in the marketplace, and we want to keep on consolidating this product that we must have, and which our customers need. It can be done in a far more efficient manner.

REDFEARN: The other issue that comes up in those committees is that there are more and more proprietary data services that each of the markets is selling separately. If New York manages Tape A and sells Tape A data, and NASDAQ manages Tape C and sells Tape C data, and so on and so forth, and each of the markets is simultaneously selling proprietary data while

[38] Anti-Money Laundering.

consolidating the public data, this raises some questions. Are there any conflicts here? Are there some synergies for primary exchanges that are not necessarily beneficial for market data consumers?

There have increasingly been calls to get one independent administrator to look over these different plans. That has not been resolved. My gut feeling is that as long as the existing governance structures remain in place within the Consolidated Tape Association and NASDAQ UTP, it is unlikely that we will see much change there.[39]

NARI JOTE [From the Floor]: Who will be the financial engineer in terms of controlling the business side of the technology? Ultimately, we are being driven by technology, and we do not want to see anything like Y2K in the future.

TURNER: On any trading floor today, the technology people are part of the business management unit because there is no other choice. If it came to market data and that was a revenue source for us, we would all be involved. Anyone thinking that technology is a separate entity from what the business is trying to do and from what trading is trying to do would be mistaken.

REDFEARN: Absolutely. The working relationship between technology and business is and must be very tight.

UNIDENTIFIED SPEAKER [From the Floor]: I have a two-part question regarding the two proposed mergers that we have been talking about. What are the odds that one of the mergers does not go through? And if that happens, how does it change the dynamics of competition?

REDFEARN: People have said that any one of these deals without the other deal would probably have been less likely to go through. But people have also suggested that one deal begets the other. If NASDAQ was not acquiring Instinet, it would be harder for New York to close its deal with Arca, and vice versa. People I have spoken to are optimistic about both deals going through because there will be two big players, not one big guy versus one small guy or somebody else. What are the rest of you hearing?[40]

LAVICKA: It is not a matter of whether it is going to go through or not, but of how long it will take. You have to deal with the Justice Department. You have to deal with the non-profit chain of the New York Stock Exchange. There are a whole host of things. I am sure that there are

[39] As of writing, the existing governance structures often require unanimity in decision-making.

[40] NYSE completed its merger with Archipelago Holdings, operator of ArcaEx, on March 7, 2006. Earlier, on December 5, 2005, NASDAQ announced it had completed its

some rules that have to be filed and changed to allow for it all to happen. It will be more a function of how long, two years versus nine months.

BROWN: Why would one of them not succeed? It seems to me that if they are both going through the SEC, and the SEC chooses to accept one and reject another, it would be very significant. That would be something to be very concerned about. But if one of the deals falls apart for its own reasons – if one of the sides in one of the deals backs out, for instance – that should not impact the other merger's chances of going forward.

MURPHY: I think that they will go through. Number one, the SEC seems to be for it, and I have heard very little discussion on the negative side. People seem, for the most part, to agree that it will be good for the industry. With that in mind, I think that it will take a while, and that it will probably affect the hybrid model that the exchange puts in place. And there are other things out there right now that will be affected because it will take a while. We will have to comment on everything.

REDFEARN: Any other questions?

UNIDENTIFIED SPEAKER [From the Floor]: Two questions. What impact do you see Reg NMS having on the regional exchanges? Does it make it more relevant because they can compete, or are they more irrelevant as a result of it? One argument that I have heard in SEC circles is that, as a result of the new duopoly from these two mergers, we will have somebody rise from the ashes and become a more effective competitor. Are any of you guys looking to invest in one of these that might become a more effective competitor?

BROWN: We already raised the idea that Reg NMS may create opportunities for bids and offers to be posted on regional exchanges because they will be protected under the trade-through rule. We will have to see when we get the final rule. But again, I am not sure that all the regionals will survive under that scenario. Whether there will be enough buy-in to pay the bills of any particular exchange remains to be seen. The regional exchanges have their own problems. Many are still brick and mortar establishments. At a time when we see the New York Stock Exchange moving to automation. A regional exchange cannot afford to remain in that type of business. It will have to automate.

REDFEARN: The pro for regionals in this environment is that, given how the trade-through rule will work, the top quote of all markets will be protected. This creates value to the franchises of regional exchanges. If regionals can attract competitive quotes, those quotes will be protected in the marketplace to a greater extent than in the past. They will not only be protected if they are at the national best bid or offer, or NBBO; they will also be protected if they are the best bid or offer, or BBO at that particular market. In other words, if an upstairs

---

acquisition of INET. The U.S. Department of Justice approved the both transactions on November 16.

trading desk is trying to put up a cross through the national best bid or offer, they will not only have to take out the NBBO quotes, they will also have to trade with all of the quotes sitting at the top of the book at regional exchanges if those quotes are better than the cross price. This dynamic of breaking up crosses will be part of the incentive for traders to quote on regional exchanges. So there is some inherent value that this rule creates for the regional stock exchanges.

The con for regionals in this environment is that one of the reasons why we are seeing these deals, specifically the NASDAQ-INET deal, is that the revenue from transaction fees in this business has shrunk, shrunk and shrunk. Look, for example, at NASDAQ's top tier pricing of 22 cents per 100 shares for adding liquidity, and 27 cents per 100 shares charge for taking liquidity. This adds up to an effective rate of two and a half mills. This is pretty small. To stay profitable in this space, markets need significant economies of scale. And it will be difficult for small regional markets to make the extensive technology investments that are required to compete and, at the same time, to grow scale and be able to turn a profit.

TURNER: If they can get pricing power, then the regionals will have a shot. Especially the electronic ones, and those with low costs.

MADOFF: Volume will flow to the most efficient markets – those with the lowest prices and the best executions. That has been the case for a while now. Reg NMS will not all of a sudden result in a regional exchange becoming a viable option simply because they can offer price protection off the book. They must also offer an efficient way of getting there. They must also offer other aspects of their system, and allow for best execution. They will have to step up to the plate and commit capital. Ultimately, committing capital – risk taking – is the only way to get an 11Ac1-5 number with a price improvement[41] that will make one execution destination different from another.

If somebody gets together with a regional and creates an entity that is willing to do that, the regional can survive. But volume will flow to the best and the most efficient. If somebody buys market share but has a poor effective spread, volume will not continue to flow to that destination.

LAVICKA: There will always be innovators out there coming up with better mousetraps to bring buyers and sellers together. Now they have a vehicle to do that if they partner up with one of the regionals. There will always be some business model that will make these regionals work.

[41] Market makers can offer price improvement by competitively using their own capital to narrow the spread between public bids and offers. The results will be reflected in data publicly disclosed by market centers under the requirements of SEC Rule 605 (formerly known as Rule 11Ac1-5). Market centers, including exchange specialists, NASDAQ market makers, ATSs and others, are subject to this disclosure on the monthly quality of their trade executions for customers.

BROWN: There is one other piece required in this, and it may be resolved in the final draft of Reg NMS. That is manual quotes, quotes that are not automated. The re-proposing release in December still maintains that, under a broker-dealer's best execution obligation, you still have to access manual quotes. If that is the case, this whole idea that we will be bouncing from automated market to automated market is not quite true. If you bypass a manual quote (which the trade-through rule says you can do), you may have violated your duty of best execution. The SEC's Office of Compliance Inspections and Examinations will be coming to your door very shortly to comment on that. The SIA as well as many people commented on this remaining element. We will see what the SEC does about it.

REDFEARN: A word regarding Liquidnet. The initial Reg NMS proposal stated that any market that grew beyond five percent market share in a given security had to provide "fair access." That is what people initially thought would happen. Then, at the open SEC meeting on April 6, the Commission came out and said that they are inclined to give Liquidnet an exception to this rule. A lot of people will be very interested in the details of that exception. Will this be an exception from five to ten percent, or will it be a blanket exception that goes up to no end? This will be debated quite a bit more. Certainly, if Liquidnet were to attract a 50 percent share in certain securities, there would be concern among other market participants who cannot see the quote and who cannot access the market. We will be watching very closely to see how this pans out. Questions? Miranda?

MIRANDA MIZEN (American Stock Exchange) [From the Floor]: There is a lot of talk about Reg NMS and its impact on the exchanges. Could you touch on how you think the proposal will affect your own upstairs business and your block trading?

LAVICKA: We are all waiting for the rule to come out. Yes, there is a trade-through rule, but there are a host of exceptions to it. That is the part that you really have to see to get into the specifics of how the rule will affect us.[42]

REDFEARN: In the listed marketplace, when upstairs firms would try to cross-large trades, these crosses could often get broken up when they went to the exchange floor. This was much less of a factor in the NASDAQ market where it was easier to cross-large trades upstairs without being broken up.

[42] As of writing, Rule 611, the order protection rule of Reg NMS, popularly known as the trade-through rule, requires that market centers route orders they receive to other markets if those other markets have superior prices. These prices must be accessible in under one second; otherwise they can be ignored. The idea of the order protection rule is to prevent market centers, such as exchange specialists, from trading-through other market centers without satisfying all 'top-of-book' quotes in the market. Therefore, limit orders with the best bids or offer are protected under this rule.

Now, with the trade-through rule applying to both listed and over the counter stocks, you have a situation where you can be broken up not only by the NYSE floor, but also by any other market. For NASDAQ stocks, as well as listed, you can be broken up by any displayed quote that resides at the top of the book of a given exchange if it is superior to the price of the cross.

Technology will have to be developed for cases where traders want to cross or print trades away from the inside market. This technology must have the functionality to take out various "top of book" quotes before such crosses can be printed. Another, second thing, as was mentioned earlier, is that the SEC has included a stop exception in the final rule. This is different from the existing block trade exception. But with this exception, the SEC is allowing upstairs firms to continue to commit capital to customers and to print large trades at prices that were agreed to earlier – the stop prices – through the NBBO quote at the time of the print, as long as the firm is "under water." For example, a trader would work a 100,000 share order for his customer at such and such agreed upon price, as long as he is working that order in the market in accordance with the order-protection rule. When the order is completed, if the trader is losing money – if he is on the down side of the trade or under water – then he can put up a print that is away from, or through, the best displayed display quote at that point in time. We are looking closely at the fine print as to how these exceptions will work in practice.

LAVICKA: There is also the VWAP exception.

REDFEARN: Yeah, the VWAP exception as well.

LAVICKA: Benchmark exception, whatever they call it.

REDFEARN: We expect to see the use of this as well. These types of trades are becoming a larger portion of the market. Tom.

RICHARDSON: I want to interject something here, Brett. We have not talked about just a simple trade. Suppose the account wants to sell 250 Microsoft, and Microsoft has five to ten quote updates in a second. The account does not want to stop. It does not want an average price. It just wants to sell the stock. It wants the price that you give them. The account does not want it in bits and pieces. It is 30 cents, 31 cents, they sold you 250 at 30. But it could take anywhere from one to five seconds to go back and forth between the sales trader, the account, and the trader, and then all the way back to the sales trader, and then the buy-side trader, and guess what? That is 25 or 30 quote updates and that means the stock is moving.

We think that that will force people from a surveillance perspective to build tech databases. You will need a tech database because you will have to snap the inside every time you are trading. We think that the $150 million figure that was thrown around for technology upgrades for Reg NMS is quite low.

REDFEARN: OK, we are out of time. Thank you very much. We appreciate it.

# CHAPTER 6: REFLECTIONS FROM THE BUY-SIDE

Moderator: Peter Jenkins, *Senior Vice President, New York Stock Exchange*
Andrew Brooks, *Vice President and Head of Equity Trading, T. Rowe Price Associates*
Paul Davis[43]
Robert Felvinci, *Senior Vice President, Alliance Capital Management*
Dan Royal, *Co-Head of Equity Trading, Janus Capital Group*
Lisa Utasi, *Legg Mason*[44]
Ken Zimmer, *Senior Trader, Frontier Capital Management*

ROBERT SCHWARTZ: As usual, I am blessed with some great moderators. I still think of this one, Peter Jenkins, as buy-side Pete (laughter). I understand he went over to the dark side (laughter). I have learned a lot from our discussions over the years, and I have taught him nothing (laughter). So Pete, you have a great group here, and guys you are in great hands.

PETER JENKINS: Thank you, Bob. When Bob asked me to moderate a buy-side panel I had to remind him that I am with the New York Stock Exchange (laughter). But all joking aside, I am the head of the NYSE's institutional client group. And I am fortunate enough to deal with these people all the time. We do not talk only about NYSE issues. Often, we also talk about market structure, and the things that the buy-side needs. On behalf of my panel in general, these are their opinions, and not necessarily the opinions of their organizations. They do not have to say that, but I want this discussion to reflect their own personal opinions.

[43] At the time of the conference, Mr. Davis was Managing Director at TIAA-CREF Investment Management.

[44] At the time of the conference, Ms. Utasi was Senior Equity Trader at Citigroup Asset Management.

We have seen a lot of change on the buy-side. There is Reg NMS, speed, connectivity, algorithmic trading, smart routers, the changing role of the intermediaries. We have NASDAQ, Instinet, the NYSE, and Arca, and we are going to hear a lot of different buy-side opinions today. These opinions should differ from those of the sell-side. And, if you have any opinions or questions, we would like to fit them in rather than hold them up for the second half.

Let's begin with a very broad question: What are the most competitive and challenging prospects for the NASDAQ market over the next few years? Andy, start us off please.

ANDREW BROOKS: A couple weeks ago I might have answered this a little differently. Clearly the integration of the INET platform into NASDAQ, and NASDAQ migrating all of their trading to the INET platform in a couple of years will be critically important. Along with that, there will be the ongoing challenge to provide a fair and competitively priced, open and transparent trading venue. Further, regulation is something that the legacy markets have had to contend with over the past few years. By legacy markets I mean NASDAQ, the NYSE, American, Chicago, and Boston. Everybody that has been around has had to bear the burden of regulation.

Some of the newer upstarts have been somewhat freer to innovate. We have all benefited from that. But as things cycle back, we will have to reaffirm the importance of regulation, oversight and compliance. One of the earlier panels talked about the fact that there are too many regulators, that regulation is redundant. I think there is still a lot of bad stuff going on, so I am hopeful we will be able to keep a close eye on all of this activity.

NASDAQ has a pretty full plate. They have a history of trying to provide a reasonable platform. I hope that they have a chance to do a better job and offer competitive pricing. I worry what that pricing will be. I hope that NASDAQ will be transparent in their pricing and, if their prices do go up, I hope that it will be because their value proposition has been improved.

JENKINS: Paul?

PAUL DAVIS: I look at it rather selfishly as a representative of a large buy-side institution. I want to know what they will do for me. That is the challenge for NASDAQ. If you look at the different sizes of orders relative to the liquidity in a stock, we can talk about small, medium and large orders. For the small and medium-sized orders, the NASDAQ structure that is emerging will handle things quite well. The large orders are a problem. Here is where I would really like to see meaningful innovation coming from NASDAQ. I could make lots of suggestions, but I would rather it came from them.

Let me just put one suggestion on the table as a way to go. Once upon a time, NASDAQ was working on a system called Liquidity Tracker,[45] and then they dropped it. I would love to see them reinstitute Liquidity Tracker. It is a way for size to find size. And with that I will turn it over to…

JENKINS: Rob?

ROBERT FELVINCI: Looking at it from a big picture perspective, what we have seen over the past two to three weeks is a major coup for the New York Stock Exchange. NASDAQ is on the defensive. This is because they have to deal with a competitor that has a huge name brand and is now in their type of marketplace. It will be challenging for NASDAQ to compete for new listings. All those listings that automatically go to NASDAQ, because they were not qualified to be on the New York, will be opened for competition. You may also see a jump from a lot of smaller companies that always wanted to be on New York but never could. So NASDAQ may lose some share in that respect.

JENKINS: Dan?

DAN ROYAL: I have two things to say in line with Rob's comment. The merger between NYSE and Arca blurs the line between what NASDAQ and the NYSE are providing. On the crossing networks these will continue –the buy-side loves them, especially when the sell-side is not involved. If that is something that this group could provide – I am not trying to provide competition for Liquidnet – but crossing network models do work, and NASDAQ may gravitate towards them.[46]

JENKINS: Lisa?

LISA UTASI: Now we must look at the landscape on a more global investment basis. That is the first thing I thought about when you asked the question. NASDAQ has for a long time battled the ECNs to trade its own issues. Now, the game is on. As for side-by-side trading, there will be a full suite of investment products – probably stocks, options, futures, maybe bonds – some of the things I have heard that the New York and Arca might try to introduce. These might take place side-by-side. We will see how forward- looking NASDAQ can be with these kinds of products. As the other gentleman mentioned, there will still be a continuing race for listings. But we have to also think about increased regulation. Today, I received the news that Fuji Photo is not going to renew its ADR program when its current

[45] NASDAQ announced it was discontinuing Liquidity Tracker in June 2003, about six months after it was launched, as part of a reduction in non-core services, such as NASDAQ Europe. Liquidity Tracker, which was accessible via NASDAQ's SuperMontage, was programmed to send orders to traders who were willing to fill them.

[46] The launch of the NASDAQ intra-day cross was expected in early November 2006. It was dependent on the integration of NASDAQ's individual trading platforms into one single book.

sponsorship expires because of some of the rules regarding Sarbanes-Oxley. That is something that NASDAQ will have to deal with for its listed companies.

Another issue is market hours. I am not much of a fan of extending hours. There is competition already out there: it starts at 4:00 a.m. and stays open until 9:00 p.m. New York now owns, or soon will own, those market hours. So what will happen at NASDAQ? They have started a voluntary session from 8:00 a.m. to 9:30 a.m., but I am not sure that there has been much of a ramp-up in trading volume.

Compliance and surveillance across markets is something that will be really important with Reg NMS. When different marketplaces start to trade the same securities we will see more cooperation among regulators. If I go into New York to trade Intel, a NASDAQ stock – perhaps on the Arca platform – I should be able to talk to their regulator if something problematic occurs. In the past, I would just talk to the NASD. Those are some of the challenges that NASDAQ –and no doubt all of the other marketplaces in the United States – will be facing in the near and longer term.

JENKINS: Ken?

KEN ZIMMER: Somebody stated in an earlier panel today that fragmentation was raised as a topic at previous Baruch Conferences. I would disagree with the idea of fragmentation being an issue. In the past, liquidity was spread out across multiple market centers including the NYSE, NASDAQ, ATSs, ECNs and crossing networks. From my perspective, it is now down to a two-man race. It is about which one of these two Trojan horses – the NYSE and NASDAQ – can de-fragment the marketplace and become the all-encompassing marketplace for liquidity. The other thing I would say is that it is not a structure issue, it is a format issue. Both of these platforms can de-fragment the industry.

JENKINS: Let me throw out a question. They discussed this in the last panel. Lisa touched on it – the international dimension. Why would there be an interest in NASDAQ trading international securities in the U.S.? Would that be important to you as a buy-side firm?

UTASI: As traders we appreciate the transparency of our markets. Moreover, the sponsorship of companies, once they are traded on our markets, goes up dramatically. It improves the research that I have available to me, and it improves the depth of the markets in which I can trade. I enjoy dually-listed securities and, for those that trade deeply in the U.S., I enjoy trading them here. It has a lot to do with currency exchange and that sort of thing. It really takes out a lot of the X factors when I am able to trade in dollars. Those are some of the reasons why I think it would be helpful if we had more listings.

JENKINS: Dan, you trade international securities pretty heavily…

ROYAL: To a certain extent. Most of that is handled overseas for us, but there is some overlap, and it provides a bit of uniformity. If you take a model that works for the U.S. and you apply it to international stocks, it creates familiarity. Like Lisa said, it creates a little more depth of liquidity.

JENKINS: Let me change the subject. I would like to get your thoughts on another thing that came up on a previous panel. The electronic markets have allowed the buy-side to reduce substantially their commission rate structure. There is a constant discussion about how far the decline in rates will go. There is product, such as research at the sell-side firms, bundled into the overall commission structure, which includes the execution cost. But clearly, the rates for trading with an exchange have declined and are now pretty low. Are we in danger of affecting, as Mike Murphy said, the portfolio manager's selection of information on the sell-side if commissions do not compensate for sell-side research? Andy?

BROOKS: I always find this an entertaining question. Order flow has value. If we were in the business of thinking what we are paying in commissions, we would sell it. We would have a lot of people willing to pay us for the knowledge that we are trading in XYZ stock today, tomorrow, and for the next week and a half in order to buy a 4% position in a company. Let's acknowledge that. Let's also acknowledge that the business is about picking good stocks and supporting the investment process. At 4 cents or 3.5 cents a share, wow, I do not think that we are center stage. It is just not that big of a deal.

But is it important to monitor transaction costs? You bet it is. Is it important to make sure that we are getting a reasonable value for a reasonable amount of commissions paid? You bet it is. But let's not lose sight of what we are trying to accomplish. We are generally moving pretty large positions in stocks that sometimes do not trade so well. Even when trading 100 shares of Microsoft, you should try and line up the venue that is consistent with your needs. We spend so much time on transaction costs as defined by explicit commissions because they are seen. We forget about things like: How is your performance? What have you done? What is your turnover? What expenses do you have? What kind of value do you provide for your shareholders? If we re-orient our thinking toward that, maybe we will get into a better discussion about market structure, public policy, etc.

JENKINS: Rob?

FELVINCI: It really is a tight rope. You are pressured by plan sponsors, by boards, and by the SEC in terms of how far you can drive down rates. On the other side you have what you are paying for – information, trading flow and research from the brokers. It is the constant battle that we are dealing with now. We are coming to an inflection point where we have the buy-side continuing to put pressure on rates, and waiting for the pushback from the sell-side. That pushback is starting to happen. We get comments every once in a while like, "Well, I do not know if we are going to be able to bring that management team in here or that research team."

Once you hear that, you know the sell-side is starting to say enough is enough. We cannot stay in business with these kinds of rates. If we continue to put pressure on rates – and we are in the driver's seat here – you may reach a situation where brokers say, "We cannot make money anymore. We cannot support our research product, and maybe we are going to go back to net markets.[47] Take these rates off the table because we are just going to start trading everything net – trading for the spreads is the only way we can make money." We are getting to that point where there is going to be pushback.

ZIMMER: It almost seems like we will go full circle. It's the same old story, implicit versus explicit costs. A client says you can get commissions down lower. I say, how low do you want them to go? I can get them to zero if you want – we can go back to net if you think that is advantageous to you. Maybe explicit commissions are just too visible to the public eye and with plan sponsors. Maybe that is where we are headed. But it is ironic. A couple of years ago, it was the move away from net. At that time we thought that we would never go back to net. It does appear that we may go full circle.

JENKINS: Somebody mentioned information flow. Some have said that information flow starts to disappear in the NASDAQ market and in electronic markets. How important is information flow in the markets?

ROYAL: I will take a stab at that. If you are comparing information flow to a New York model, what is the value of some of the flow you get off of New York? The information flow will go upstairs, and you will get it in either market. So, are you really losing much in a NASDAQ model in terms of information from a trader's perspective? In my opinion you are not. I really do not think that we receive a lot of value from the other models right now.

FELVINCI: You have to look at this in terms of best execution. The order flow and information that you are getting from the sell-side is very valuable. I need it to carry out my best execution responsibilities. If I am hiding in a box all day–I mean an aggregator, crossing network or ECN– I will not get that information from the sell-side. I am not paying for it. I may

[47] With the introduction of penny pricing in the U.S. equity markets, explicit fees – commissions – for sell-side institutional stock executions became more popular in NASDAQ transactions. In 2002, many NASDAQ market makers shifted from net – spread-based trading – to charging commissions, in response to the impact of penny increments. In a net trade, a dealer aims to buy shares of stock at one price and sell them at a higher price to his customer.

be missing a very large trade away from me, or information that will help me achieve best execution, as I am supposed to.

UTASI: One difference to note is that, if you are trading with NASDAQ and you are using the market maker model that is part of NASDAQ, you still get an awful lot of information. In fact, sometimes you get more information because there are multiple market makers, or people who are trading a stock. So, there are a lot of people watching a stock, and you can get a large amount of information as a result. Compare that with one market maker who is called a specialist on the NYSE. At the New York, there is only one flow of information – what the specialist tells people on the floor and in the crowd. You start to lose some of the flow of information that is so important when you trade away from NASDAQ, away from market makers, when you use an electronic model, perhaps an electronic crossing network, or perhaps one of the solely electronic networks without market makers.

BROOKS: We might observe in the very liquid NASDAQ stocks that there is so much liquidity around the inside, that information is often less important. Information is more important for the secondary and tertiary names where perhaps the NASADAQ model is weaker here than the specialist model. A good specialist in a thin name can actually give you some information that helps you analyze supply and demand. It is harder to get that kind of information in the secondary and tertiary NASDAQ names. So, in some respects, they each have a possible advantage.

JENKINS: Capital usage in the NASDAQ market used to be obviously very important. It does not seem like it is very important today. Does anybody want to comment on that? Lisa?

UTASI: I am ready (laughter). A little due diligence from this side. OK, here it goes, it depends (laughter). I talk to my peers, buy-side and sell-side, and I would say that there are different types of investors, different categories of investors if you will. Perhaps the hedge funds were more aggressive capital users in the past than they are today. You might suggest that they are willing to work with the people who will give them a bit more capital, which I think is fine. Regarding the plain vanilla mutual fund world that I have more experience in, I think that we have more or less shied away from capital for a while, but have come back in some way. It is not necessary to start off with in a trade, but along the way you sometime have to have it. We have used it in over-the-counter NASDAQ trades. I think that there is capital available there. It depends on what the investor needs, and who is asking for it.

JENKINS: At these rates, capital is available?

UTASI: I think so. Given the way that you are dividing your business up, you could move rates down maybe one or two cents, or even to zero. But that is a blended rate. Many of us are still paying full-service research brokers commission rates that might be 5, 7 cents a share, whether it is for research, capital, or whatever other services such as clearing you get from them. Blended rates can be brought down. There are other tools that we use such as algorithmic trading, which tend to be less costly, depending on what is appropriate. But there is the ability to pay, at least with certain firms, the per share prices that allow you to have capital.

FELVINCI: Also, remember the sell-side position trader. He is paid to take positions, not just to trade stocks on an agency basis. He will not make any incremental money just sitting there trading as agent all day long. He wants to take a position, he wants to trade with risk, because that is how he will make money. Whether we are paying him 4 or 5 cents a share does not really matter to him. He wants a position because he wants to make a bet on that stock. We are the facilitators of that.

ROYAL: For a variety of reasons, including dwindling commissions, we are typically not a capital-intensive shop. The last thing you want to do is to put someone in a position where you stick them with a trade and, all of a sudden, it changes your budget for the year. But I am finding, especially in the middle tier of brokers, that they are becoming more aggressive with capital just to buy the business. That goes back to Andy's and to Rob's comments. These guys want the flow. They are willing to pay a price to get it. If they take a hit on it, they say, "Oh no, I am OK," but it always comes back to haunt you.

ROYAL: So the capital is there. It is almost being offered to us more than in the past, just because they are trying to buy the business…

DAVIS: Yeah, we are using it more and more.

ZIMMER: You see less of the big bids and offers now. Brokers, from what I have seen, are reluctant to get smacked around and take that risk just to drum up business. I mean certainly, if they know the order is in hand and they can tie you in, that is one thing. But just to go out fishing? I think that there has been a bit of a reduction in that.

JENKINS: The merger: What does the NASDAQ merger do for you? How does it impact your life? Who wants to go first?

ZIMMER: Does anybody know (laughter)? Do we know the answer to that?

JENKINS: Well, how could it impact your life? Is it good from your perspective?

ROYAL: It concentrates a pool of liquidity. That is what we are trying to do. We want to decrease some of the fragmentation that is out there. But with smart routers I will hopefully get routed ultimately to where the liquidity is. But is there an advantage starting at the right place? Yeah, you would think so. Maybe just the fact that you have fewer players means that liquidity will eventually be concentrated in fewer places.

ZIMMER: We may see bigger pools of liquidity if these are gobble-up mergers where one takes the other whole and a competitor is taken out. That would be great. It may not have a huge effect on us if it is a standalone arrangement where the two operations run in parallel and they sort of share revenues and synergies. But this remains to be seen.

UTASI: It may give us another venue for trading listed equities. No one has really mentioned this from the buy-side. We know when we heard about the potential NYSE-Arca merger, that the NYSE would automatically gain 25% of NASDAQ listed trading volume. But nobody thinks that NASDAQ-Instinet could own some of the listed trading volume. So it may give us a whole different venue to trade listed securities, which would be interesting.

ROBERT SCHWARTZ [From the Floor]: I have an observation and a question. The observation, if I am not mistaken, is (and I have heard it for the second time on this panel) recognition of the fact that our markets really are fragmented, and that there could be benefits from this type of consolidation. I have certainly heard from regulators (and from some of my academic colleagues) that the markets in the past were really not fragmented because we have had connectivity. I have heard that connectivity is a good substitute for having one liquidity pool. And yet you are saying that one liquidity pool is better. My question is, do you agree?

DAVIS: Let me take a crack at that. I have a little different slant on this fragmentation issue. Markets are still very fragmented. They are fragmented in time. Focusing on the NASDAQ-Instinet merger, yes, there is less fragmentation, but the focus of the new entity will be on enhancing the order-driven electronic marketplace that they currently have. What I am looking for from this new entity is real innovation in terms of what they will do for me.

FELVINCI: When we talk about fragmentation, we are not thinking only of stocks that are trading on Arca and NASDAQ and the P-Coast and so on. We are also thinking about stocks that are trading in the crossing networks, POSIT and Liquidnet. Everybody would like to bring that order flow that has hit those crossing networks, – which is where the real fragmentation is – back onto a regular exchange, into a regular pool of liquidity. That is some of the fragmentation that people speak of.

BROOKS: There is another thing about fragmentation. When you talk about our jobs, one of the most important things that we do is assess supply and demand. If you cannot figure that out, you are in a box. You are disadvantaged and not very well informed. So one of the challenges on Rob's point is to put all these pieces back together and look at the aggregated, but now fragmented, liquidity.

SCHWARTZ [From the Floor]: That could have implications for this reduction of the average order size reversing itself and increasing back to where it once was.

JENKINS: This gets back to my other question: What design is there for immediacy, for block trading in size? It seems that the tools are disappearing. That is why orders are being broken up. So, what would you like to see here?

UTASI: I do not think the connectivity we have is great. This is one of the problems. We have spent the last two years debating the SEC about Reg NMS, and the most important component of Reg NMS was the connectivity and access portion. One reason in my opinion is that the SEC wanted to extend the rule to the top of the book of all markets because there isn't great connectivity. We cannot get to all those price points that we need. If we had looked at connectivity first – and if we had that connectivity in place among marketplaces –then I am not sure we would need Reg NMS which aims to make more liquidity across the markets more accessible. That is part of the problem. I do not know many buy-siders, except for some of the larger firms, who even have smart order routing, or who have started to incorporate it until they had to, which is just recently. Let's go back to the real issue. There is no great connectivity.

WAYNE WAGNER, (ITG, Inc.)[48] [From the Floor]: I want to take Rob on a little bit about Liquidnet and Pipeline. The reason they exist is that they are offering a service that is appealing to the people here. The reason that it is appealing is that it differs from what you can get from other organizations. I do not think that you would want to give up the kind of anonymity that you can get on those systems in exchange for having liquidity all in one place. If that were true, they wouldn't exist, right?

FELVINCI: I agree. But I think that these ATSs came about because people lost confidence in the NYSE. They lost confidence in displaying orders because they always felt that someone was trying to steal from them. That someone could be a specialist or just a local broker on the floor. There was a general breakdown in confidence and, while it was not the only reason, the breakdown helped to facilitate a lot of these crossing networks. It helped to facilitate algorithms. Algorithms are the reason why the average trade size has dropped as much as it has. Everybody is putting these orders into the algorithms, and they are chopping it up over the day.

It is a fear of being wrong. Some people are happy about getting VWAP, the volume weighted average price of the day, in exchange for not being wrong. It was a lack of confidence that helped to drive it. It may not have

[48] At the time of the conference, Mr. Wagner was Chairman of Plexus Group. On January 3, 2006, Plexus Group was acquired by ITG, with whom Mr. Wagner is now a consultant.

been the only reason, but it helped to drive some of us to some of the crossing networks.

ROYAL: But even if you concentrate liquidity in the exchange, nothing really changes. You still have the ability to be gamed. It is still all there. It does not really re-instill confidence. It just says, OK, here is the liquidity. Maybe you can access it a little bit easier. Maybe you can get a little better feel for the flow. But the crossing networks at least give you an option if you want to put up a piece of stock and not break it up into 375 share segments and work it over 92 hours.

FELVINCI: If you pool liquidity, you have more confidence to trade. You are more likely to go down to the NYSE, or trade a liquid stock on NASDAQ where there is a pool of liquidity, rather than going into a box.

BROOKS: There is a corollary to this. In some respects, the sales trading function has broken down on the sell-side, or it has not been supported. I have been doing this for almost 25 years and, when I started, that sure was one important group of people. They were talented, they were charismatic, and they could hold you to the table. They could make you feel confident enough to open up, to expose what you were trying to do, and to trust them.

By and large, those talented people have not been replaced as broadly as they should have been. There are still a lot of really talented sales traders, but one of the things I always tell the sell-side is to employ very good sales traders. The sell-side should do this to give Dan and me the confidence to open up through an intermediary and trade. I am happy to trade anonymously in a crossing network, but it is more fulfilling most of the time to trade where it might actually feel like you had some dialogue, where you could understand the rationale and why the price was reasonably derived.

JENKINS: Question in the back.

CHRIS CHURCH, (Radianz, Inc) [From the Floor]: I wanted to pick up on Lisa's point about the connectivity angle. You say that there is not enough connectivity. Could you elaborate on what you are referring to here? What do you think Reg NMS will do to connectivity? How will that drive the connectivity changes that perhaps you are looking for?

UTASI: In the listed markets, there has always been a connectivity system called ITS. I do not think that it has kept up with the times. It has turnaround times that are way too long for the kind of trading that we do now, which is nearly instantaneous. We have a much better ability to connect to each other in the electronic markets. There is much better connectivity between the players who want to put their liquidity into NASDAQ's SuperMontage. Obviously the people who decided to be outliers were difficult to reach, so there you have a problem. Going forward, one of the things that we expect to see in Reg NMS when it comes out as a rule is that the SEC will at least promote private connectivity[49] to the liquidity points. And anything built now will obviously be state of the art.

CHURCH [From the Floor]: Do you think that what is built will connect the buy-side to the market centers, or will it be through the brokers?

UTASI: It could be either way. It could be sponsored by site access to those market centers. Because we are not members of any of those marketplaces, we will not be able to do business directly. But perhaps we could do business in a sponsored way, yes.

JENKINS: Question over here.

KIM BANG, (Bloomberg Tradebook) [From the Floor]: In the previous sell-side panel we heard that there is an unbundling process going on with different pricing points for different sorts of executions, with and without research and capital commitments, and so forth. I am interested in hearing from the panel about the extent to which you have gone through that unbundling process? How much of your business is execution only?

Also, when you get down to evaluating executions only, do you provide certain transaction cost analysis measures and benchmarks? The next part of my question is, if you find superior execution – which is typically imbedded in the implicit part of the equation – how much are you willing to pay for that? Are you willing to pay a premium for that? Are you willing to direct more of your flow to a venue that you deem will provide superior execution?

JENKINS: Who wants to touch that (laughter)?

DAVIS: I will give you some of our specifics at TIAA/CREF. For over ten years we have done over 50% of our business as execution only. As for the other 50%, we are now moving roughly 30% to 40% of it to execution only. That does not leave much of the pot for research. But we are willing to pay up for research now.

ZIMMER: It sounded like it was implied in your question that the premium would be on the rate. At least in our case, that is not so. The premium is on the flow. Namely, it is on the total amount of execution business. So, if the execution is superior or there are benefits to the execution, that is where the business flows to. It does not come from the rate. And I do not think that it should.

FELVINCI: On the unbundling part of your question, we did a dry run. We went to a number of our firms and asked them, "OK, we are going to start writing checks out for your research. What do you think is the value of your research? We did a survey, and it is still ongoing, but it is amazing

[49] The NYSE and the regional exchanges have spent budgets on technology to comply with Reg NMS's trade-through rule. The rule, in effect, has forced the exchanges to develop their electronic 'connectivity' so that orders can be routed from one exchange to another exchange if it has a superior price.

what we got back from the sell-side. It was everything from exactly what we paid them last year to three times what we paid them last year (laughter).

It was really hard to judge it. But it is something that we must take seriously. At the very least we must start disclosing everything about what we are paying for, and how and why we pay for the research, as the FSA has required in the UK. We may go to full unbundling. We do not know, so we have to be prepared for that. Am I willing to pay up for better execution? Yes, definitely. Pay up for capital? If I can justify why I am paying up, then that is OK. But I must be able to justify that the reason why I am paying up is to get best execution.

ZIMMER: It is just a matter of time. I know that there are systems out there already, and that we do not use them. But until evaluating research becomes just as important as evaluating transaction costs in the eyes of the regulators, firms won't spend explicit commission dollars to use those systems. I would not be surprised if the SEC moves in that direction. I do not think you can put a flat rate on research and say that reports cost $1,000 each, and that company visits cost $2,000 each, and so on. It varies based on how good the research is and on what you get in return for that research. Down the road this will have to be evaluated and monitored.

BROOKS: I would echo that. In fact, I think that the SEC is already going down that road. They are expecting us to have a frank conversation with our sell-side constituency in order to understand the profitability of that relationship, and to make sure that we are paying a reasonable amount for what we think is the value we derive from that relationship. As for execution only, hopefully, going into a trade, you are not sacrificing best execution by choice of venue. At the same time as you are concerned about the value of research and relationships, it is important to remember that there are different kinds of trades. There are various sizes and prices involved. So, if I have 1,000 shares of Intel to buy, for example, there is a good chance that I ought to be doing it at a penny in B-Trade, or in a similar venue. There is not a lot of value to be had for executing that kind of trade at 5 cents a share.

ROYAL: We are all under pressure to bring our blended costs down, that is, the blend, or combined costs of the high-touch trades of the full-service broker, and the low-touch trades of an electronic venue. If you are trading a liquid stock, why would you pay a full-service rate of 4 cents a share when you can pay a penny for a low-touch trade in the same stock? Our boards are saying that we need to reduce our blended rate. There are certain trades, like Andy pointed out – Intel or Cisco trades, for example – where we would question paying 4 cents, or whatever the full-service research rate is, on these liquid names. What happens is that some of the difficult trades, the smaller ones that do not have a lot of trading volume, go to the full-service brokers. But it is tough to justify a 4-cent commission in some of the liquid names. With these trades, you need to send them to an electronic venue.

But best execution trumps everything in terms of what we are looking for. Do we tend to gravitate towards venues that are providing best execution? Yes. One of the things we are struggling with is the effectiveness of trade-cost analysis because the data used are somewhat stale when they are analyzed. We are still trying to find a good model. We use ITG and Plexus, but a more real-time analysis of what our trades are costing is needed. Sometimes the data are a week or a month-old. Stale data become difficult to analyze. Sometimes it is difficult to compare different venues in this situation. Often we spend more time just assessing whether the data are valid than we actually spend assessing the results. I do not know if anybody else is having the same issues with transaction-cost analysis, but there is a market out there and it might be imbedded within the Order Management System. The OMSs are operating broker neutral platforms that buy-side firms are subscribing to. These OMSs are grabbing every trade tick already, so it is a logical step for them to come into this space and provide real-time trade cost analysis.

JENKINS: Let's switch gears a bit here. I have to do some research for the NYSE as well. About the voluntary early opening, is it a success? I want your feedback on this. Is it a good thing? Should we just open earlier? I have not heard a lot of cries on voluntary, but…

BROOKS: I have been waiting for this one (laughter). One of the things that Bob challenges us to do is to be somewhat outrageous in our commentary. I will try to be outrageous here because it is important. It is fair to say that most pre- and pos *t* hour trading is parasitic in nature. Somebody is trying to take a conscious advantage of somebody else. There is incomplete information. Often there is misinformation, or information that is not fully disseminated, that has not been properly analyzed by most market participants. A lot of people get picked off. Let's talk about this.

What is the advantage of opening at 8:00 a.m.? What is the advantage of having 24X7 in trading? From a public policy standpoint, a market should be like a pharmacy – you know when it is open, you rely on it, and you can count on it. It is a huge disservice to the people on the West Coast. It is a huge disservice to everyone who is in the business.

We need some time to assess what has happened overnight, to gather together, to have a cup of coffee, to think about our investment strategy. This is not day trading. I do not care about that. I am not sure that we should facilitate mis-information, and things like that. Take Pfizer, for instance. When 12 million shares of Pfizer trade before 8:30 a.m., that is a problem. Of course, you could also make the case that maybe on that day, we should have held up all trading until there was proper information dissemination.

The SEC should look at this issue and think about whether all markets should not be required to operate during specific market hours. That is my announcement. I do not represent the NYSE or any other venue (laughter).

JENKINS: How about the voluntary part of the question…

UTASI: I have to agree with Andy to some extent. It would be important for the regulators to look at least at a uniform opening time. Of course, if markets want to trade voluntarily they should be allowed to. From what I can tell from talking to several of the major market makers who make lots of names, they have not seen a huge pick up in activity between 8:00 a.m. and 9:30 a.m. Obviously for story stocks, and when there is news, there is activity. But, in general, how many stocks really trade pre-opening? We have not seen a lot of them. We have been watching. We have been looking at who has been opening their markets. We have not seen that many people open their markets at 8:00 a.m.

I agree that there is something to be said for a unified market open. Whether you trade voluntarily before or not, if 9:30 a.m. is the spin, then I think that everybody should spin at the same time. One should not effectively have their opening spin at 8:00 a.m. and another few have theirs at 9:30. Listen, we are institutional investors, we can roll with anything. Our desk sizes are not that huge, so in two seconds we can tell our room if we want to open tomorrow at 9:00 a.m. People will come in early. We will be able to have our trades in order. We will be able to open at 9:00.

But what about all of the retail investors? What about people who cannot get hold of their brokers? We sometimes think that institutional investors rule the world –although I do not think so! But for the retail investors, it would be really hard to communicate. Even different order types are confusing when you get to the retail level. I definitely believe that if there is no uniform open and close time there will be chaos.

DAVIS: I applaud the NASDAQ for having their new opening call auction and closing call auction. It is a little inconsistent to have these call auctions along with all this trading that is going on earlier than the open and after the close. A challenge would be, can we shrink the trading day (laughter)?

JENKINS: Let me see a show of hands. Is there support for earlier hours out there? Is there a lack of support? That is interesting, I see a lot of "I do not cares" (laughter).

UNIDENTIFIED SPEAKER [From the Floor]: I would like to ask a question about your comment that early trading is parasitic. First of all, wouldn't you agree that both parasites think that they are picking off the other guy, or they wouldn't be doing it?

BROOKS: Yes, and occasionally we are right and occasionally we are wrong.

UNIDENTIFIED SPEAKER [From the Floor]: That is true but both guys are trying to pick off the other guy.

BROOKS: Gus Sauter from Vanguard[50] made a really interesting assessment on this. He said that opening early will not cause us to trade one more share. People think that they are going to gain market share by opening earlier. That is a fallacy.

UNIDENTIFIED SPEAKER [From the Floor]: But again, from the perspective of the two parasites, each one believes he is picking off the other guy. Let 'em go at it! A second thing: Isn't research generally speaking intended to be parasitic? Aren't you trying to gain an advantage in trading a stock? You just want to pick them off slow, but these guys just want to pick them off fast (laughter).

BROOKS: Good point, I am in the slow pick-off game (laughter).

UTASI: You have to look at it in two ways. We are talking about it as investors. But when you look at the bigger picture (I am sure that Pete will appreciate this) you have to look at it from a business model perspective. Pete just tossed this out, what do you think about the NYSE opening earlier? There was a pretty big outcry from us and many people on the West Coast. This is not something that we would like to see come to pass. But then again, other markets might take market share away from a traditional market like the NYSE that opens at 9:30 a.m. This is something else to think about. I am not sure who will win in this debate, the investors or the business modelers.

MATTHEW LAVICKA, (Goldman Sachs) [From the Floor]: I was intrigued by the earlier comments on net trading. In light of the existing best execution rules and the forthcoming Reg NMS, the question is, is net trading still alive or is it being regulated to death? If you think it is still alive, how do you think it will work in the new environment?

FELVINCI: We were talking in the context of commissions coming under pressure to such a degree that it is no longer viable for a sell-side firm to stay in business trading for 2 cents a share, or 1 cent a share, or whatever that number is. The sell-side firms may decide the only way that they will be able to stay in business is to go to a net market that gives them a chance to trade for a spread of probably more than 2 or 3 cents a share. We have to get there first. Is it viable? Sure it is. If they all decide they want to do it, then that is where the market will go. Is it likely? Probably not, but again it depends on where commission rates are going.

BROOKS: Net markets are probably not so good for us. It might be good for dealers, but probably not so good for us.

[50] George U. (Gus) Sauter, Managing Director, Vanguard Quantitative Equity Group.

LAVICKA [From the Floor]: How you can co-exist is really the problem. You say if we all go there, right, but how do you have a net market and an agency market co-existing with best execution rules?

BROOKS: You sort of have that now on certain block trades, sometimes, for example, on take-downs – in which an investment bank buys a block of stock and re-offers it – as well as on overnight offerings of stock which are announced at 4:00 p.m. by banks and completed the next morning.

ZIMMER: Andy said not so good for us. I do not believe net trades are so good for investors either. The investor is far better off to have explicit costs on the commission side so that they can at least quantify and monitor them. It is worse if these expenses are buried in implicit costs. I do not think an investor realizes that. He can see commission go out the door, but he cannot see a couple of basis points.

ROYAL: That is why I believe commission rates have bottomed to a certain extent. I do not think that there is a big push from the buy-side to go to a net model. Knowing basically what the cost can be, I would rather have an agency situation and know with more clarity what is occurring. I am not in favor of a net market and think that commissions are about where they are going to get to.

NARI JOTE, (Baruch College) [From the Floor]: My question concerns mergers and acquisitions. A recent BusinessWeek article said that M&As are not always good from the investor's point of view. If a merger takes place, what are the long-term consequences for the investors? In the future, the regulators may have to come up with acts and laws in this area. Also, exchange mergers raise concerns about monopoly pricing for customers of exchanges. Are we prepared for that?

JENKINS: Andy? (laughter).

BROOKS: On the question about monopoly pricing of exchange products and services for customers, we certainly need to be careful. We must make sure that the prices charged continue to be transparent and reasonable. That is one of the things that I am anxious about as this consolidation is being announced.

ZIMMER: I will throw out an answer to what I think the question is. I am worried about competition. The industry right now is going through a process that is natural for any industry. You go through innovation. We had that for years while all the ECNs sprang up. Now we are beginning to go through consolidation, which is natural. Then we will go through maturity, and then the decay of the industry. The only thing that can really kill competition is regulation. Hopefully that will not happen. But as long as there is money to be made, in the absence of aggressive regulation, competition will take care of itself.

ROYAL: Consolidation is good up to a point. If one of the few remaining market centers drops the ball, someone could step into the space relatively easily and keep innovation at the forefront. The cost of entering the space – the cost of introducing a new ATS or ECN, for example – is relatively low.

FELVINCI: The SEC and U.S. government will not countenance a market, which has no competition. They showed in Reg NMS that they do not want a central limit order book. They do not want one market. They want more than one market; they want competition. I would be really surprised if they permitted something that was not competitive.

UTASI: We should not just think about the equity markets. If the equity markets are going to try to reach out and trade other products side-by-side, how long will it be before the Chicago Mercantile Exchange's of this world want to trade equities? There are plenty of competitors that we are not thinking about. We are thinking about new ECNs, but there are established markets that need only turn on a machine to trade an equity side-by-side with their bonds or options. There is plenty of competition that is already built and already out there. They only have to flip a switch.

BROOKS: I also wonder at what point the specialists are going to start to say, look at this bond market, those are pretty wide spreads, there is an opportunity for us (laughter) here. It might cause the regulators to shift their focus away from us (where we have had a reasonable amount of change forced upon our marketplace) to other markets that are less transparent. I am excited about that opportunity (laughter).

JENKINS: Question here.

ANTHONY FORTUNATO,(Instinet, LLC)[51] [From the Floor]: How do the investors benefit when a market participant's mandate is to target an index?

JENKINS: Can you elaborate?

FORTUNATO [From the Floor]: I am talking about an S&P 500, or any other index change where a broker will come to the indexer on the buy-side, offering to execute his order, say at 1 cent, or 2 cents better than the close. The point is, the indexer does not necessarily care what the closing price is. He wants to match the closing price.

JENKINS: Okay, I understand.

FORTUNATO [From the Floor]: Do you see that going away? And how does the investor benefit from that?

FELVINCI: Personally, we do not do a lot of that. I do not believe that anybody can consistently guarantee me better prices. When people say that

[51] At the time of the conference, Mr. Fortunato was Director, US Equity Sales & Trading at Nomura Securities International.

we will guarantee you 2 cents better than VWAP, do not believe it. You cannot do that consistently. It is just not possible. It is the same thing with market on-close. Those two cents are coming from somewhere. I do not know from where, and I think that I do not want to know (laughter). But I am very suspect of that.

ROYAL: I am not getting those calls (laughter).

BROOKS: We used to get more of those calls. If the point is that somebody guarantees you the closing price and you take a profit split on the order that, in effect, incentivizes this participant to get an inferior execution price for you, then net net you are worse off in the end. Even though you are splitting the difference between the closing price and the execution price actually achieved, you are still not getting 100 percent of the difference. That would be a bad trade in my view. Hopefully, if you engage in a profit split it is because there is enough offsetting liquidity to minimize your exposure, and it is a reasonable trade in contrast to a terrible trade at an inferior price.

UNIDENTIFIED SPEAKER [From the Floor]: I recall a time when people felt that the NYSE was clearly the place to trade, that you could get more blocks done there. Then there has been an evolution to NASDAQ with limit order handling and enforcement against backing away. Is NASDAQ better now than it had been for institutional investors? Will the enforcement of Reg NMS that is being able to trade at the best price, automatically validate the limit order book? Is electronic automatic execution a better model than the auction model for institutional investors?

FELVINCI: Each model has its place. And it depends on each situation. It is very subjective. You always want to go to the place that will provide you with the best execution. On the New York, you go down there for the information advantages, the color from human floor traders and other services. Lately, you have not gotten a lot of these same advantages from the New York. NASDAQ operates a different model, an electronic dealer market. I would have to agree that NASDAQ has improved. And yes, the electronic-model had been validated by the NYSE-Arca merger. But there is still value for the traditional type of New York model. By pooling liquidity, hopefully, we will get back to the value that used to be there.

UTASI: Reg NMS says it is important to keep up with the available technology. If electronic trading is available and people find it important, then it should be used. Not being able to trade-through an accessible electronic quote – versus being able to avoid a manual quote – in accordance with your best execution obligations and Reg NMS validates what NASDAQ is doing all along. But only time will tell if the NYSE hybrid system works. If it succeeds, won't that tell us there is still a place for the auction market and the benefits of the specialist, in addition to the electronic model provided by NASDAQ?

ZIMMER: Let us not forget that there is an inherent benefit to the auction market that the dealer market does not have – a centralized location. Granted, there is a lot of noise in the auction market – leakage of information, slowness, etc., etc. But perhaps the worst thing that could happen to NASDAQ would be if the NYSE said, "you win, we are going completely electronic, keep a centralized trading position, but get rid of the specialists, get rid of the things that are causing a drag on us." Then you would have an electronic marketplace that traded in one centralized location that would bring the benefits of the auction market into play. That could be a very fearsome competitor for the NASDAQ.

UTASI: There is something to be said for having somebody involved in a trade. If you look at the volatility statistics within the trades at the New York, they are a lot lower than at NASDAQ. I am sure that NASDAQ would be a lot less volatile than a fully electronic system that does not have market makers. I know it depends on the stock. I know they trade differently, and I will offer that caveat. If you compared apples to apples, it would not be that way. There are a lot of stocks that are listed on the NASDAQ that make them more volatile because of their spreads, etc. Nevertheless, the point is, when there is somebody involved in the trades, whether it is a market maker or a specialist, there is less volatility in the market. If we go completely electronic, there will be more volatility. Arca just asked that market makers come into tits system. If it was not something that institutions wanted, Arca probably wouldn't have offered that invitation.

JENKINS: That is a perfect way to end this panel. Thank you very much everybody (applause).

# CHAPTER 7: DIALOG WITH ROBERT GREIFELD

Robert Greifeld, *President and CEO, The NASDAQ Stock Market, Inc.*
Robert Schwartz, *Marvin M. Speiser Professor of Finance, Zicklin School of Business, Baruch College, CUNY*

ROBERT SCHWARTZ: It is with great pleasure that I welcome Bob Greifeld to Baruch College.

ROBERT GREIFELD: I thank you.

SCHWARTZ: It is an honor to have you with us. I have to thank you for making such a magnificent announcement two weeks before this conference.

GREIFELD: It is not a coincidence. I met with the professor right before we went into the final stage of negotiations. He said that the attendance for the conference was good, but that he was hoping for more. We did the deal just to make sure there would be a big turnout (laughter).

SCHWARTZ: It certainly is appreciated.

GREIFELD: The first thing I want to say about our transaction is that we will have INET integrated into NASDAQ within 12 months. There are no market structure issues with respect to this transaction. They run a very efficient order matching system. So do we. We will clearly recognize synergies through consolidating down to one platform. This transaction is straightforward. We will get it done. INET has about 80 people, so there are certain social issues, but nothing that is overwhelming, nothing that is beyond our competence to manage.

However, putting the deal together, I have to admit, was very complicated. There was a three-part deal.[52] We went in with the strategy to

[52] NASDAQ's acquisition of Instinet Group Inc. involved three transactions; NASDAQ purchased and retained INET ECN, there was a concurrent sale by NASDAQ of Instinet's institutional brokerage division to Silver Lake Partners, and Instinet separately entered into a definitive agreement to sell its Lynch, Jones and Ryan subsidiary to Bank of New York.

bid on all three. We had the great pleasure of working with two leading private equity firms and they redefined the term "negotiation." Every word was negotiated thoroughly. It was a hard slog. We also had a number of banks involved with the process, and that involved its own set of dynamics. In addition, we had people who were bidding on other assets, and that had yet another set of dynamics. Then we had to come up with what we call "intramural agreements" that had to exist pos *t* acquisition, and that had its own set of dynamics. All that being said, we spent a lot of time in lawyers' conference rooms over a period of weeks. Now, with that hard work behind us, we have a clear path. We will not own the Instinet broker-dealer, except for maybe three milliseconds. We will be non-conflicted right from the get go.

What does the transaction mean to the industry? There will be two leading pools of liquidity for equity trading here in the United States. That is a very good thing for us as we look globally at the London Stock Exchange or at the Deutsche Börse. London in particular is a very aggressive competitor for international listings. Clearly the size and the breadth of the equity players here in the US have been used against us in those types of situations in the past.[53] That is good. But we also recognize that there are constraints upon the behavior of the duopoly competitors. The first is that Reg NMS essentially establishes nine competitors in this space. With the application of the trade-through rule, for both NASDAQ and listed, the barrier to entry is very, very low. All one has to do is post one bid at Boston and we or New York cannot trade-through that bid.

When I think back to my entrepreneurial days starting up Brut, when I compare the set of challenges faced then to the entrepreneurial challenge of taking one of the regionals and competing with one of the duopoly competitors, I like that set of circumstances better. I am not announcing that I am resigning from NASDAQ to try to compete. I am saying that the opportunities are out there. The other key factor is that everything we do – and I have to keep reminding myself of this – everything we do has to be approved by the SEC. Every single pricing action that we take, every single

[53] NASDAQ lost some bids in the past to the NYSE and other markets in the competition for listings of non-U.S. companies. The NYSE, for instance, was viewed as a more prestigious route to the world's largest capital market. The total capitalization of NYSE-listed companies, combined with the liquidity and visibility of a Big Board listing, were strong attractions. However, as Robert Greifeld notes, London has become "a very aggressive competitor." In 2005, for example, the Big Board and NASDAQ combined listed 28 new international companies. By contrast, London and Luxembourg Stock Exchange landed 50 between them. In recent years, in a reversal of an earlier trend, the U.S. has been losing more listings to overseas markets. Analysts blame the 2002 Sarbanes-Oxley U.S. corporate governance rules, but also note that overseas markets are becoming major hubs of capital.

feature that we bring to market, requires us to file with the Commission. We have a natural market setup, based upon the rules of Reg NMS, in which you have seven other competitors besides the two largest, plus an SEC that is actively and intimately engaged in every aspect of our daily market operations.

SCHWARTZ: When you get to talking about the SEC and regulating the markets, I always feel a twinge of micro-management. My opinion is you regulate the markets with respect to abuses of power and position and stuff like that, but that market structure should not be micro-managed.

GREIFELD: It is not the way the world works today, professor.

SCHWARTZ: Sad but true. Talking about the SEC and regulation, what is the latest on being an exchange?

GREIFELD: A number of months ago, we reached what I call a policy agreement with the commission. Today – and it is a very active process – we are going through the ministerial efforts. That means that we have a 500-page rulebook as NASDAQ the stock market. Every line in that rulebook has to be mapped to our existence as NASDAQ the exchange. We have made great progress on that.

SCHWARTZ: Sounds like it might be a rather fast track.

GREIFELD: It has been over four years in process, so it would be hard to call that fast (laughter).

SCHWARTZ: Yes, but is the finish line coming into sight?

GREIFELD: We are getting closer.

SCHWARTZ: That is good news. How will it work with internalization? Is that the biggest problem?

GREIFELD: I have said in the past that we would not sacrifice good market practice just to be called an exchange. And that was basically the competing debate. So we have solved our exchange application not through a market structure solution per se, but through a corporate structure solution. You will see us come out with an exchange that is an operating company that has its own SRO license. You will see a separate operating company that will house the internalization business, and that will be continued under the regulatory aspect of an exchange.

SCHWARTZ: So is it a device to get around this notion…

GREIFELD: It is a corporate structure solution.

SCHWARTZ: It will get you what you want?

GREIFELD: Right, and to the extent that there are issues with internalization in the minds of the SEC, which at this point we do not believe there are, then they still have the ability to address that.

SCHWARTZ: Internalization is certainly a part of our environment. Here and in Europe, it is just a part of how things work.

GREIFELD: It brings value to the market.

SCHWARTZ: Yes.

GREIFELD: Every study shows that. As I said, we would not have agreed to an exchange deal had it limited our ability to support internalization.

SCHWARTZ: As I see it, transparency is a wonderful thing for my order of a couple hundred shares. But what if you are TIAA-CREF? Do you want to put your order on the limit order book? Probably not. So how do you work it? You have price discovery and you have quantity discovery. They are really, for the most part, handled separately. They may be coordinated, but they are separated out. A lot of the quantity discovery is off of the main market.

GREIFELD: You have seen that the markets here in the States have gotten incredibly effective at handling a fairly large number of small orders in rapid succession. The average trade size has declined to around 400 shares. Clearly the large blocks are being discovered away from the electronic markets.

SCHWARTZ: Yes, that came up in the last panel. We have questions from the audience. Wayne?

WAYNE WAGNER (ITG, Inc.)[54] [From the Floor]: I heard you say that the price is discovered first and then the quantity. When you think of it in terms of large orders it works in a different manner. First it is interest, then quantity, and then price. That is working in a different dimension. I cannot believe that the answer is tinier and tinier trade executions.

GREIFELD: I agree. When we look at the market innovation that is required in the years to come, we have to address large size orders. As I said, we have gotten incredibly efficient in all markets, so that part of the puzzle is being perfected. But clearly innovation in market structure that addresses the larger size trades is very important.

SCHWARTZ: Benn Steil.

BENN STEIL (Council on Foreign Relations) [From the Floor]: Bill Donaldson has graciously taken credit for both of the momentous transactions we have seen in the past few weeks. He said that both of them were driven by the Reg NMS reforms that were recently instituted. Was he justified?

GREIFELD: Benn, you are trying to get me in trouble now, aren't you? My general comment on NMS is that the trade-through rule applied to NASDAQ is essentially a tax on the industry. But it did not have a dramatic effect on trading, because we do not have trade-throughs on the market today. So it is an unnecessary tax. Where there is truth to his statement is

[54] At the time of the conference, Mr. Wagner was Chairman of Plexus Group. On January 3, 2006, Plexus Group was acquired by ITG, with whom Mr. Wagner is now a consultant.

that we want to have a full frontal attack on trading New York Stock Exchange listed stocks. We think that Reg NMS opens trading up in a major way, and our capital assessment of how to maximize our opportunity to achieve those goals would be through this transaction. So, in a way, I guess that I am agreeing with the chairman.

SCHWARTZ: Kim?

KIM BANG (Bloomberg Tradebook) [From the Floor]: I am interested in what the opportunity is that you see for NASDAQ to trade New York listed stocks. You have NASDAQ InterMarket, which is a very viable venue in its own right. You are talking about porting technology over to the Instinet platform. Does that include the New York Stock Exchange listed securities? What does the opportunity to compete in that business mean for NASDAQ?

GREIFELD: First, on the technology side, we believe in having one order-matching system that handles both NASDAQ and New York for all our business. You will see us focus on having one platform. With respect to trading unlisted stocks, as most folks know, we became a member of the New York Stock Exchange through our Brut broker-dealer not too long ago. We got a pretty good rate on the lease rental, and we are happy to have that (laughter). I think it was $60,000 a year. Under REG NMS, we see the broker-dealer access to other market centers as being the predominant way to reach New York, and we will still maintain linkages through InterMarket agreements, but we do think the dealer way is the predominant way.

SCHWARTZ: Brett Redfearn.

BRETT REDFEARN (Bear Stearns) [From the Floor]: It sounds like the exchange application is impending and I am sure you are excited about that. Once you become an exchange, what do you see as the real benefits with respect to regaining control of the board? Are there any market data opportunities there, or is there anything else that is a real benefit of getting exchange status?

GREIFELD: Regaining control of the board – now that is a thought. When I first came to NASDAQ a few years ago, one of the top action items being discussed was gaining this exchange registration. After getting educated on the issue, I told folks that I did not want to hear about it. It really was not among the top 10 or 20 things that we had to do. Our exchange registration achieves certain things but it does not change our day-to-day operations. From a strict operational point of-view, when we get the exchange application approved, the Level Two market data goes out of the plan[55] and becomes a product of the NASDAQ stock market. So it has

[55] This is the UTP, or Unlisted Trading Privileges Plan. Level Two data is no longer shared with other exchanges in the UTP plan.

financial benefits for us, and we certainly look forward to it. It also simplifies our approval process in that we will no longer have to go through the NASD.

Today, if we come up with a thought for a product or feature, we have to get it approved by the policy committee of our board. It generally takes us a couple of days to get that done. Then we have to forward it to the NASD, and they have to approve it since we share the license with the SEC. That takes a couple more days. Then it goes down to the commission. There it takes a couple of months. Pos *t* exchange registration, it goes straight from my board to the SEC. So, it is a nice thing to have, but it is not critical.

The other thing is, the Golden Chair[56] that the NASD currently has disappears. They essentially have voting control (we truly are a sub of the NASD today). It is hard-wired in, but upon exchange registration that disappears. So the Golden Chair is theirs – it has never been used, never been exercised, but it is there in theory, and that disappears. Those are the three known things that happen when our exchange status comes through.

SCHWARTZ: I always get confused about this trade-through thing. The desire to link markets and have pricing uniformity, and stuff like that, sounds like consolidation. But on the other hand, it can result in fragmentation. Which is going to dominate? Consolidation or fragmentation?

GREIFELD: The way I look at it is, if we as one of the two large players in the space execute our business plan and provide to the market a deep liquidity pool at a very attractive place with easy access, there will be less fragmentation. To the extent that we do not do that, then there will be more fragmentation. The burden comes back to us.

In time, REG NMS may cause the most dramatic change on the listing business. Chairman Donaldson said on CNBC the other day that NASDAQ will trade New York, and that New York will trade NASDAQ stocks. If I am a CEO of a listed organization, I see that, regardless of where I am listed, X percent of my volume will be on NASDAQ, and Y percent will be on New York. That, in time, will change the dynamics of competition in the listing business. We will be prepared for that eventuality. Today, the listing business is more firmly wrapped up than the trading business. That will be a fundamental shift when it happens. We must be prepared for the event, just as New York has to be prepared for it. Today, the listing business is a duopoly competition that is extremely competitive. If you were to see how we competed for Sears, or competed for the Google listing, it was quite intense. It was a good endeavor. We see that level of competition continuing for the foreseeable future.

[56] The Golden Chair refers to the one share of Series D preferred stock that NASD owned. NASD essentially had voting control of NASDAQ, i.e., 50.1% of the vote.

CHRIS CHURCH (Radianz, Inc.) [From the Floor]: My question is about DMA.[57] It is a very hot topic. What are your thoughts on what would happen to the pace of DMA. Will it accelerate, because of the mergers and because of Reg NMS? Will we see more of it? Will it be adopted faster? And if so, why?

GREIFELD: Electronic liquidity pools are good for DMA providers. These transactions and the advent of New York going electronic as a result of REG NMS is a positive for DMA providers. On the flip side, DMA providers have part of their value proposition in the complexity of reaching out to multiple liquidity pools. So long as there are more than one or two, DMA providers have a strong value proposition.

STEPHEN SAX (Floor Brokers Network) [From the Floor]: One of the area's that will benefit the whole economy is the creation of new products. One of the products I know that NASDAQ was involved in was a very early proposal in the ETF world. The ETF space has grown from almost zero to $227 billion, and it is anticipated that it will go substantially higher. Is that an area that you are looking to get more involved in? I see an opportunity there that will benefit everyone.

GREIFELD: I could not agree with you more. As a point of reference, the ETF is a very portable product internationally. It is hard for an international investor to want to take just one stock, but to the extent that you can buy an ETF based on some index, we see a lot of take with that. We are in the process of rolling the Qs out on a global basis and the pick-up internationally is very strong. Just today, I was meeting with the Mexican Exchange. They took the Qs on late last year and it has done very well. The ETF product has a lot of appeal. It has appeal in a pension account, and we are interested and excited about growing that business. We had some work to do internally to build the technical architecture that would allow us to create these products and that work is almost done. So I agree with you completely. There are winners all around, because it obviously generates enormous trading.

UNIDENTIFIED SPEAKER [From the Floor]: Given that NASDAQ will be using INET's order matching platform going forward, can you tell us what, if any, of Brut's technology will survive?

GREIFELD: Good question. We are making a statement to our customers that they will not be impacted by this series of transactions between Brut and INET. So if we have a customer who comes to us today through a Brut fix engine, a NASDAQ fix engine, or an INET fix engine, they will not have to do anything. The back end match will change and it will be transparent to them. As a second stage, the customer will say, "OK, I

[57] DMA stands for direct market access.

know that I am going to one match engine and that I have three circuits. I have a legacy Brut, a legacy Montage and a legacy INET transaction," and we will give them a patch to rationalize that. But that will be a self-selected model, where they are doing it for their own benefit. That certainly sets us up to have a commitment to the fix engines of all three players for a longer period of time, and also the routing technology. As we said before, Brut was our chosen technology for routing, prior to the INET acquisition. We have not finalized plans, but we are very excited about the performance we have received from the Brut routing technology. That probably has a strong chance of being a long-term survivor.

SCHWARTZ: I have a question on behalf of myself and Holly Stark. We were both on The Opening and Closing Cross committees. I am hearing from Frank Hatheway that both crosses are doing well. It was a good design, and he gets much credit for the design. My question is, do you have plans to extend it? Will you use it during the day if there is a big volatility event? Will you halt trading and then reopen the market using an intra-day cross?

GREIFELD: The answer is yes. First up would be to use that technology for IPOs. Not the Dutch auction part of the IPOs, but the secondary trading in the IPOs. It would be a great way. That would be the next supplement. After that would be certain types of pre-defined market imbalance situations.

SCHWARTZ: In Europe, Deutsche Börse put in what they called a volatility interruption. On a stock-by-stock basis, they halt trading for a brief period of time (on the order of a minute or two), and then restart it with a call auction. It is a very good procedure.

GREIFELD: I remember when I saw that, probably back in '96 or '97. A bolt of lightning struck. I realized that other markets were far ahead of ours in terms of technology. It is an impressive system. The key point that I would leave you with is that the volatility indicators, or whatever the trigger points are, will be objective. They must be transparent so that everybody will know what the triggers are. They will have warnings to know that they are coming.

SCHWARTZ: Yes.

BRETT REDFEARN (Bear Stearns) [From the Floor]: This is very interesting to me. The idea of the liquidity replenishment fund was something that was talked about in New York. One of the concerns that we have is that, in the REG NMS framework, if there is excessive volatility in the market and one market stops their trading, and the SEC rules say that everybody else can trade-through a slow quote during that period of time. People have started to suggest that it might make sense to have inter-market rules if there is a point in-time where the markets are taking off. Because otherwise, if one market stops and everybody else keeps trading, we will have a problem. If you are looking at this, which I suggest is a very good idea, does it make sense for markets to try to get together to find an overall standard for dealing with a technological glitch or some other imbalanced condition?

GREIFELD: We have thought about it. The practicality of having eight markets agree to stop trading is low – I would not say impossible, but it is certainly very low. What it means is that, if you are going to halt the market, you had better have a compelling reason to do so. You must establish that a vast majority of investors will be better served by going into your electronic auction. With regard to the SEC mandating it? Number one we are anxious to see REG NMS in its full form, and we are not saying at this stage that we could use a refinement that we have not yet asked for.

SCHWARTZ: We owe Bob Greifeld a great big hand. Very, very informative. Thanks! (applause).

# CHAPTER 8: NASDAQ'S ELECTRONIC CLOSING CROSS: AN EMPIRICAL ANALYSIS[58]

Jeffrey W. Smith, *NASDAQ Economic Research, The NASDAQ Stock Market, Inc.*[59]

## 1. Institutional Background

In April 2004, NASDAQ introduced a new feature to its electronic stock market—a closing call auction. In brief, the auction accepts special order types that participate in the closing call only. As the close approaches, buy/sell imbalances of these orders are disseminated electronically, and market participants have the option of reacting by entering another type of on-close order that buffers the imbalance. At the 4:00 p.m. close, the crossing algorithm then finds that price that first maximizes the number of shares that can trade then second minimizes the residual imbalance. The shares are crossed at this price, which is then disseminated over the Tape as the NASDAQ Official Closing Price (NOCP). This paper presents an in-depth analysis of the functioning of the closing cross, focusing on how on-close orders are filled, and how the imbalance dissemination draws in liquidity. Whether and how the enhancement has improved market quality is also addressed.[60]

[58] This article is reprinted with permission from Institutional Investor, Inc. It originally appeared in the Summer 2006 issue of the Journal of Trading. It is illegal to make unauthorized copies of this article. For more information please visit www.iijournals.com. All Rights Reserved.

[59] NASDAQ Economic Research, The NASDAQ Stock Market, Inc., 9600 Blackwell Road, Rockville, MD 20850, jeffrey.w.smith@NASDAQ.com. The views expressed herein are those of the author only, and do not represent an official position of the NASDAQ Stock Market, Inc., nor any of its affiliates. The author thanks Frank Hatheway, George Sofianos, Bob Schwartz, and Jamie Selway for useful comments.

[60] See also Pagano, M. and Schwartz, R., "NASDAQ's Closing Cross: Has its new call auction given NASDAQ better closing prices? Early Findings," Journal of Portfolio Management, Volume 31, Number 4, Summer 2005, pp. 100-111. Pagano and Schwartz

The closing cross is a culmination of a multiyear effort by NASDAQ to enhance the quality of the closing process for NASDAQ-listed securities. As is well known, stock market activity is highest at the beginning and the end of the day. At least part of the reason for the surge in trading at day's end stems from the importance of the closing price. This price is widely used as a reference for a variety of purposes. Perhaps the most common purpose is the calculation of Net Asset Values (NAVs) for mutual funds, which provide the fund share price for redemption and purchase orders received that day. Many derivative contracts have final expiration values that are tied to the closing price on the day of expiration. These contracts include stock options and single stock futures. Finally, closing prices are used in the rebalancing of indexes. For example, when one stock leaves an index and another replaces it, the closing prices of the two issues are used in the calculation of the new index divisor in a way that the index value is not changed by the addition/deletion.

Because of the importance of the closing price, many market participants have a desire to trade at exactly the closing price. Traditionally, this objective has been somewhat difficult for NASDAQ-listed stocks because of uncertainty as to the precise value of the NASDAQ closing price. Prior to April 2003, neither NASDAQ nor any other market center designated an official closing price for NASDAQ-listed stocks. An informal process often used involved identifying on the Last Sale tape the last, non-modified trade reported prior to 4:01:30.[61] The trade used to determine the closing price could have been for any size and reported to markets other than NASDAQ. It may have been non-representative of trading done immediately prior to the close. Concerns were raised that firms might game or manipulate the process by attempting to print a trade at a non-representative price an instant before the 4:01:30 cutoff, or that out of-sequence trades reported with substantial lag could set the closing price, creating apparent volatility.[62]

Seeking to improve the close, NASDAQ implemented in April 2003 a process for determining and disseminating an official closing price, the

---

compare the quality of the price discovery process between the June 2003, pre-cross, and June 2004, pos *t* cross, Russell Index rebalance events.

[61] Trades in NASDAQ-listed stocks executed after 4:00 p.m. are required to carry a ".T" modifier. The additional minute and one-half after 4:00 was intended to take into consideration the 90-second trade-reporting requirement of NASD Rules. That is, unless a trade is automatically reported by a trading system, the firm obligated to report the trade to the Tape has 90 seconds to do so before the trade is to be marked late (with a ".SLD" modifier).

[62] NASDAQ's MarketWatch department and the Market Regulation division of NASD provide regulatory services designed to prevent, detect, and deter inappropriate conduct that generates non-representative closing prices.

NASDAQ Official Closing Price (NOCP).[63] First, the trade setting the NOCP would be the last one reported to NASDAQ—not other markets—before 4:00:02. Further, the price would be bounded by the NASDAQ inside quotes at the time of the trade report. For example, suppose the trade eligible for determining the NOCP had a price of $20.00, but at the time of the trade report the prevailing NASDAQ inside quotes were $20.05 bid, $20.10 offered. In this case the NOCP price would be adjusted to $20.05. The NOCP was disseminated over the Tape at about 4:01:30 carrying a ".M" modifier. Other markets authorized to trade NASDAQ stocks, such as the Cincinnati and Pacific exchanges, were free to, and in fact did, disseminate their own official closing prices.[64] These exchanges' closing prices also carried the .M modifier, but could be distinguished from the NOCP by virtue of the market center code that is part of the trade report (e.g. Q=NASDAQ, C=Cincinnati, P=Pacific).

NASDAQ's NOCP initiative and the response of competing exchanges illustrates the competitive dimension to the business of designating an official closing reference price. To the extent that traders care about a particular market's closing price, they will have a strong incentive to do their end-of-day trading at that market. Hence, a marketplace has a strong incentive to generate a closing reference price that will be widely accepted by the industry. This level of competition greatly intensified in October 2003, when Standard and Poor's (S&P) announced a pilot program for determining their pricing of the NASDAQ-listed stocks in the S&P 500 index. Under the pilot, for a sample of twelve stocks, S&P would use the closing prices as determined by the closing auction operated at the American Stock Exchange (Amex). S&P stated that it was responding to "concerns expressed by some in the investor community about the reliability of the closing prices for NASDAQ-listed securities."[65] S&P evidently believed that the agency-auction market structure of the Amex provided a better process for determining the closing price. Since 2000, NASDAQ had been in the process of developing an electronic call auction, though anticipated that its first purpose would be to open the market. With the S&P announcement, however, NASDAQ accelerated the development of the

[63] For details see the SEC order approving the NOCP at 68 FR 14446-14451 (March 25, 2003). See also NASDAQ Head Trader Alert 2003-9, January 24, 2003.

[64] Registered securities exchanges are authorized to trade NASDAQ-listed stocks, which from a legal perspective are "Over-the-Counter" securities, pursuant to the SEC-approved Unlisted Trading Privileges (UTP) plan. UTP participants include the American, Boston, Philadelphia, National, Chicago, and Pacific Exchanges. The National Stock Exchange was formerly known as the Cincinnati Stock Exchange.

[65] S&P Press Release Jan. 29, 2004, available at www.indexnews.standardandpoors.com.

cross, and decided to roll it out for the close rather than the open.[66] The S&P pilot was put into place from March 1, 2004 through July 2, 2004, after which time S&P reverted back to using NASDAQ closing prices, as NASDAQ's closing auction had been implemented by that time.

Another competitor, ArcaEx, also responded with the roll-out of its own closing auction in January 2004. To date, this auction has failed to generate substantial trading interest.

The roll-out of NASDAQ's closing cross began in April 2004 with a small set of pilot stocks. More stocks progressively became cross-eligible until mid-June at which point approximately 1670 stocks were cross-eligible. Included in this list were all active NASDAQ stocks as well as those to be added or deleted from the Russell 3000 index during its 2004 annual reconstitution. By mid-December all NASDAQ stocks became eligible to participate in the closing cross. On any given day, a closing auction can be held for a stock if eligible crossed orders are in the system at 4:00. The auction-clearing price will determine the NOCP if the number of executed shares is 100 or more. Otherwise, the NOCP is determined as it was before the cross existed.

## • FUNCTIONING OF CROSS MECHANISM

The closing cross mechanism operates as follows.[67] The core of the closing process is a new order type designed to execute at the market close at the closing price, or not at all. Traders may submit these on-close (OC) orders with a limit price (limit on-close (LOC)) or without (market on-close (MOC)). Submission of on-close orders to NASDAQ is done over the same channels as other orders or quotes, with an order modifier indicating its special status. On-close orders may not be submitted after 3:50:00 p.m., nor may pending on-close orders be cancelled after that time.

At closing, the on-close orders may balance each other exactly at a price inside the NASDAQ spread, which price would be the NOCP. More likely, the on-close orders will not be in perfect balance. Two provisions are made for the buffering of OC imbalances: interaction with orders/quotes on the continuous-market NASDAQ book; and a new order type termed "Imbalance Only" (IO). Imbalance Only orders augment the liquidity already provided on the NASDAQ book. IO orders always fill, if executed, at the NOCP on the passive side of the market. For example, in the case of a

[66] The NASDAQ opening cross was first operated with 10 pilot stocks on October 25, 2004.

[67] The legal description of the closing cross is NASD Rule 4709. See also the SEC approval order at 69 FR 12879-12881 (March 18, 2004).

sell imbalance among OC orders, sufficiently aggressive buy IO orders would execute at or below the 4:00 p.m. NASDAQ inside bid. Likewise sell IO orders can only execute at or above the NASDAQ closing inside ask. Obviously, then, buy and sell IO orders cannot interact with each other. IO orders may be thought of as a type of on-close quote with a pegged price that moves with the inside market, subject to a global limit price set by the submitter. IO orders may be entered anytime after 3:30 p.m. They cannot be cancelled outright, but they can be "improved," i.e., the limit price can be made more aggressive, or the size can be increased.

The incentive to submit IO orders comes from the dissemination of the Net Order Imbalance Indicator (NOII). The NOII indicates the state of the on-close book, relative to the continuous book, as of each dissemination time. The first NOII message is sent at 3:50:00. Messages follow every 30 seconds until 3:55:00. At this time, the frequency increases to every 15 seconds until 3:59:00. The frequency increases again to every 5 seconds. The last NOII message is sent at 3:59:50, for a total of 37 NOII messages. NOII messages are broadcast over the Internet[68] as well as the data vendor lines customarily used by traders.

The content of NOII messages provides information on the direction of the imbalance, three price indicators, and two volume indicators as follows.

**Direction** of the imbalance is calculated with respect to the "inside" price (defined below). Its values are: B (buy), S (sell), N (crossed on-close orders, but no imbalance at the inside price), or O (no crossed on-close orders).

The **Current Reference Price** indicates the state of the continuous market, and is at or inside the prevailing NASDAQ inside quotes. If the on-close orders, including the IOs, balance at a price inside the spread or on one of the inside quotes, that price is the Reference Price. (The imbalance direction would be N.) If, however, there is sell imbalance as calculated using the inside bid, that bid is the Reference Price. The inside ask is the corresponding Reference Price for buy imbalances.

The **Far Price** is the hypothetical auction-clearing price for the on-close orders only, including both OC and IO orders. If there is no non-zero, non-infinite price at which the on-close book clears, the Far Price is set to zero.

The **Near Price** is the hypothetical auction-clearing price that includes both the on-close book and the continuous book. In other words, it is the price that would emerge if the closing cross were to occur at the NOII message time. Again, if there is no price that clears both books, the Near Price is set to zero.

[68] Daily, real-time NOII access is available to the general public. Registration is available at www.noii.NASDAQtrader.com.

The **Price Variance** indicator provides a discrete characterization of the percentage difference in the Far and Inside Prices.

The **Paired Shares** indicator shows the number of on-close shares that can be paired at the Current Reference Price.

The **Imbalance Shares** indicator shows the number of on-close shares that are not paired at the Inside Price.

A typical scenario for a sell imbalance might proceed as follows. At the first NOII message, the Far Price would be below, perhaps well below, the current NASDAQ inside bid, which would be the Reference Price. The Near Price would be between the two. A fraction of the on-close shares could be paired at the Reference Price, but an imbalance would remain. As IO orders to buy were entered to buffer the imbalance, or the continuous market bid fell, the difference between the Reference and Far Prices would diminish. Imbalance shares would move into the paired category. Ideally, by the time of the final NOII message, the Reference, Near, and Far Prices would be close to each other, and most if not all of the imbalance shares would have become paired. The Near Price at the last NOII message should be a good predictor of the eventual cross price. (Empirical results regarding the rate of imbalance resolution will be presented below.)

NASDAQ's crossing algorithm follows the traditional call auction model. The process begins by integrating all OC, IO, and continuous market "auto-ex" orders and quotes into a single book. The quotes of ECNs displayed in SuperMontage are not, for the most part, subject to automatic execution (auto-ex). ECN quoting participants generally chose order "delivery," meaning that orders routed to them may be declined. (The delivery option prevents ECNs from double execution risk.) NASDAQ, in designing the auction, determined that it would be infeasible to include in the call the quotes of delivery participants. If such a participant were to decline an order in the cross, the entire process for discovering the clearing price, and the allocation of executions, would have to be re-processed.

The (single) clearing price is determined as the price at which the bid and offer curves intersect, equivalently, where cross volume is maximized. Because of the discrete penny ticksize, and the fact that orders may not be placed at all price points, the bid and offer curves are not continuous, but are step functions. Thus, it can happen that multiple prices maximize volume. A secondary criterion is to select the price that minimizes the order imbalance, i.e, the number of non-filled shares of orders whose limit price makes them eligible to be filled. In general the minimal imbalance will not be zero. A third price-determining criterion may be needed when multiple prices yield equal imbalances. This criterion is to select the price closest to the closing NASDAQ inside quote midpoint.

The three criteria just enumerated are sufficient for determining a unique auction-clearing price, which serves as the NOCP if the number of shares exceeds 99 shares. Note that by construction, the clearing price will always be at or inside the closing NASDAQ inside quotes (as set by auto-ex participants) coming out of the auction. If at the close there are no crossed on-close orders the auction is not conducted, and the NOCP is set using the pre-auction method: the last trade price reported to NASDAQ before 4:00:02, bounded by the NASDAQ inside quoted prevailing at the time of the trade report.

The criteria for determining which orders have execution priority are based on the order price and the time of submission. Regarding order price, MOC orders are deemed to have the most aggressive possible price, and hence always have the highest priority for execution. LOCs with prices more aggressive than the auction-clearing price are also granted priority. Time priority determines execution priority for LOCs priced at the clearing price, as well as eligible IO orders and orders/quotes in the continuous market priced at the auction-clearing price. There is no special order type priority for the LOCs and IOs. If an IO order is improved by the addition of size, the incremental size receives time priority based on the time of its submission. The original size keeps its original time priority. For orders in the continuous market, reserve size has lower priority than displayed size. For example, suppose a buy order priced at $20.00 has displayed size of 100 shares, reserve of 1000 shares. It arrives before another order with the same price that displays 200 shares. If the auction price is $20.00, the 200 shares of the second order have priority over the 1000 shares of reserve of the first.

Special mention should be made regarding short sale restrictions. During the continuous market, a bid direction arrow monitors the direction of the inside bid based on the most recent bid change. When the arrow points down—a down-bid situation—a non-exempted short seller must trade at a price at least one cent higher than the inside bid.[69] For practical considerations, the closing cross algorithm assumes that the arrow is "stuck" in the down position at the time of the cross. Thus, non-exempted submitters of MOC and LOC orders are unable to trade at the inside bid. Therefore, the algorithm treats short MOCs as LOCs with a floating price set one cent above the bid. Short LOCs may need to be adjusted so that the limit price is always at or above one cent above the bid. If the cross price is at the bid, short MOC/LOC orders cannot be executed. Short sale

[69] NASD Rule 3350 governs short sale restrictions on NASDAQ. All registered market makers are exempt from short sale restrictions, but many non-market maker firms participate in the cross.

restrictions are moot for selling IOs and continuous market offers, since these orders by construction cannot trade at the bid.

The cross employs global limits on the deviation of the auction price and a pre-close reference price. The reference price is the Volume Weighted Average Price (VWAP) of NASDAQ Market Center trades from 3:59:55 to 4:00:00. If there are no trades, the NASDAQ bid/ask midpoint immediately before the processing of the cross is used. The maximum deviation is 10% if the reference price is above $5, $0.50 otherwise. Technically speaking, then, the price-clearing algorithm described above actually maximizes volume and minimizes imbalances subject to a price deviation constraint. Price-constrained auctions are very rare, but they have occurred. Their occurrence may prevent all price-eligible orders from filling completely.

## • EMPIRICAL ANALYSIS OF CROSS

### 1.1 Incidence and Size of Cross

The closing cross first operated on April 12, 2004 with 10 pilot stocks. During successive weeks, stocks were progressively added to the list of those eligible for the cross. By mid June, approximately 1670 stocks were cross eligible, including active NASDAQ stocks, and all those likely to be part of the upcoming Russell index reconstitution to be held in late June. Since that time, stocks have been added to the list on an as-needed basis, with provision made for stocks being added to or deleted from indexes. Finally, in mid December, all remaining NASDAQ-listed stocks were added.

Exhibit 3 presents a graphical depiction of the total volume for all cross-eligible stocks, from mid June 2004 through the end of December 2004.The graph illustrates the remarkable daily variation that has occurred in total auction activity. Most days have volume in the range of 3 – 8 million shares. Other days have much more volume. By far, the June 25 Russell rebalance led to the highest number of shares crossed, 333 million in total. Beyond that, the graph indicates other groups of days that have generated high cross activity. The next highest group is made up of dates representing the so-called Quad Witch days, the third Friday on the last month of the quarter. The three Quad Witch days in the sample—June 18, September 17, and December 17—had average cross volume of 64 million shares, driven largely by December's 141 million shares. The next group is dates that are the last trading dates of the quarter: June 30, September 30, and December 31 in this sample, with average cross volume of 26 million shares. End-of-month days that are not also end-of-quarter also have higher than average

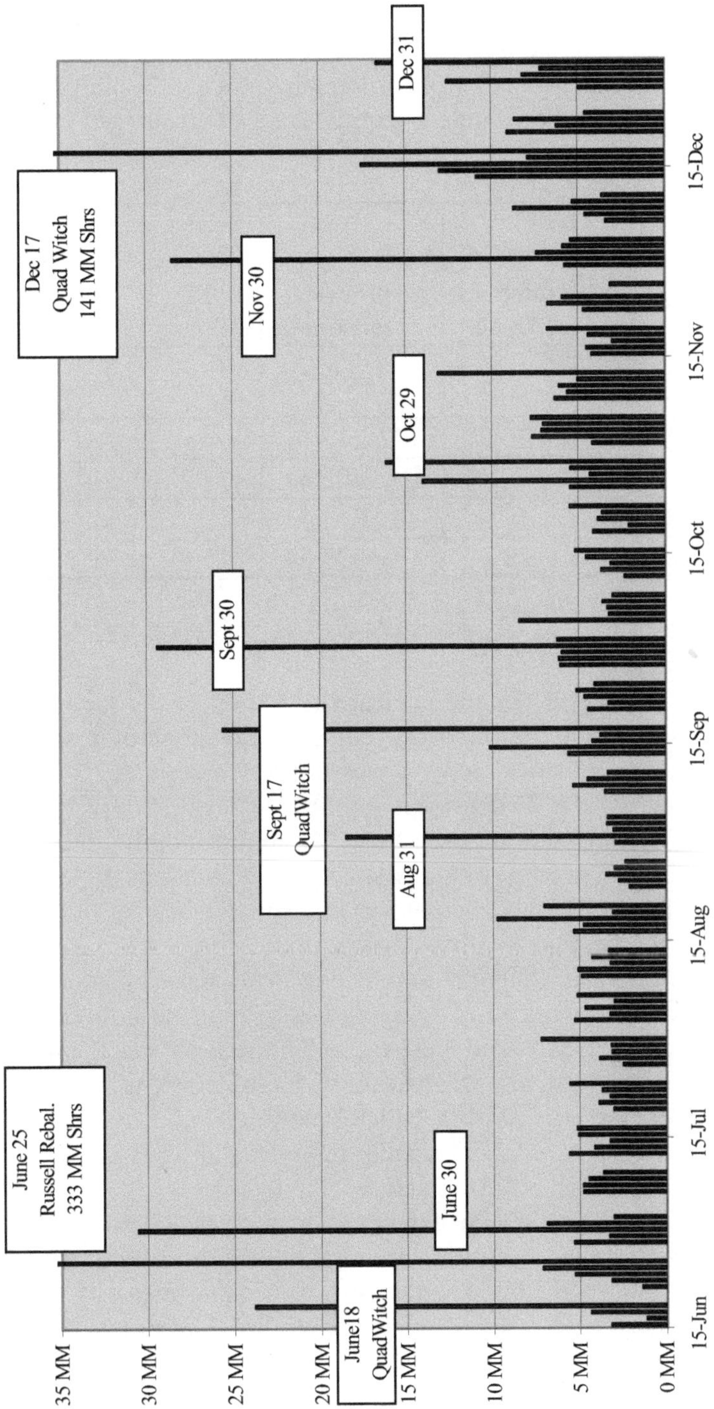


Exhibit 3. Total Volume in NASDAQ Closing Cross, 15 June – 31 December 2004

volume. July 30, August 31, October 29, and November averaged 18 million shares, though July 30 only had 7 million shares.

An overall summary of cross volume is shown in Exhibit 4. In addition to the share volume, the volume is expressed as a percentage of total NASDAQ share volume for the dates indicated.

| Dates | Number of Dates | Average Cross Volume | Percent of Total NASDAQ Volume | Avg. No. of Stocks with Cross Volume |
|---|---|---|---|---|
| Russell Rebalance | 1 | 333,385,707 | 11.96% | 1,637 |
| Quad Witch | 3 | 63,527,374 | 2.92% | 1,595 |
| End of Quarter | 3 | 25,500,540 | 1.55% | 1,490 |
| End of Month | 4 | 17,562,475 | 1.08% | 1,459 |
| All Other | 129 | 5,139,264 | 0.30% | 1,302 |

Exhibit 4. Volume in the NASDAQ Closing Cross: June 15 – Dec. 31, 2004

The difference in volume is clear illustration of the fact that the closing reference price is more important on some days than others. Exhibit 4 also shows that not all stocks have a cross on any given day. By the December Quad Witch, all NASDAQ stocks (approximately 3,300) were cross-eligible, and 2,488 had executions in the cross. By contrast, during the last two weeks in December, an average of 1,359 stocks had executions in the cross.

The NASDAQ market structure is characterized by the extensive role played by market makers, firms that commit risk capital in filling customers' orders as principal. Many market making firms agree to accept customer on-close orders. It is the firms' responsibility as to how to fill these orders, whether to represent them in the closing cross or fill them proprietarily. Executions that represent the execution, as principal, of on-close orders are indicated on the Tape with a ".PRP" modifier indicating "Prior Reference Price."[70] The .PRP trades are usually reported shortly after the dissemination of the NOCP, which occurs at about 4:01:30.

It is interesting to see the extent to which on-close orders are filled either through the auction or through principal trading. A reasonable strategy for a firm to follow might be to enter into the closing cross its own imbalance shares. For example, if for a given stock a firm had orders of 60,000 shares

[70] Some Last Sale data feeds/products (e.g. the NYSE TAQ database) use a "P" modifier to represent a Prior Reference Price trade.

to buy, 40,000 to sell, it could risklessly cross 40,000 shares internally and place the 20,000 buy imbalance into the auction. In a sense, then, the NASDAQ closing cross may constitute an auction of net imbalances.

Exhibit 5 below presents aggregate volume statistics comparing the volume done in the call auction with that done internally by market makers (at the NOCP), as indicated on the Tape as a Prior Reference Price trade.

| Dates | Average Cross Volume | Average .PRP Volume | Ratio of .PRP to Cross Vol. |
|---|---|---|---|
| Russell Rebalance | 333,385,707 | 9,609,325 | 0.03 |
| Quad Witch | 29,947,572 | 29,181,726 | 0.97 |
| End of Quarter | 24,710,565 | 21,343,547 | 0.86 |
| End of Month | 13,939,524 | 21,771,548 | 1.56 |
| All Other | 4,637,673 | 7,609,939 | 1.64 |

Exhibit 5. Volume in the NASDAQ Closing Cross and PRP Volume: June 15 – December 31, 2004

During a regular trading day, there is more volume internalized at the NOCP than is executed in the cross, by an average factor of 1.64. It appears, though, that on days in which the closing price is more important, a relatively higher share of volume is done through the auction. At the extreme date in the sample, the Russell rebalance, virtually all on-close volume was done in the auction.

## 1.2 Order Type Participation in Cross

As indicated above, the on-close order, particularly the MOC, can be thought of as the primary "customer" of the closing auction. IO and continuous book orders provide a buffer to absorb imbalances. To what extent is the liquidity provided by IO and continuous book orders needed? The shares of executed OC (MOC/LOC) orders can be broken into three categories: shares filled by OC orders going the opposite way; shares filled by IO orders; and shares filled by orders/quotes on the continuous book.

Exhibit 6 provides an aggregate breakdown on how OC orders are filled.

| Dates | OC Shares Filled by OC Shares | OC Shares Filled by IO Shares | OC Shares Filled by Continuous Book |
|---|---|---|---|
| Russell Rebalance | 78.6% | 16.1% | 5.3% |
| Quad Witch | 65.6% | 27.7% | 6.7% |
| End of Quarter | 55.5% | 42.3% | 2.2% |
| End of Month | 59.7% | 37.3% | 3.1% |
| All Other | 45.4% | 49.9% | 4.7% |

Exhibit 6. Aggregate Breakdown of the Order Type, providing Liquidity in the Closing Cross: June 15 – December 31, 2004

High volume days are characterized by a high incidence of naturally crossing OC orders. As the volume declines, IO orders play an increasingly important role in providing liquidity to imbalances. In all cases, the liquidity on the continuous book plays a minor role in absorbing imbalances. Data like that in Exhibit 6 from periods before mid-June show, however, a much greater role for the continuous book. Evidently, during the first few months of operation, IO orders had not yet attained their eventual level of usage. This seems a natural consequence of the industry learning how to interpret and react to the NOII messages.

An interesting cross-sectional relationship emerges with respect to the role played by IO and continuous book orders. The relationship, shown in Exhibit 7 starts by categorizing each stock according to the *total* cross volume obtained during September – October 2004. The categories are 0-9 shares, 10-99 shares, 100-999 shares, etc. As shown in Exhibit 7, at the extreme low end, 35 stocks had total two-month cross volume of less than 10 shares. These stocks likely had only a single, tiny OC order during the two-month period. The exhibit shows that the continuous book was the primary source of liquidity for these orders, though IO orders also play a secondary role. As activity level increases, the continuous book plays a reduced role; at the high end it provides almost no liquidity. IO orders and other OC orders play a more important role, with the latter dominating at the high end.

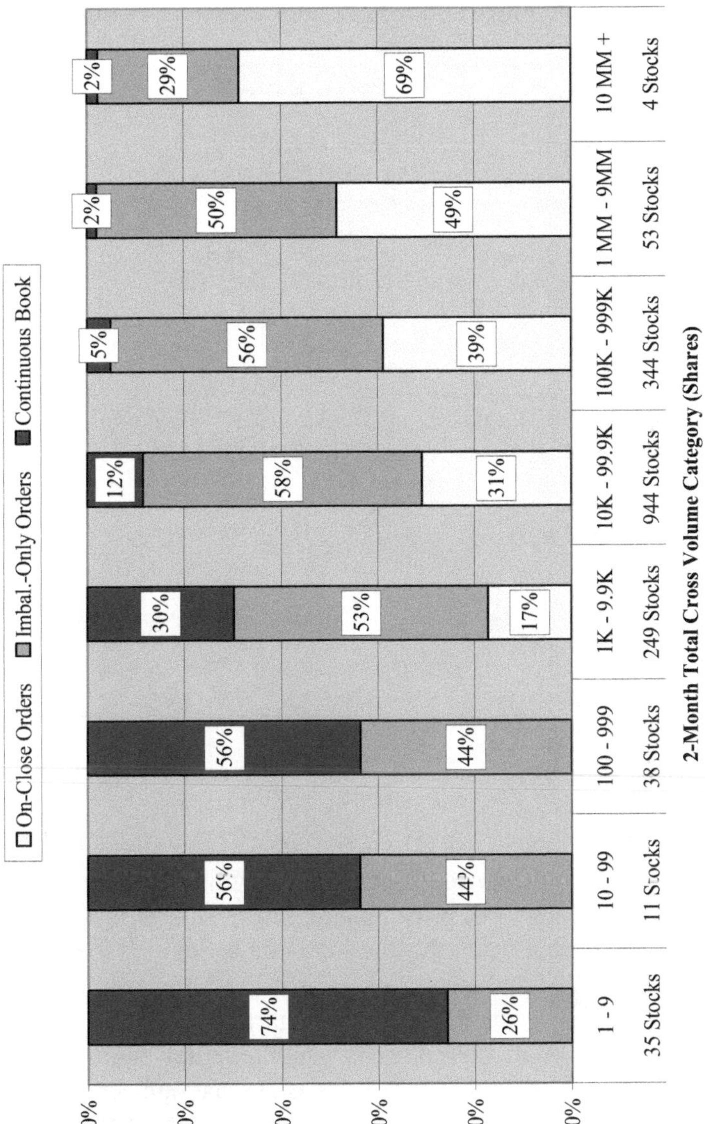


Exhibit 7. Liquidity Provision in the NASDAQ Cross: Cross-Sectional Breakdown for Sept-Oct 2004

## 1.3 Fill Rates

Overall rates of order entry and fill rates are shown in Exhibit 8.

| | MOC Orders | | | | LOC Orders | | | | IO Orders | | |
|---|---|---|---|---|---|---|---|---|---|---|---|
| | Average Daily Shares (MM) | | Fill Rate | | Average Daily Shares (MM) | | Fill Rate | | Average Daily Shares (MM) | | |
| Date | Entered | Executed | Non-short | Short | Entered | Executed | Non-short | Short | Entered | Executed | Fill Rate |
| Russell Rebal. | 407.2 | 402.5 | 99.9% | 36.6% | 805.2 | 146.6 | 21.5% | 6.0% | 179.1 | 88.3 | 49.3% |
| Quad Witch | 86.3 | 85.0 | 100% | 53.1% | 168.3 | 9.0 | 6.6% | 2.5% | 52.6 | 24.9 | 47.3% |
| End of Quarter | 20.5 | 20.2 | 100% | 39.5% | 142.0 | 15.2 | 13.9% | 1.0% | 58.3 | 14.8 | 25.4% |
| End of Month | 22.6 | 21.9 | 100% | 39.2% | 109.5 | 3.0 | 3.7% | 0.6% | 21.5 | 9.4 | 43.7% |
| All Other | 5.6 | 5.5 | 100% | 41.6% | 81.8 | 1.3 | 2.2% | 0.1% | 9.3 | 3.1 | 33.3% |

Exhibit 8. Fill Rates for On-Close Order Types: June 15 – December 31, 2004

As would be expected, MOC orders have essentially a 100% fill rate. If an MOC is not an order to sell short, the only thing preventing a guaranteed fill at the NOCP is the 10% price change limit. Time priority will determine which MOCs are filled when the auction price is not able to clear the market. During the Russell Rebalance cross, a small number of stocks reached the price threshold, preventing the aggregate fill rate to fall short of 100%. In the case in which an MOC submitter is a non-exempt short seller, the order cannot be filled unless the clearing price is at least one cent above the inside bid. For the most part, such an outcome requires that there be a net buy imbalance. Exhibit 8 indicates fill rates for non-exempt, short selling orders fluctuating from between about 35% and 50%. The fact that the fill rate tends to be less than 50% suggests that the submission of short sale MOC orders seems to be positively correlated with the occurrence of a sell imbalance in the auction.

The aggregate size of entered LOC orders is much larger than that of MOC orders, but they exhibit much lower fill rates than MOCs. Further, the

LOC fill rate has variation across the date categories under consideration. For the Russell date, non-short LOCs had a fill rate of about one-fifth. The end-of quarter dates had LOC fill rates of about 15%. On the other dates, the fill rate was much lower, especially for non-special dates. The key determinant of fill, of course, is the aggressiveness of the limit price. Evidently, on the Russell and end-of-quarter dates, LOC submitters were relatively more aggressive in their pricing, submitting more of what would turn out to be marketable limit orders. On the other dates, however, the pricing of the LOCs was extremely non-aggressive. Analysis of the distribution of order prices suggests that some firms seem to use LOCs as a type of imbalance buffering order—filling only when a substantial spike in price occurs. It seems, then, that the LOC order type is more commonly used by opportunistic traders. Those who truly wish to trade on the close use the MOC order.

Short LOC orders have very low fill rates. On a typical day, a short sell LOC is almost never filled. This is suggestive of two possibilities: short sell LOC orders are less aggressive than non-short orders, or, as is the case with MOCs, short sell LOC orders tend to be submitted in auctions in which there is a sell imbalance, leading to a clearing price at the bid, preventing the order from executing.

IO orders have fill rates fluctuating between one-half and one-quarter. On a regular day, about one-third of entered IO shares are filled. Additional analysis (not shown in the table) indicates a gradual fall in IO fill rates over time. Combined with increases in the sizes of the auctions, this fall indicates a growing surplus of on-close liquidity at the close.

## 1.4 Resolution of Imbalances

An important characteristic of the NASDAQ closing cross is the high degree of transparency regarding the level of imbalance on the on-close book. As described above, from 3:50:00 to 3:59:50 a sequence of 37 NOII messages are disseminated. This section provides an empirical analysis regarding the way in which imbalances are resolved during this time frame.

Consider the observed change in imbalance direction between the first and final NOII messages (Exhibit 9). There are four values taken by the imbalance direction indicator: buy (B), sell (S), no imbalance with crossed on-close orders (N), and no crossing on-close orders (O). The values are calculated with respect to the current state of the MOC/LOC order book, which cannot change, and the IO book and continuous book, both of which can change. Exhibit 4 presents results from all cross-eligible stocks during all trading days in September and October 2004. The table indicates the percentage breakdown of the four possible initial NOII values. The percentages are calculated in an unweighted fashion, in which each stock/day auction is an observation, as well as where each auction is weighted by the number of executed shares—more active stocks are given more weight. Then, for each value of the initial imbalance, the final imbalance is shown.

| | Percent of Auctions | | | Percent of Auctions | |
|---|---|---|---|---|---|
| Initial Imbalance | Un-weighted | Volume Weighted | Final Imbalance | Un-weighted | Volume Weighted |
| B | 46.9% | 56.4% | B | 36.5% | 43.6% |
| | | | N | 62.3% | 55.8% |
| | | | O | 0.0% | 0.0% |
| | | | S | 1.2% | 0.7% |
| S | 33.1% | 43.1% | B | 1.2% | 1.0% |
| | | | N | 56.7% | 60.4% |
| | | | O | 2.4% | 0.0% |
| | | | S | 39.7% | 38.6% |
| N | 0.4% | 0.5% | B | 0.4% | 3.3% |
| | | | N | 98.9% | 96.6% |
| | | | O | 0.0% | 0.0% |
| | | | S | 0.7% | 0.1% |
| O | 19.6% | 0.0% | B | 0.2% | 84.5% |
| | | | N | 0.0% | 1.4% |
| | | | O | 98.1% | 3.8% |
| | | | S | 1.7% | 10.3% |

Exhibit 9. Comparison of Initial and Final NOII Imbalance Indicators All Cross Eligible Stocks: September-October 2004

The table indicates that initially, buy imbalances are more common than sell imbalances. The short sell restrictions described above may be largely responsible for this difference. Very few sessions begin with a state of balance (status N), while about one fifth begin with no crossing orders (status O).

Roughly one-third (36.5%) of initial Buy imbalances remain Buy imbalances by the time of the last NOII message, with almost all of the remainder having been resolved to a state of balance (N). Initial Buy imbalances very rarely become either Sell imbalances (S) or non-crossed (O). On a share weighted basis, the likelihood of moving from B to N is lower than the unweighted likelihood, indicative of the fact that the larger auctions are less likely to be completely resolved as of 3:59:50.

The outcome of Sell imbalances is similar—the majority of imbalances and shares of imbalances are balanced by the time of the last NOII messages, but a large incidence of sell imbalances remain. If a stock starts the close with an N or an O, it will very likely remain that way during the remainder of the auction.

The impact of the resolution of imbalances on the clearing price can be seen by comparing the Current Reference Price, indicating the current state of the continuous book, and the Far Price, which indicates the current state of the on-close book in isolation. Exhibits 10 and 11 present a graphical representation of the convergence of the two prices for stocks with initial buy and sell imbalances, respectively.

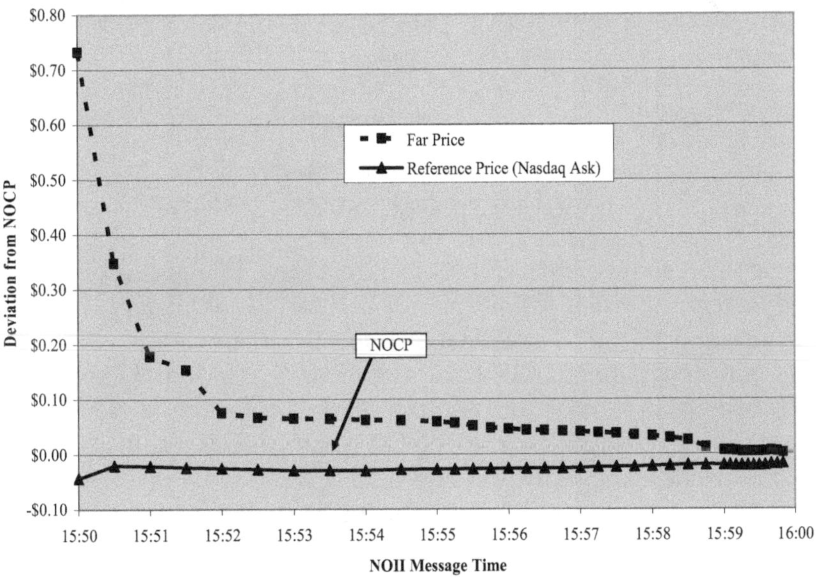


Exhibit 10. Convergence of Far Price and Continuous Market Price: Weighted Average of Stocks with Initial Buy Imbalances, Sept – Oct 2004

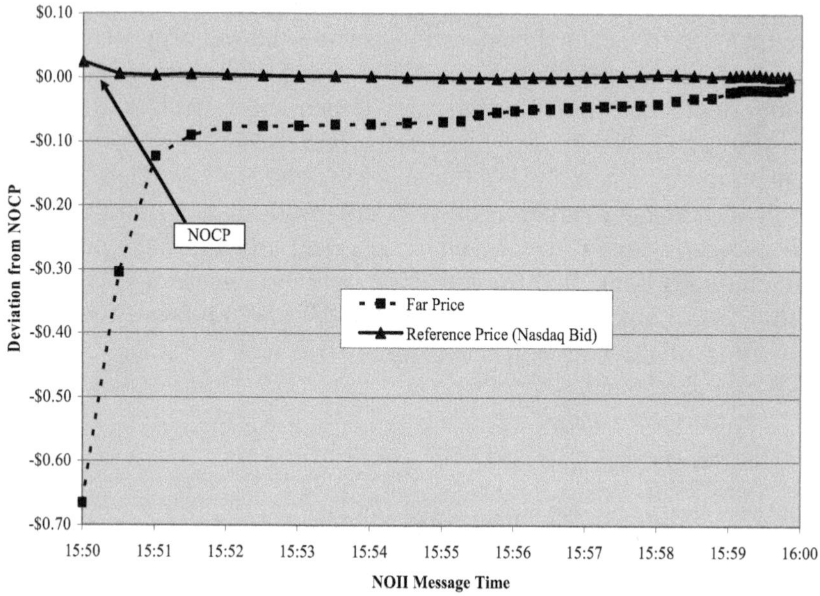


Exhibit 11. Convergence of Far Price and Continuous Market Price: Weighted Average of Stocks with initial Sell Imbalances, Sept – Oct 2004

Each exhibit shows, at each NOII dissemination time, the deviation of the Far and Reference Prices from the price that would (ultimately) become the auction-clearing NOCP. The deviation shown in the exhibits is a weighted average of the deviation of all stocks with the indicated initial imbalance, the weights being the number of executed shares in the cross. Note from the exhibits the way in which the rate of NOII messages increases.

As one would expect, for the buy imbalances shown in Exhibit 10, the initial Far Price exceeds the NOCP. The initial Reference Price, in this case the NASDAQ inside ask, is less than the NOCP. The deviation is much larger, though, for the Far Price, averaging about 73 cents. By the time of the next NOII message at 3:50:30, the average deviation has been about cut in half, to 34 cents. Thirty seconds later, it is cut in half again to 18 cents. Convergence to the NOCP seems to level out a bit at 3:52:00, though it accelerates again as 3:59:00 approaches, by which time the convergence has been achieved. The initial Reference Price averages about four cents less than the NOCP. It moves up to within about two cents below, but then basically stays there for the remainder of the NOII dissemination period. In sum, a buy imbalance in the on-close book, on average, results in the submission of IO orders that bring the clearing price back into line with the continuous market. The imbalance does, though, exert a small upward push on the continuous market price.

The situation for sell imbalances shown in Exhibit 11 is very similar to that of buy imbalances, with the obvious change in sign. Far prices are well below the NOCP but they quickly and steadily converge to the NOCP. In contrast to buy imbalances, the initial Reference Price of sell imbalances is only a bit more than two cents above the NOCP, and it quickly converges to a level that ultimately becomes the NOCP.

In sum, the empirical results show substantial industry reaction to the NOII message data. At the time of the cross, market participants have a very good idea of what the clearing price will be. Buy and sell imbalances in the on-close order book are effectively buffered by participants responding to the imbalance indicators. This finding does not, of course, mean that the price discovered in the auction is a "good" one. That topic will be taken up in the subsequent section.

## • IMPACT ON MARKET QUALITY

The previous section dealt with the functioning of the closing cross mechanism. This section addresses a more challenging question: the impact of NASDAQ closing cross on market quality. Specifically, three issues are addressed: the dispersion of prices at the close, the degree of fragmentation at the close, and the quality of NOCP price discovery. The analysis is based on making comparisons over three periods: the last month prior to the implementation of the NOCP, March 2003; the last month prior to the implementation of the closing cross, March 2004; and a month for which the closing cross was fully implemented, and market participants had adapted to it, September 2004. Each of these months contained a QuadWitch Friday as well as an end-of-quarter date, both of which were shown above to be of particular importance to the close. As with any analysis of this nature, the impact of the cross may be confused with other coincident trends in the marketplace. One such trend was a decline in stock price volatility generally. For example, the NASDAQ Composite Volatility Index of the Chicago Board Options Exchange (VXN) had the following values for the three sample months: 46.5, 24.9, and 21.7. The results shown below should be viewed with this caveat in mind.

## 1.5 Dispersion of Prices at Close

A classic complaint regarding the traditional, informal NASDAQ close was that there was no clear sense as to which of the many prices observed at the close of the day represented a suitable closing reference. Rather than a clearly predominant price at the close of the day, NASDAQ trading produced a "cloud" of end-of-day prices. As discussed above, many observers adopted an informal last sale rule to identify a closing reference price, but this price may not have represented the majority of trading done at the end of the day. Indeed, it may have been, and sometimes was, quite removed from the bulk of trading.

To assess the impact of the closing enhancements, end-of-day trading is analyzed for the three sample periods. Specifically, all non-late (.SLD), non extended-hours (.T) trades reported by all UTP market centers from 3:59:45 through 4:03:00 are identified. Prior Reference Price (.PRP) trades from the same timeframe are also identified. Technically speaking, while .PRP trades are effected after the market has closed, from the customers' perspective they are not viewed as extended hours trades. Finally, from the pos *t* closing cross month, the trades executed in the cross are identified. These trades should also be viewed as regular market open trades.

For each of the end-of-day trades in the sample, the difference between the trade price and the closing reference price is determined. For the March 2003 period, the closing reference is the price of the last non-modified trade before 4:01:30 from any market center. For the other two periods, the NOCP is used as the closing reference price. The price difference is rounded to the nearest cent. The shares of each trade are used as a weighting variable in determining the dispersion of trading around the closing price.

Exhibit 12 below provides some measures of dispersion of trading around the closing price.

| | March 2003 Pre NOCP | March 2004 Pre Cross | Sept. 2004 Post Cross |
|---|---|---|---|
| Share-weighted Mean Absolute Deviation[71] | \$0.022 | \$0.021 | \$0.012 |
| Percent of Volume at Closing Price | 38.6% | 56.0% | 72.7% |
| Volume within 2 cents of Closing Price | 74.0% | 75.7% | 86.1% |
| Volume within 5 cents of Closing Price | 89.5% | 87.6% | 94.1% |

Exhibit 12. Dispersion of End-of-Day Prices Around Closing Reference Price

By any of the dispersion measures shown in the table, the concentration of trading around the closing reference price has progressively tightened with each successive enhancement. The closing cross, though, appears to have had a larger impact than the NOCP introduction.

A graphical representation of the concentration of trading at the close is provided in Exhibits 13, 14 and 15 which provide share-weighted histograms of the end-of-day prices for each of the sample periods. The figures indicate the volume from the regular market open session, that reported .PRP, and, for September 2004, that done in the closing cross. Exhibit 13 shows that even though there was no formally designated closing price in March 2003, volume did tend to concentrate on the price determined by the informal rule. There was a comparatively small amount of volume marked .PRP done at the closing reference. Not readily visible from the graph are very small amounts of .PRP trades done at other prices.

Exhibit 14, illustrating the situation pos *t* NOCP but pre-Cross, indicates less dispersion. Trading done at the NOCP was predominately internalized .PRP trades, presumably done by market makers with customers. The addition of this segment of trading is the main contributor to the tighter distribution of trade prices at the end of the trading day. Finally, Exhibit 15 exhibits the tightest concentration of trading at the closing price. Trading done during the regular session, in the cross, and done .PRP all contributed to the shares done at the NOCP. During this month, virtually no .PRP trades were done at prices other than the NOCP.

[71] The formula for the mean absolute deviation is

$\sum volume_{i,j} \cdot \left| price_{i,j} - close_i \right| \div \sum volume_{i,j}$ for sample end-of-day trade *j* of stock *i*.

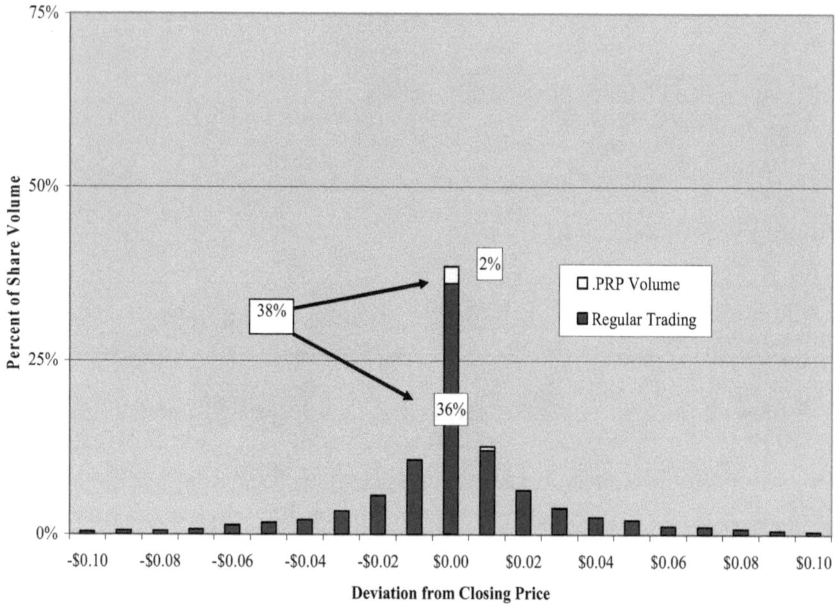


Exhibit 13. Dispersion of Prices at Close of Day: March 2003

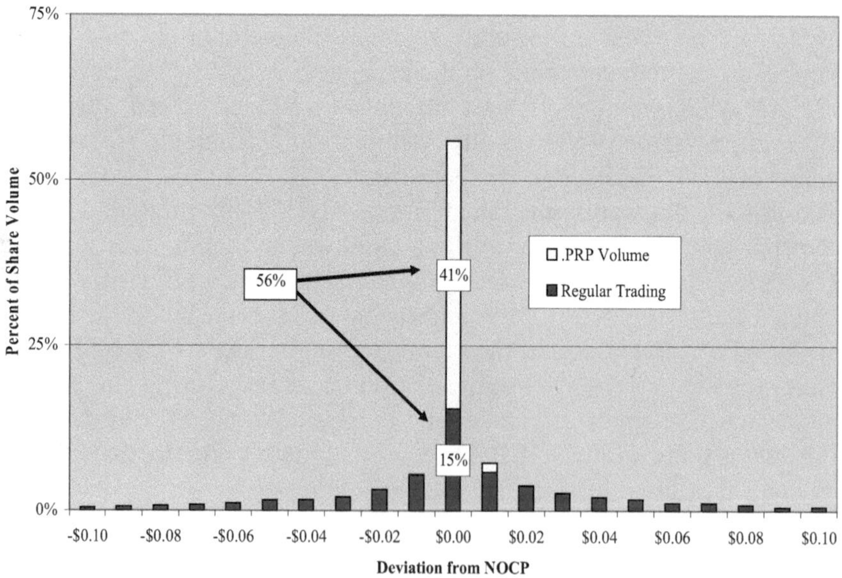


Exhibit 14. Dispersion of Prices at Close of Day March 2004

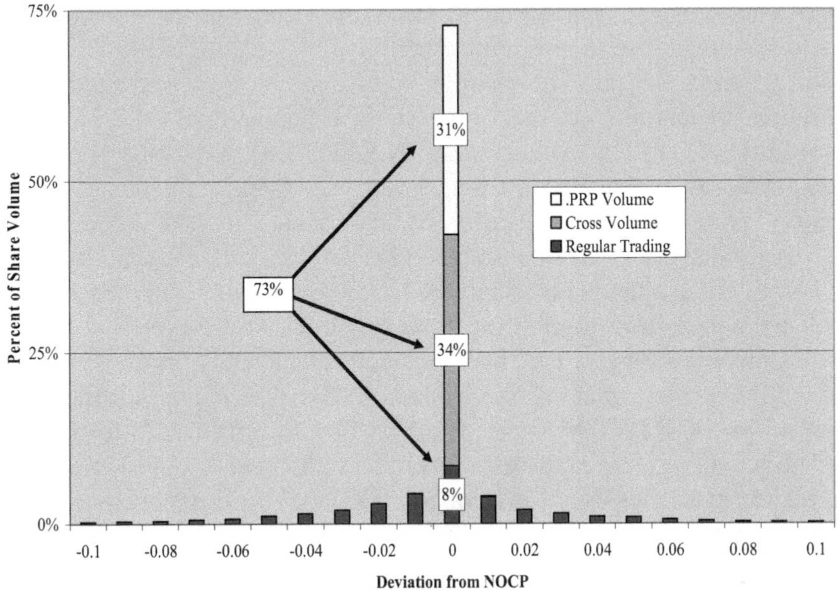


Exhibit 15. Dispersion of Prices at Close of Day: September 2004

## 1.6 Dispersion of Trading Across Venues

Another common complaint regarding end-of-day trading on NASDAQ stems from its "fragmentated" structure, i.e., liquidity spread over a number of venues. During the sample periods under consideration, trading in NASDAQ-listed stocks was largely dominated by trading within four electronic venues: Instinet/Island, Archipelago, BRUT, and NASDAQ's SuperMontage platform.[72] In addition to trading in these venues, there was a large segment of dealerized trading, sometimes broadly referred to as internalization. While important for the addition of liquidity it represents, internalization relies, for pricing purposes, on trading done in the electronic venues, which sets the inside quotes.

The electronic venues are tightly linked with each other; either through systems provided by the venue itself, or by third-party service bureaus.

[72] The Island and Instinet books were merged during the sample period of this study. The combined entity is called the INET ATS. There are other electronic venues trading NASDAQ stocks, Bloomberg TradeBook and the Attain ECN. These two venues have comparatively small amounts of volume compared to the other four. SuperMontage is now termed the NASDAQ Market Center.

Nevertheless, it is arguable that price discovery at the close, and the determination of an appropriate reference price, are hampered by the existing fragmentation. The fragmentation has perhaps worsened with the affiliation of certain of the above-named venues with Self-Regulatory Organizations (SROs) other than NASD/NASDAQ. Specifically, the Archipelago ECN became affiliated with the Pacific Exchange, and was formally recognized as a facility of that exchange and named ArcaEx. Starting in the spring of 2003, trades done on ArcaEx were reported through the Pacific Exchange. The Island ECN affiliated itself with the Cincinnati Stock Exchange (now named the National Stock Exchange), and registered as a Cincinnati specialist. Instinet, before its integration into Island, frequently reported trades through the NASD's Alternative Display Facility (ADF). The BRUT ECN began in early 2004 to print trades to the Boston Stock Exchange rather than NASDAQ. This changed, though, in September 2004 after NASDAQ's acquisition of BRUT. The fragmentation of trade reporting across various SROs meant that there was no single SRO responsible for maintaining the integrity of the Tape, e.g., ensuring that trades were reported properly, and that bad prints were pulled off the Tape. Further, fragmentation hampers the determination of an officially-recognized closing reference price.

While there are a number of ways to measure fragmentation, the simplest is to look at the market share of trading across the SROs trading NASDAQ-listed stocks. Exhibit 16 presents market shares for the five reporting venues that have made up the majority of reported trading during the three sample periods under consideration. Market share is computed for the end-of-day trading as well as for the full day. End-of-day trades are identified as was done in the analysis of the previous subsection: trades done during the last 15 seconds of the day, .PRP trades, and trades done in the closing cross. Market share can be measured by share of trades or share of share volume. For convenience, the table presents the simple average of the two market share metrics.[73] Also for convenience, two market share subtotals are shown representing the merger of Island and Instinet into INET, and the departure and subsequent return of BRUT to NASDAQ.

[73] The results shown in the Table are similar if one uses trade share or volume shares. Interestingly, pursuant to the data revenue sharing plan markets trading NASDAQ-listed stocks (UTP Plan), data revenue is allocated according to the simple average of trade market share and share volume market share. Thus, the figures in Table 7 represent revenue sharing percentages, which revenue constitutes a sizeable fraction of each market's total revenue.

| | March 2003 Pre NOCP | | March 2004 Pre Cross | | September 2004 Post Cross | |
|---|---|---|---|---|---|---|
| | End-of-Day | Full Day | End-of-Day | Full Day | End-of-Day | Full Day |
| Pacific (ArcaEx) | 0.4% | 0.3% | 13.1% | 22.7% | 9.2% | 22.8% |
| Cincinnati (Island/INET) | 16.1% | 12.5% | 10.6% | 26.7% | 11.4% | 27.5% |
| NASD/ADF (Instinet) | 3.9% | 6.0% | 0.0% | 0.1% | 0.0% | 0.2% |
| **Cincinnati + ADF** | 20.0% | 18.5% | 10.6% | 26.8% | 11.5% | 27.7% |
| Boston (BRUT) | 0.0% | 0.0% | 3.6% | 10.1% | 0.0% | 0.0% |
| NASDAQ | 78.9% | 80.5% | 72.3% | 40.0% | 79.1% | 49.2% |
| **NASDAQ + Boston** | 78.9% | 80.5% | 75.9% | 50.1% | 79.1% | 49.2% |

Exhibit 16. SRO-Reported Market Share for NASDAQ-Listed Stocks

It was during March 2003 that ArcaEx began migrating it's trading of NASDAQ stocks to the Pacific Exchange, hence there is not much to be learned by observing the Pacific's share of trading for that month. By contrast, Island was reporting all of its trading to Cincinnati during that month. Its share of trading was higher at the end of the day than during the day generally. Instinet was reporting trades to both NASDAQ and the NASD's Alternative Display Facility (ADF). The ADF share was a bit lower at the end of the day. The Cincinnati/ADF combination had slightly higher market share at the close than during the day generally: 20.0% compared to 18.5%. On net, NASDAQ's market share was a bit lower at the close.

By March 2004, after nearly a year's experience with the NOCP, the story was quite different. NASDAQ's market share was much higher at the close than during the rest of the day, and the three competing electronic venues' shares were roughly half of their full-day value at the close. The initiation of the closing cross seems to have advanced NASDAQ's market share a bit more. While the combined NASDAQ/BRUT full-day share fell about one percentage point between March and September 2004 (50.1% to 49.2%), the share at the close increased by about three points (75.9% to 79.1%). NASDAQ is now the dominant SRO venue at the close. While this development undoubtedly benefits NASDAQ's commercial interests, to the extent that fragmentation at the close was bad for traders, the situation is now much improved. The NOCP as promulgated by NASDAQ has clear claim as a representative closing reference price.

## 1.7 Quality of Price Discovery

Perhaps the most interesting but difficult question regarding the benefits of the NASDAQ closing process is its impact on the quality of the closing price. Is the new NOCP as determined by the closing call auction a "good" price, better than what had been used before? Obviously, sellers prefer a higher price, buyers a lower one. Is there an objective standard, though, for determining whether a price is at the right level? An approach espoused in the academic literature on market microstructure starts with the idea that efficient price discovery results in stock prices following a random walk. Changes in efficient prices should be unforcastable. Otherwise, the price does not impound all available information regarding the value of the stock. Applying this concept, one would conclude that the NOCP is good to the extent that it conforms to the properties of a random walk process.

There are two ways that a deviation from a random walk can occur: overshooting and undershooting. To illustrate, suppose that the auction process begins with a buy imbalance. If there were insufficient liquidity to buffer the imbalance, the auction would clear at a price that is "too high" in the sense that in a predictable fashion it will revert back to a lower level in subsequent trading. Consistent and predictable overshooting of the NOCP — rising too much or falling too much—is a violation of a random walk. A second deviation from a random walk is undershooting. This could happen if for some reason the NOCP were prevented from rising, say, as much as it should to accommodate a buy imbalance. The NOCP would be "too low" in the sense that price would predictably rise in subsequent trading. Price deviation collars set too tightly could create an undershooting problem.

Empirically, the typical deviation from random walk in a short horizon microstructure setting is overshooting. The overshoot occurs because liquidity-demanding orders (e.g. market orders, large institutional orders) will temporarily push the price up (for buys) or down (for sells). While this price movement is buffered by liquidity suppliers (dealers, limit order investors), these suppliers typically require compensation—the spread—in return for the risk they bear in having exposed their trading commitment to the market. Generally, spreads will always be non-zero, leading to non-random overshooting of prices, often referred to as "bid-ask bounce." Inevitable as spreads are, any market structure innovation that allows liquidity to be marshaled in such a way as to lower spreads represents an unambiguous improvement in market quality.

Evaluation of the closing enhancements, then, involves measuring the implicit "spread" impounded in the closing price. Does the closing price, if higher than the average level of prior trading, tend to fall back? If lower than prior trading, does it bounce back up? With a perfect closing price discovery process, there would be no relationship between the pre-close price change, and the pos *t* close change.

Within the current closing auction process, it is easy to grasp the idea that imbalances in on-close order flow could cause temporary dislocations in price. That is, a buy imbalance may be expected to exert upward pressure on prices. Would the same thing have happened under the two previous closing-price regimes? Prior to the implementation of the auction, imbalances in on-close order flow could indeed have occurred, putting pressure on prices, but they would have been far less transparent. For example, suppose market making firms had received an imbalance of on-close buy orders from customers. In response, they would have likely started to pre-position themselves to fill these orders by buying in the continuous market in the minutes leading up to the close. This buying would have put upward pressure in the market, resulting in a closing reference price higher than would have been the case without the imbalance. The presence of the imbalance would not have been as widely known, however.

While comparing the implicit spread of the closing price is an interesting issue, one caveat should be kept in mind. The new closing auction may have made investors more comfortable with the idea of submitting on-close orders for NASDAQ stocks. This could have led to an increase in on-close order submissions that, all-else equal, would increase the spread. Thus, finding that spreads are higher under the closing cross is not necessarily proof that market quality for investors has not improved.

There exist a variety of ways for measuring spreads. The method presented here fits nicely with the previous discussion on the quality of price discovery. Further it does not require knowledge of whether the closing process for a given stock and day had a buy or a sell imbalance.[74] (While imbalance direction is now known, thanks to NOII dissemination, it was not

[74] If imbalance direction is know, the well-known "effective" and "realized" spread measures can be computed. These measures are based on a direct comparison of the closing price with pre- and pos *t* close reference values. When one has estimates of effective and realized spreads, a determination of the so-called "information content" of the on-close order flow is possible. The information content is identified by gauging the extent to which price dislocations caused by the closing process are permanent or transitory. The spread measure using in this study is not able to made this determination.

known prior to the implementation of the cross.) The spread measure is based on comparing the pre-close price change with the pos *t* close change. Let $V_{pre}$ represent a pre-close reference value, $P_{close}$ the closing price (NOCP after April 2003), and $V_{post}$ a pos *t* close reference value. The spread measure starts with the following computation:

$\mathrm{Cov}[\log(P_{close}) - \log(V_{pre}), \log(V_{post}) - \log(P_{close})]$, where $\mathrm{Cov}[\cdot]$ represents the covariance measure from basic statistics, and $\log(\cdot)$ is the natural logarithm. The covariance measures whether successive price returns are correlated or not. Under a random walk, the covariance of successive returns is zero. It was shown by Richard Roll[75] that the typical overshoot (bid-ask bounce) scenario leads to the covariance being negative. For example, a buy imbalance leads to a price increase, but this is typically followed by a price decrease. Roll further suggested that the square root of the negative of the covariance ($\sqrt{-Cov}$) is a reasonable measure of the implicit spread, expressed in basis points.

The pre- and pos *t* close reference values should be chosen to be near the 4:00 closing, yet be totally free from the influence of any temporary price dislocation stemming from the closing process. Results shown below are based on using as $V_{pre}$ the 3:00 p.m. bid-ask midpoint of the NBBO (including all markets, not just NASDAQ), and $V_{post}$ as the 10:00 a.m. NBBO.

| | | March 2003 Pre NOCP | March 2004 Pre Cross | Sept. 2004 Post Cross |
|---|---|---|---|---|
| 1,459 Cross-Eligible Stocks | Unweighted | 88.4 bp | 68.6 bp | 52.5 bp |
| | Dollar-Volume Weighted | 35.4 bp | 35.5 bp | 28.6 bp |
| NASDAQ-100 Stocks | Unweighted | 37.7 bp | 39.6 bp | 29.4 bp |
| | Dollar-Volume Weighted | 37.4 bp | 32.0 bp | 27.0 bp |

Exhibit 17: Implicit Spreads of Closing Prices

75 Richard Roll, "A Simple Implicit Measure of the Effective Bid-Ask Spread in an Efficient Market," *Journal of Finance*, 39, 1127-1139, (1984).

midpoint of the day following the close. September 2004 is used as the pos *t* cross reference month because it, like March 2003 and March 2004, includes a quad-witch expiration date and an end-of-quarter date. Two groups of stocks are considered: all those that were cross-eligible during the pos *t* cross period, and the NASDAQ-100 stocks. To enhance the comparability, only those stocks listed during each the three sample periods under consideration are used. This restriction results in a full sample of 1,459 stocks, and a NASDAQ-100 sample of 97 stocks. The results for a given month are presented two ways: one in which each stock is weighted equally in computing the average spread, and one in which each stock is weighted by its daily average dollar volume. The weighted average is the preferred measure, as it is more indicative of the average experience of investors, who trade some stocks more heavily than others.

The results indicate that the closing prices in September 2004 were more efficient than those of the previous months. That is, the closing prices of September 2004 deviated less from a random walk than did the prices of the pre-cross sample months. The results are somewhat mixed as to whether pricing in March 2004 was better than March 2003. Comparing the weighted and unweighted results, and the results for all cross-eligible stocks with the NASDAQ-100 demonstrates that more active stocks tend to have better price discovery at the close. This result is not at all surprising, since spreads are generally tighter for active stocks. As noted above, interpretation of the foregoing results may be due to other confounding factors such as the decline in stock price volatility generally.

In sum, then, it appears that NASDAQ's new closing cross has contributed to improved market quality at the close. It has created a venue by which traders can focus their on-close activity, assured of obtaining a price that has become the industry standard reference. The system further provides a vehicle by which other traders can provide liquidity needed to fill imbalances arising from the on-close order flow.

The results indicate that the closing prices in September 2004 were more efficient than those of the previous months. That is, the closing prices of September 2004 deviated less from a random walk than did the prices of the pre-cross sample months. The results are somewhat mixed as to whether pricing in March 2004 was better than March 2003. Comparing the weighted and unweighted results, and the results for all cross-eligible stocks with the NASDAQ-100 demonstrates that more active stocks tend to have better price discovery at the close. This result is not at all surprising, since spreads are generally tighter for active stocks. As noted above, interpretation of the foregoing results may be due to other confounding factors such as the decline in stock price volatility generally.

In sum, then, it appears that NASDAQ's new closing cross has contributed to improved market quality at the close. It has created a venue by which traders can focus their on-close activity, assured of obtaining a price that has become the industry standard reference. The system further provides a vehicle by which other traders can provide liquidity needed to fill imbalances arising from the on-close order flow.

# CHAPTER 9: NASDAQ'S CLOSING CROSS: HAS ITS NEW CALL AUCTION GIVEN NASDAQ BETTER CLOSING PRICES? EARLY FINDINGS[76]

Michael S. Pagano, *Associate of Professor of Finance, Villanova University*
Robert A. Schwartz, *Marvin M. Speiser Professor of Finance, Zicklin School of Business, Baruch College, CUNY*[77]

On March 29, 2004, the NASDAQ Stock Market expanded its hybrid market structure by introducing a price discovery call auction. The call is run daily at 4:00 pm to close the normal NASDAQ trading day. NASDAQ refers to this as "closing cross," but the facility is in fact a call auction because it provides price discovery.[78]

We assess the impact that the call has had on NASDAQ's official closing prices. The assessment should be considered preliminary because relatively little time has passed since the call has been instituted. Time is required for participants to learn how best to use any new system, and for sufficient data to be generated for a more complete analysis. Nevertheless, we have undertaken this early assessment in view of the importance of the innovation.

[76] Reprinted, with permission, from Pagano, M. and Schwartz, R., "NASDAQ's Closing Cross: Has its new call auction given NASDAQ better closing prices? Early Findings," Journal of Portfolio Management, Volume 31, Number 4, Summer 2005, pp. 100-111.

[77] We are grateful to Frank Hatheway and Tim McCormick for their insights and factual information that they have provided us. We also thank Yakov Amihud, Corinne Bronfman, Lin Peng, George Sofianos, and Steve Wunsch for their very helpful comments.

[78] Crossing networks such as ITG's Posit and Instinet's after hours cross, do not provide price discovery. Rather, they match crossing buy and sell orders at a price (either the mid-point of a stock's bid-ask spread or a stock's closing transaction price) that is set in a major market center.

A call auction differs from continuous trading in the following way. In a continuous market, a trade is made whenever a bid and offer match or cross each other in price. In a call auction, the buy and sell orders are cumulated for each stock for simultaneous execution in a multilateral, batched trade, at a single price, at a predetermined time. By consolidating liquidity at specific times, a call auction is intended to reduce execution costs for individual participants, and to sharpen the accuracy of price discovery for the broad market.[79]

Call auctions have historically been a standard part of the French and German exchanges. The Deutsche Börse holds three calls a day for its large market capitalization stocks. Closing call auctions were introduced in Europe (including London, Paris, and Germany) specifically because of customer demands for improved price discovery at market closings. Most important, trading in derivatives such as equity options was being adversely affected by the ease with which only a relatively small number of orders could cause price dislocations in the equity market (the motivation for introducing the closing calls, according to senior officials at the Paris Bourse). The situation was making it difficult for traders to unwind their positions, and for positions to be marked-to-market at appropriate prices.

Indexers have their own needs to trade with certainty and precision at the closing prices that are used to compute the index values that they are seeking to track. The difficulty of doing this is particularly acute on days when firms are being added to and deleted from an index. Blume and Edelen [2004], in an insightful paper that pre-dates NASDAQ's Closing Cross, note that "NASDAQ has no formal mechanism to assure that a non-prearranged trade would take place at the closing price." The formal mechanism that would give this assurance is a closing call auction.[80]

Fully electronic call auctions have long been the standard procedure for opening the electronic order book markets of Canada, Europe, and the Far East (see Schwartz and Francioni, 2004). Until recently, however, they have been neither widely used nor well understood in the United States. The New York Stock Exchange opens and informally closes with calls that are not fully electronic and, until its expected introduction of an opening call in late 2004 / early 2005, NASDAQ has had no special opening facility at all.

Because of the importance of a single price opening procedure, Arthur Levitt, then chairman of the U.S. Securities and Exchange Commission,

[79] For additional discussion and further references, see Economides and Schwartz (1995), and Schwartz and Francioni (2004).

[80] The prearranged trades are the product of bilateral agreements with counterparties who are commonly hedge funds or dealers.

pressured NASDAQ in May 2000 to introduce call auction trading.[81] NASDAQ responded by establishing a special committee to consider the procedure, but the committee ended its work with no plans to introduce a call into its market model.

At the time, introduction of a periodic, batched auction into NASDAQ's sequential execution system would have presented a formidable challenge (as we learned from Frank Hatheway). Subsequently, the introduction of SuperMontage in Summer 2002 made the prospect of running a price discovery auction feasible, and NASDAQ's incentive to proceed with the innovation intensified in the Fall of 2003 when the American Stock Exchange, responding to Standard and Poor's expressed needs for better closing prices, announced that it would introduce a closing call auction.[82] The Amex call started as a pilot program in December 2003, and NASDAQ's Closing Cross, as noted, began operations on March 29, 2004.

Any market structure change can leave footprints in the data that, given the myriad of factors that impact security prices, are very difficult to detect. Detection at this time would be especially difficult with regard to NASDAQ's introduction of the Closing Cross. For one thing, the time-series data available for the analysis are limited. More importantly, participants have had very little time to become accustomed to the new facility and to establish their procedures for responding to imbalance information. Nevertheless, the closing cross is a major change in the NASDAQ market, and an attempt to assess its impact carries with it an effort to better understand the innovation.

Our assessment focuses on Closing Cross's impact on price determination at the June 25, 2004 Russell 2000 index rebalancing. Because of the importance of efficiently handling the Russell rebalancing, NASDAQ had accelerated its roll-out of Closing Cross so that all of the almost 1,700 NASDAQ stocks in the index would be in it by June 25. This daring move led Sofianos and Su [2004b] to write, "...it will take time and experience for NASDAQ to fine-tune its Closing Cross and for all market participants to fully incorporate it in their trading routines and systems. The Russell

[81] In a letter dated May 16, 2000 to Frank Zarb, then-chairman and chief executive officer of the National Association of Securities Dealers (NASD), Arthur Levitt wrote, "I urge the NASD to pursue a unified opening procedure, and in the interim, to press forward with measures to make the opening process more reliable and fair to investors."

[82] It was reported in *Securities Industry News*, October 13, 2003, that, according to David Blitzer, managing director and chairman of the S&P index committee, "S&P has been unhappy with Nasdaq delays in providing a final closing price, particularly on days with higher-than-normal volumes, cancelled trades that cause delay and uncertainty, and unusual price movement around the close."

rebalancing is happening too soon, before NASDAQ had the chance to gradually build full confidence in its new closing procedures for such a large number of stocks."

Key features of Closing Cross are the transparency it provides and the opportunity participants have to enter imbalance orders. But these features will work only if enough participants are watching the screens and entering these orders. Sofianos and Su [2004b] further wrote, "On June 25, many passive indexers will be demanding liquidity in the same direction. This will cause large imbalance announcements and profit opportunities for liquidity suppliers. The NASDAQ Closing Cross will make it easier for liquidity suppliers to identify these opportunities and provide liquidity, reducing closing price dislocation." Then the authors added a caveat: "The imbalance announcements will not work if nobody is watching."

In Pagano and Schwartz [2003], we assess the impact on price determination at the close that attended the Paris Bourse's inclusion of electronic call auctions at market closings in 1996 (for one set of stocks) and in 1998 (for a second set of stocks). The findings yielded by our Paris study indicated that the innovation significantly improved market quality at closings, and that the new procedure was a good complement to its electronic call auction openings.

We use a similar methodology here. We use the well-known market model to analyze the relationships between returns on individual stocks and the returns on a market index. Various researchers have found that the relationship between stock and index returns becomes much fuzzier when short run (e.g., daily) returns are used in place of longer-run returns (e.g., monthly) (see for example, Fisher [1966] for early work in this area, as well as Cohen et al. [1983a, b]). This deterioration has been attributed to price dislocations and other sources of noise in the price discovery process. Accordingly, any sharpening of price discovery following the introduction of the closing call should be reflected in more accurate market model estimates being obtained from daily data.

Extensive calendar data are needed, however, to contrast the goodness of market model estimates obtained using short return intervals with estimates obtained using long intervals, and relatively little time has passed since NASDAQ instituted their closing cross. We overcome this problem by using market model parameters estimated from prior data, and by focusing on two days when the market closing was under particular stress: the annual Russell 2000 index rebalancing on June 30, 2003 and the Russell rebalancing on June 25, 2004. We also analyze price determination on several surrounding days (one trading day before and after, and seven trading days before and after each of the two rebalancing days).

## DESCRIPTION OF CROSS PROCESS

NASDAQ's Closing Cross is an intricate facility that includes new types of orders; new order handling, display, and price determination procedures; and safeguards against unduly large price changes. But its fundamental functionality is straightforward.[83]

The key to NASDAQ's closing cross is the interaction of its continuous market with three types of close specific orders: market on-close (MOC) orders, limit on-close (LOC) orders, and imbalance orders (IO). The MOC and LOC orders are standard market and limit orders, except that they are to be executed in Closing Cross only. These on-close orders can be entered or cancelled at any time from the market's 9:30 am opening until 3:50 pm, ten minutes before the market's close.

At 3:30 pm, the facility starts accepting imbalance orders. As the name implies, IO orders are designed to reduce any imbalances that may exist between the market orders and limit orders that have been entered for the cross. All IO orders must be priced. An IO sell is executable only if it is priced at or above the 4:00 pm NASDAQ offer, and an IO buy is executable only if it is priced at or below the 4:00 pm NASDAQ bid.[84]

Because they are prevented from being priced aggressively, IO orders will never trade against each other. Rather, IO sells will execute against any buy imbalance (that drives price up), and IO buys will execute against any sell imbalance (that drives price down). IO orders can be entered until the time of the cross but, like the MOC and LOC orders, cannot be cancelled after 3:50 pm.

Transparency is critical to making the cross work. The driving force behind good price discovery at the close is for participants to see any buy or sell imbalances, and to benefit from an imbalance by entering an order that offsets it. Accordingly, between 3:50 pm and 4:00 pm, NASDAQ disseminates information about imbalances, indicative clearing prices, and the number of on-close and IO shares that the market is able to match at an indicative clearing price as the close approaches. The frequency of information dissemination increases from every 30 seconds (starting at 3:50), to every 15 seconds (at 3:55), to every 5 seconds (at 3:59). In total, users have ten minutes to check 1,500 issues for order imbalances and to respond. Order entry mistakes and the infeasibility of taking multiple looks

[83] Our description is based on information provided on Nasdaq's websites, MKTDATASVC@nasdaq.com and www.NASDAQTrader.com/close, as well as Sofianos and Su [2004a and 2004b].

[84] IOs that have been priced more aggressively are repriced for the cross at the best 4:00 p.m. bid or offer.

at a stock will limit the effectiveness of Closing Cross until appropriate order management systems for doing this electronically are put in place.

At 4:00 pm, no further orders are accepted, and the determination of the closing prices begins. At the cross, the MOC, LOC, and IO orders are brought together, along with limit orders and quotes from SuperMontage. A fairly complex algorithm is then used to determine the clearing price and the specific orders that trade.

The first criterion used for selecting the clearing price is to maximize the number of shares that will trade at the cross.[85] Time and price priorities are used to determine the specific orders that execute given the clearing price. In the determination, MOC orders receive the highest priority, which makes them highly likely to execute, although their certainty of execution is not guaranteed.

In general, buy orders at the clearing price and higher execute, as do sell orders at the clearing price and lower. All of the executed orders for a stock clear at a single price. Because of the transparency of the system, the pooling of all orders for a stock, and the inclusion of imbalance only orders, these single price auctions are expected to generate values that are less subject to price dislocations and are more in tune with the broad market's demand to hold shares.[86]

Closing Cross has been stress tested at various rebalancings and expiration days since its March 29th introduction. Not only are the event days stressful, but so too are surrounding days as participants pre-position and pos *t* position their holdings. Executives at the NASDAQ Stock Market have found that, by and large, the new facility has risen to the task from technical, user, and broader economic perspectives. Complexity does not appear to have been a drawback, heavy volumes have been adequately handled, and closing price behavior has seemingly improved.

The biggest test thus far for Closing Cross was on June 25, 2004, the day of the Russell 2000 rebalancing. 1,637 NASDAQ stocks participated in the rebalancing. Aggregate trading volume on that day was 2.54 billion shares, a total that exceeded NASDAQ's average daily trading volume by roughly

[85] If two or more prices result in an identical maximum number of shares that will trade, the algorithm for selecting a clearing price includes additional criteria: first, minimize the LOC imbalance and then, if a unique price still cannot be found, minimize the distance from the final mid-quote value in SuperMontage.

[86] The Nasdaq computer sets the closing price stock-by-stock and reports all of the orders that execute for a stock as a single print. Generally, the reports are completed within 4 seconds of the 4:00 pm cross, and Nasdaq Official Closing Prices (NOCPs) are disseminated at 4:01:30 pm. The process took 10 seconds at the Russell rebalancing because of the heavy volume on that day.

72%. Of the 2.54 billion shares, 333.39 million (13.14%) were in the cross.[87]

The median price difference between the volume-weighted average price (VWAP) for the 5-second interval preceding the cross and the price set at the cross was 16 cents (roughly 1.0% of price). Our analysis suggests that this average pricing difference might, in part at least, be mitigating dislocations experienced in the continuous market at this stressful time.

## METHOD FOR ASSESSING MARKET QUALITY

Our assessment of the closing call's impact is based on a methodology that we used for the Paris study (Pagano and Schwartz, [2003]). The key to our methodology is recognition that inaccuracies in price discovery for individual stocks are reflected in non-synchronous price adjustments across stocks and that, because of this, we can gain insight into the sharpness of price discovery by studying the co-movements of security prices in relatively brief intervals of time (i.e., one-day). That is, our procedure enables us to infer market quality from the synchronicity of price changes across a set of stocks.

To this end, we use the well-known market model to infer the quality of price discovery at market closings. The market model simply regresses a company's stock returns on the returns for a market portfolio using equation:

$$\kappa_{j,t} = \alpha_j + \beta_j \kappa_{m,t} + \varepsilon_{j,t}$$

where,

$\kappa_{j,t}$ = daily stock return for the company j at time $t$,

$\kappa_{m,t}$ = daily stock return on the systematic risk factor, i.e., the "market" return at time $t$,

$\alpha_j$ = intercept term,

$\beta_j$ = a measure of the $j^{th}$ stock's sensitivity to the systematic market risk factor, and

$\varepsilon_{j,t}$ = random error term (market model residual) at time $t$ with zero mean.

Drawing on work by Cohen, Hawawini, Maier, Schwartz, and Whitcomb [1983a, 1983b], we use the market model to contrast the short-run and long-run relations between individual stock returns and broad market index returns. Factors such as bid-ask spreads, market impact, and inaccuracies in price discovery all affect the very short interval (i.e., daily) returns. More importantly, short-term stock price adjustments across a set of stocks are

[87] The most heavily traded stock in the cross was Cisco (7.45 million shares).

expected to be non-synchronous if price discovery for individual equity shares is a protracted process (as prior research suggests).

Our methodology is designed to capture this non-synchronicity. The key is observing the extent to which residual variance (the variance of the $\varepsilon_{j,t}$) is higher when returns are measured using a daily interval in place of a longer interval (e.g., one month). We assess residual variance by examining its converse, the square of the market model correlation coefficient $R^2$, a statistic that measures the percentage of variation in the dependent variable ($\kappa_{j,t}$) that is explained by variation in the dependent variable, $\kappa_{m,t}$. Higher values of $R^2$ indicate that a stock's price movements are more closely aligned with changes in the broad market.

This methodology provided the basis for our previous study of the introduction of the closing call in the Paris market. The Paris Bourse (now known as Euronext Paris) provided an exceptionally rigorous environment for assessing the efficiency of call auction trading. Because the Bourse introduced its closing call at two different dates for two different sets of companies, we were able to test the robustness of our analysis through replication. In addition, we contrasted changes in the quality of the market at closings with changes in the quality of the Paris Bourse's market openings.

This gave us reasonable assurance that our findings were not attributable to the particular time period used or to the specific sample of stocks selected. We have reasonable confidence that our statistical findings are attributable to the call itself, not to some other factor.

The Paris study, however, required a relatively extensive set of calendar data. We used 500 trading days' worth of data to estimate the requisite market model parameters spanning the periods May 1995 – April 1997 and June 1997 – May 1999 for the two closing call event dates. A similar test design for our current Nasdaq study would have required a data set that extended to June 2005. We expedite the estimation process by using a modified methodology to focus on just a few days of particular stress, at and around the day of the Russell 2000 index rebalancing in 2003 and in 2004.

Amihud, Mendelson, and Lauterbach [1997] describes a relative return dispersion (RRD) measure that can be computed using the residuals from a market model. Using the market model run on daily data, the statistic is calculated for day $t$ as:

$$\mathrm{RRD}_t = \Sigma_j \varepsilon_{jt}^2 / n$$

where $\mathrm{RRD}_t$ is the relative return dispersion for the entire sample of securities at day $t$; $\varepsilon_{jt}^2$ is the squared market model residual for security $j$ at time $t$; and $n$ is the number of securities in the sample at day $t$.

The relative return dispersion measure incorporates market frictions from a different perspective than the conventional market model $R^2$ statistic. The $R^2$ statistic captures the magnitude of market model residuals over time for a particular stock. Amihud, Mendelson, and Lauterbach's RRD measure depicts the magnitude of the market model residuals across stocks for a particular trading day. The two measures provide complementary methods for examining market-wide changes in trading costs and the accuracy of price determination.

The RRDs should be higher on days when the market faces large buy or sell order imbalances but, for any given level of stress, it should be lower if the trading system is better able to cope with these imbalances. For this reason, the measure is particularly suitable for analyzing the quality of price determination at Russell index rebalancings (days of particular stress), and for contrasting the 2003 rebalancing (before Closing Cross was introduced) with the 2004 rebalancing (after Closing Cross had been put in use). If the new facility has in fact increased the accuracy of price determination, price adjustments across stocks should be more synchronous, and the RRD statistic for the 2004 rebalancing should be *lower* than it was for the 2003 rebalancing.

## ANALYSIS OF THE PARIS CLOSING CALL

Our analysis of price behavior at the Paris Bourse was based on two samples of firms (50 relatively small cap "B" stocks, and 50 large cap "A" stocks) for two different event dates (the closing call was introduced on May 13, 1996 for the B stocks, and on June 2, 1998 for the A stocks). We summarize the findings in this section of the paper. Our market model tests indicated that price adjustments, for these stocks, were more synchronized after the closing call's implementation. The clarity of the results obtained provides confidence that the basic methodology employed can be used to assess the impact of NASDAQ's Closing Cross.

| | Smaller Cap Stocks | | | Larger Cap Stocks | | |
|---|---|---|---|---|---|---|
| Average $R^2$ | Pre-event | Post event | % Diff. | Pre-event | Post event | % Diff. |
| 1-day interval | 0.005 | 0.012 | **140.0** | 0.101 | 0.120 | 18.8 |
| 20-day interval | 0.050 | 0.094 | 88.0 | 0.177 | 0.275 | 55.4 |
| Change in $R^2$ (20-day minus 1-day) | 0.045 | 0.082 | 140.0 | 0.076 | 0.155 | 103.9 |
| Pctg. Difference (%) | **900.0** | **683.3** | | **75.3** | **129.2** | |

Exhibit 18. Comparison of Adjusted $R^2$ Statistics over Different Return Intervals before and after Implementation of the Closing Call Auction Mechanism at the Paris Bourse. Note: Boldface identifies the differences between the average $R^2$ statistics that are significant at the .01 level.

Exhibit 18 shows sample average $R^2$s for the two sets of stocks (the less-liquid, small cap B shares, and the more-liquid, large cap A shares), for two measurement intervals, the shortest being 1 day and the longest being 20 days.[88] The individual $R^2$s shown in Exhibit 1 display considerable variation across measurement intervals and between the large and small cap stocks. Nevertheless, they provide a good overview of the closing call's impact on the synchronicity of price movements across stocks.

For the small cap B stocks, the pre-event $R^2$s average 0.050 for the 20-day interval and 0.005 for the 1-day interval, a 900 percent difference. The comparable values for the large cap A stocks are 0.177 for the 20-day interval and 0.101 for the 1-day interval, a 75.3 percent difference. After the event dates, the across-firm, average 1-day $R^2$s increase 140% for the B stocks and 19% for the A stocks. The jump is very clear for the small cap stocks but less so for the large caps, especially given the underlying variability in the $R^2$ measurements.

We further found that improving market quality at the close had broader impacts on the Paris market. Spreads tightened during the final hour of trading in the Bourse's continuous B market (not tabulated here). Presumably, knowing that they could always go into the closing call, traders were more willing to place limit orders and to run the risk of not executing in the closing minutes of the continuous market. Further, the quality of price formation improved at next day openings (although not as much as at the close itself). Apparently, sharpened price formation at the close has a

[88] Returns are measured using closing prices. We report changes in the market model's beta parameter in Pagano and Schwartz [2003], but omit them here to conserve space.

positive spillover that translates into more accurate price determination at next day openings.

The results for the Paris study were consistent for two independent events that involved two different samples of stocks and that occurred on two different dates. They were also robust to the possible confounding effects of sample wide changes in return volatility and trading volume during the periods surrounding the closing call's two implementation dates. Our findings were further supported by the lack of any material changes in the test statistics for two control samples for both opening and closing prices. This gave us further confidence that our results were not attributable to the specific samples of stocks, time periods, or methodology that we used.

## MARKET MODEL RESULTS FOR NASDAQ STOCKS

We run a comparable market model test that we ran on 50 NASDAQ stocks for the periods January 2000 – December 2001 and January 2002 – December 2003. Our objective is to assess changes in the market model $R^2$ statistic for the NASDAQ stocks as we switch from a 20-day to a 1-day measurement interval. We wish to determine whether or not non-synchronicity characterizes daily closing prices in the NASDAQ market as it does in the Paris market.

Our two NASDAQ samples captured two different sets of market conditions. During 2000-2001, the stock market bubble burst and the U.S. economy entered its first recession in over a decade (March 2001 – November 2001, per the NBER cycle dating methodology). In the following period, 2002 – 2003, macroeconomic growth rebounded and, as it did, the market bottomed out and rallied strongly.

We apply the methodology described in Pagano and Schwartz [2003] to a stratified sample of 50 NASDAQ stocks using daily closing prices. The sample included the 10 most actively traded NASDAQ stocks for 2003 plus 40 stocks that were randomly selected from size-ranked deciles (we randomly chose 4 stocks from each of the 10 deciles created by the Center for Research in Security Prices.

We then run market model regressions for each stock for 12 different return intervals (1 – 10, 15, and 20 days). These 600 regressions (50 stocks x 12 intervals) were estimated for both sample periods (2000 – 2001 and 2002 – 2003, respectively). This yields 1,200 regressions in total (600 x 2 periods). For the most part, the results for $R^2$ were similar in magnitude to those reported in Pagano and Schwartz [2003].[89]

Exhibit 19 shows the $R^2$ values for just two of the measurement intervals (1-day and 20-day) and for the two time periods. For the earlier period, $R^2$ increased 35.1% (from 0.074 to 0.100) as we move from the 1-day interval to the 20-day interval. Surprisingly, in the later period, average $R^2$ is actually higher for the 1-day interval than for the 20-day interval, although the two values are virtually identical (0.134 and 0.157 for the 20-day and 1-day intervals, respectively). Apparently, the rapidly rising tide of the market during the rebound period carried a broad array of NASDAQ stocks along with it on a daily basis.

| Average $R^2$ | Earlier | Later | % Diff. |
|---|---|---|---|
| 1-day interval | 0.074 | 0.157 | **112.2** |
| 20-day interval | 0.100 | 0.134 | 34.0 |
| Change in $R^2$ statistic (20-day minus 1-day) | 0.026 | -0.023 | n.m. |
| Pctg. Difference (%) | 35.1 | -14.6 | |

Exhibit 19. Comparison of Adjusted $R^2$ Statistics over Different Return Intervals for 2000 – 2003 at the NASDAQ Stock Market. Note: Boldface identifies the differences between the *Earlier* and *Later* periods' average $R^2$ statistics that are significant at the .01 level. n.m. denotes not meaningful.

## RUSSELL REBALANCING

The 1996 and 1998 results for the Paris Bourse stocks, coupled with the 2000 – 2003 evidence for the NASDAQ stocks, suggest that market frictions perturb the synchronicity of intra-day price movements, and that the introduction of a closing call auction has the potential to improve market quality for NASDAQ. To test this hypothesis, we examine some of the most stressful trading days of the year on NASDAQ, the days surrounding the Russell 2000 index rebalancing.

Our test focuses on the relative return dispersion statistic (RRD) described by Equation (2). If Closing Cross has had a beneficial effect, RRD should be lower during the 2004 rebalancing compared with the 2003

[89] The changes in the market model beta between the 1-day and 20-day measurement intervals were also similar to what we observed for the French stocks. To conserve space, we report only results for the 50-stock averages of the 1- and 20-day return intervals rather for all 12 return intervals.

rebalancing. This, however, is a tough test given that the 2004 rebalancing occurred only three months after the introduction of the Closing Cross. Sofianos and Su [2004b], writing before the rebalancing, put it this way: "But on June 25, traders will be stress testing a complicated closing mechanism that has been up and running for only a few months."

Over the next several years, more extensive time series data will be available and, more importantly, NASDAQ's closing call will have become more familiar to traders and portfolio managers. Nevertheless, a preliminary assessment is possible today.

- Rebalancing

The rebalancing of the Russell 2000 index is an annual event that has taken place toward the end of June each year since 1990.[90] This index is comprised of small- to mid-cap U.S. stocks, and the rebalancing (or "reconstitution" as Russell Inc. calls it) is a stressful event for portfolio managers and NASDAQ, the market where most of the stocks in the index trade. As Russell's website, www.russell.com, notes, "over $300 billion is invested in funds that rely on Russell's U.S. indexes as investment models." (see www.russell.com)

Russell ranks the largest 3,000 U.S. stocks by their market capitalizations as of the end of May, starting with the largest. The Russell 2000 contains the smaller two-thirds of this set (i.e., stocks ranked 1,001 – 3,000). The Russell 1000 index represents the top 1,000 U.S. stocks, but portfolio managers generally concentrate more on the Russell 2000, possibly because the large cap stocks are in other widely tracked indexes such as the S&P 500 and Dow Jones Industrial Average. Preliminary lists of additions, deletions, and weight changes to the Russell 2000 are circulated during June prior to the official, effective date of the index's rebalancing.

Trading is unusually heavy on the rebalancing day and the surrounding days. Portfolio managers sell the stocks that are being dropped from the index or that are being given a reduced weight in it, and buy those stocks that are being added or given a greater weight. Managers who want to minimize "tracking error" relative to the index typically concentrate their trades on the official rebalancing date and, because one closing price is used to compute two returns, a larger return variance (measured using closing

[90] Before to 1990, the rebalancings were more frequent (quarterly during 1979-1986 and semi-annually from 1987 to June 30, 1989).

prices) may be observed on the day of the rebalancing and on the following day.[91]

The additions and deletions from the index are announced earlier in June, and some managers choose to adjust their portfolios closer to the announcement date than to the implementation date. We have been advised that some managers traded in advance of the 2004 rebalancing for another reason: to guard against the possibility of a technical failure preventing them from executing in Closing Cross on June 25.

Before 2004, the annual rebalancing occurred on the last trading day of June (typically June 30th). In 2004, Russell moved the rebalancing date up to the last Friday in June to allow more time before the next trading day to alleviate potential trade processing concerns. In a Russell Press Release dated February 5, 2004, Sandy Rattray, a managing director at Goldman, Sachs & Co., was quoted as saying, "The Russell index reconstitution day is one of the busiest trading days in the U.S. equity market, particularly because passive managers are rebalancing small cap portfolios. Occasionally closing prices can be difficult to immediately determine on the rebalance day. Moving the date to the last Friday in June allows exchanges, asset managers and brokers plenty of time to be ready for the next trading day if operational issues arise." Accordingly, the Russell 2000 rebalancing, which was on June 30 in 2003, was moved to June 25 in 2004. We use these two event dates as the primary focus of our analysis.

- Data

For our RRD tests, we first compute the residuals from the market model described by Equation (1) for the specific event dates in question. These residuals, the $\varepsilon_{j,t}$ (also known as "abnormal returns"), are squared and averaged across stocks for a specific day (e.g., June 25, 2004 for the 2004 "event," and June 30, 2003 for the 2003 "event"). The cross-sectional average is our RRD statistic.

We compare the RRD for June 30, 2003 with the RRD for June 25, 2004, and we test the hypothesis that NASDAQ's closing call improved market quality. For this purpose, we apply difference-in-means statistical tests for the overall sample of stocks, and for quartiles broken down by market

[91] Approximately 275-450 stocks are either added or deleted from the Russell 2000 during a typical rebalancing and thus there are 600-900 stocks in total affected by this event. Approximately 1,500-1,700 stocks remain within the index from one year to the next. A Tuesday closing price is used to measure the Tuesday return (Tuesday's closing price relative to Monday's closing price) as well as the Wednesday return (Wednesday's closing price relative to Tuesday's closing price).

capitalization. If the call was successful, we expect, all else equal, that the RRD for 2004 will be smaller than the RRD for 2003.

Daily returns were computed using Reuters' Bridgestation service for the relevant days surrounding the 2003 and 2004 rebalancings. The assessment covered 1,488 stocks in 2003 and 1,550 stocks in 2004. Along with the daily returns for the individual stocks, market index returns and beta estimates are needed to calculate the market model residuals. For this purpose, we used the daily return on the S&P 500 stock index and the 60-month beta estimates pre-computed by Standard & Poor's Compustat service. The beta estimates are based on monthly return data for the individual stocks and for the S&P 500 stock index during the 60-month period ending in April of each of the two years.[92]

Using the data described above, we compute the market model residual for each of the stocks for each of the days in our analysis. To examine the immediate effect of the two rebalancings, we calculate the market model residuals and average RRD statistic for the day before the event ( *t* 1 in our notation), the actual day of the rebalancing (t), and the day following the event ( *t* 1). Recognizing that the rebalancing has an even more protracted impact as some managers pre-position well before the event while some who have over-compensated subsequently reverse out of their unbalanced positions, we also compute the market model residuals and RRD statistics for the seventh trading day preceding and the seventh trading day following the 2003 and 2004 events.[93]

In all, we have five RRD statistics for each of the two years: days *t* 7, *t* 1, t, *t* 1, and *t* 7. The RRD statistics are computed for the full sample of stocks, and for four quartiles that are based on the market capitalization of the stocks at the end of April for each year.

- Findings

[92] Specifically, the beta estimates for the 2003 event are based on data from May 1998 to April 2003, and the 2004 beta estimate is based data from May 1999 to April 2004. We ended each computation period in April so that the estimates would not be biased by potentially confounding effects associated with the Russell 2000 rebalancing activity that begins at the end of May each year.

[93] The -7/+ 7 trading days were chosen to avoid the potentially confounding effects caused by "triple witching" expiration dates earlier in June, and the Fourth of July weekend in early July. Days yet farther away from the event dates were not considered because there is a greater chance that, as the "event window" is lengthened, confounding effects related to changes in market wide conditions and/or macroeconomic news might influence the results. The -7/+ 7 trading days represent a reasonable trade-off between the conflicting effects.

The RRD statistics are given in Exhibit 20. The first two columns report the cross-sectional means for 2003 and 2004, respectively. The actual difference and percentage difference between these averages are presented in the third and fourth columns, respectively, and the last two columns display the related *t* statistics and p values associated with a difference-in-means test. Panel A gives the results for the full sample, and Panels B – E show the results for each of the four market cap quartiles, from the lowest to the highest.[94]

**A. 2003 to 2004 Difference in Means Test Results for Full Sample**

| Variable | 2003 Mean | 2004 Mean | Difference | Pct. Diff. | t Value | Pr > \|t\| |
|---|---|---|---|---|---|---|
| RRD (-7) | **0.000858** | **0.000432** | **-0.000426** | -49.6% | **-5.95** | 0.0001 |
| RRD (-1) | **0.000733** | **0.000583** | -0.000150 | -20.5% | -1.48 | 0.1389 |
| RRD (0) | **0.000968** | **0.000842** | -0.000126 | -13.0% | -1.26 | 0.2067 |
| RRD (+1) | **0.000899** | **0.000653** | **-0.000246** | -27.4% | **-3.21** | 0.0015 |
| RRD (+7) | **0.000750** | **0.000402** | **-0.000348** | -46.4% | **-4.05** | 0.0002 |
| RRD (-1 to +1) | **0.002089** | **0.001673** | **-0.000416** | -19.9% | **-2.06** | 0.0401 |

Exhibit 20. Relative Return Dispersion (RRD) Test Results. Note: Boldface items denote statistically significant differences from 0 at the .05 or lower level

[94] Non-parametric Wilcoxon tests and tests based on medians yield essentially the same results reported in Exhibit 3 based on the *t* statistic. To conserve space, we report only the *t* statistics here. We also report the median RRD estimates across size-based quartiles in Exhibit 23 and discuss this graph in this section.

**B. 2003 to 2004 Difference in Means Test Results Ranked by Market Capitalization (First/Smallest Quartile)**

| Variable | 2003 Mean | 2004 Mean | Difference | Pct. Diff. | t Value | Pr > \|t\| |
|---|---|---|---|---|---|---|
| RRD (-7) | **0.001332** | **0.000417** | **-0.000915** | -68.7% | **-5.49** | 0.0001 |
| RRD (-1) | **0.001129** | **0.000709** | **-0.000419** | -37.2% | **-2.12** | 0.0347 |
| RRD (0) | **0.002035** | **0.001338** | **-0.000697** | -34.2% | **-2.33** | 0.0206 |
| RRD (+1) | **0.001378** | **0.000895** | **-0.000483** | -35.0% | **-2.62** | 0.0093 |
| RRD (+7) | **0.001234** | **0.000580** | **-0.000654** | -53.0% | **-3.09** | 0.0023 |
| RRD (-1 to +1) | **0.004226** | **0.002492** | **-0.001734** | -41.0% | **-2.97** | 0.0033 |

**C. 2003 to 2004 Difference in Means Test Results Ranked by Market Capitalization (Second Quartile)**

| Variable | 2003 Mean | 2004 Mean | Difference | Pct. Diff. | t Value | Pr > \|t\| |
|---|---|---|---|---|---|---|
| RRD (-7) | **0.000879** | **0.000473** | **-0.000406** | -46.1% | **-3.41** | 0.0008 |
| RRD (-1) | **0.000755** | **0.000593** | -0.000162 | -21.5% | -1.20 | 0.2316 |
| RRD (0) | **0.000914** | **0.000842** | -0.000072 | -7.9% | -0.54 | 0.5893 |
| RRD (+1) | **0.001027** | **0.000661** | **-0.000366** | -35.6% | **-2.21** | 0.0276 |
| RRD (+7) | **0.000643** | **0.000380** | **-0.000263** | -40.9% | **-2.72** | 0.0070 |
| RRD (-1 to +1) | **0.001684** | **0.001493** | -0.000190 | -11.3% | -0.83 | 0.4084 |

**D. 2003 to 2004 Difference in Means Test Results Ranked by Market Capitalization (Third Quartile)**

| Variable | 2003 Mean | 2004 Mean | Difference | Pct. Diff. | t Value | Pr > \|t\| |
|---|---|---|---|---|---|---|
| RRD (-7) | **0.000736** | **0.000449** | **-0.000287** | -39.0% | **-1.99** | 0.0476 |
| RRD (-1) | **0.000664** | **0.000297** | **-0.000367** | -55.3% | **-4.11** | 0.0001 |
| RRD (0) | **0.000610** | **0.000673** | 0.000063 | 10.3% | 0.39 | 0.6989 |
| RRD (+1) | **0.000694** | **0.000580** | -0.000115 | -16.5% | -0.75 | 0.4544 |
| RRD (+7) | **0.000779** | **0.000281** | **-0.000498** | -63.9% | **-2.15** | 0.0323 |
| RRD (-1 to +1) | **0.001533** | **0.001043** | **-0.000490** | -32.0% | **-2.26** | 0.0243 |

**E. 2003 to 2004 Difference in Means Test Results Ranked by Market Capitalization (Fourth/Largest Quartile)**

| Variable | 2003 Mean | 2004 Mean | Difference | Pct. Diff. | t Value | Pr > \|t\| |
|---|---|---|---|---|---|---|
| RRD (-7) | **0.000483** | **0.000388** | -0.000095 | -19.8% | -0.70 | 0.4819 |
| RRD (-1) | **0.000386** | **0.000723** | 0.000336 | 87.1% | 1.07 | 0.2852 |
| RRD (0) | **0.000316** | **0.000476** | 0.000160 | 50.6% | 1.16 | 0.2481 |
| RRD (+1) | **0.000499** | **0.000457** | -0.000042 | -8.5% | -0.48 | 0.6285 |
| RRD (+7) | **0.000346** | **0.000362** | 0.000016 | 4.6% | 0.16 | 0.8765 |
| RRD (-1 to +1) | **0.000917** | **0.001597** | 0.000681 | 74.2% | 1.56 | 0.1201 |

Exhibit 20 (cont.). Relative Return Dispersion (RRD) Test Results Note: Bold face items denote statistically significant differences from 0 at the .05 or lower level

Panel A shows that, for the full sample, the RRD statistics are uniformly lower in 2004 than in 2003. The largest reductions (in percentage terms)

occurred during trading days *t* 7 and *t* 7. The RRD statistics for the three days surrounding the 2004 event are also lower than their 2003 counterparts (e.g., 13% – 27% lower), but only the *t* 1 day's difference is statistically significant. The lack of statistical significance on days *t* 1 and *t* may not be surprising given the accentuated volatility leading up to and including the official index rebalancing date.

We examine the three days surrounding the event because the Russell 2000 rebalancing appears to create price dislocations for the day before, the day during, and the day after the event and because, as we have noted, a price dislocation on any day *t* affects the return computed for days *t* and *t* 1 For example, increased buying for a stock that is included in the Russell 2000 index could cause a positive price dislocation at the time of the rebalancing (day t) that might be repaired (at least partially) on the following day (day *t* 1). For this reason, we expect RRD to be highest for days *t* and *t* 1.

Also shown in Panel A of Exhibit 20 is the RRD statistic over the three-day event window [referred to as RRD (-1 to +1) in the exhibit]. This measure is also significantly smaller for 2004 (.001673 for 2004 vs .002089 for 2003, or 19.9% less). The cross-sectional standard deviation of the individual stocks in our sample was 3.1% for the 2003 event day and 3.2% for the 2004 event day, and hence the appreciable decrease in the RRD statistic could not be attributable to an overall difference in the daily returns volatility of individual stocks for the two days.[95]

The story told by the RRD statistics can be seen in the graphical form displayed in Exhibit 21.

[95] Along similar lines, one might argue that a substantial difference in the overall market's volatility during the 2003 and 2004 event days could affect our results. For example, if the underlying return volatility of the Russell 2000 index is much lower in 2004 than in 2003, then the 2004 RRDs might be smaller than the 2003 RRDs even without the introduction of the Nasdaq Closing Cross. We checked for this possibility by computing the High-Low range for the Russell 2000 index (as a percentage of the closing index value) for both event days. The percentage ranges are essentially the same for both years (1.43% and 1.49% for 2003 and 2004, respectively). Thus, a substantial drop in volatility within the Russell 2000 index during the 2004 event did not occur, and our findings are more likely to be attributable to the introduction of the closing call.

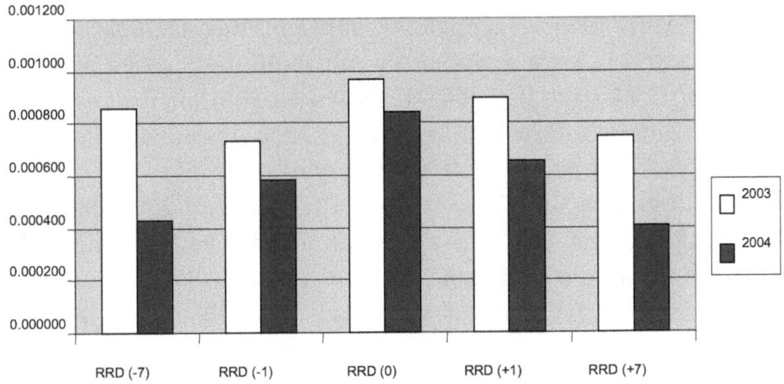


Exhibit 21. Relative Return Dispersions for the Russell 2000 Rebalancings: 2003-2004

The exhibit reveals a distinct pattern. The 2004 RRDs for the full sample rise until the rebalancing day, and then decline sharply over the "pos *t* event" days. The 2003 RRDs display a similar pattern, but are consistently higher than the 2004 values across the five days. The sizable peaks in RRD observed on the official rebalancing days underscore that the 2004 Russell 2000 index rebalancing was indeed a stressful, economically significant event, as was the 2003 event.

The market cap sub-sets tell a more striking story. The RRD statistics for the four sub-samples are reported in Panels B-E of Exhibit 3. Interestingly, the smallest market cap quartile (the first) shows the largest decreases in RRD during the 2004 event. The RRDs for each of the five days are significantly smaller in 2004 than in 2003, with the declines ranging from 34% on the event day to 69% on day *t* 7. The cumulative decline, for the three day period -1 to +1, was 41%.

Turning to the second and third quartiles, we see in Panels C and D of Exhibit 3 that the decreases in the 2004 RRD statistics during the event window conform to the general pattern described for the first (smallest) quartile stocks, but that the decreases are not as large and are generally less significant than they are for stocks in the first quartile. Panel E shows, for the largest stocks (the fourth quartile, E), that the 2004 RRDs actually exceeded their 2003 values, although the increases are statistically insignificant. The 2004 RRDs for days -7 and +7 are less than the comparable 2003 values, but these differences also are not statistically significant.

The average RRDs and median RRDs across the four quartiles are shown graphically in Exhibits 5 and 6, respectively. We report both the means and the medians because the average RRD results could be influenced by outliers (i.e., stocks that might have experienced unusually large price dislocations at the rebalancing). The median RRDs shown in Exhibit 6 conforms to our mean RRD findings and, in fact, present clearer support for the hypothesis that Closing Cross sharpened price discovery.

Overall, both graphs show two things: (i) that the smallest cap stocks had the highest RRDs, and (ii) that the small caps benefited the most from Closing Cross at the 2004 rebalancing. This result, which is consistent with our findings for the Paris study, is very plausible – the small, illiquid stocks are most likely to experience price dislocations when under stress, and the Russell rebalance is especially stressful for the small cap stocks (stocks that are added to the index are generally small, as are the "fallen angels" that are deleted from the index). The large cap stocks are basically affected by the re-weightings.

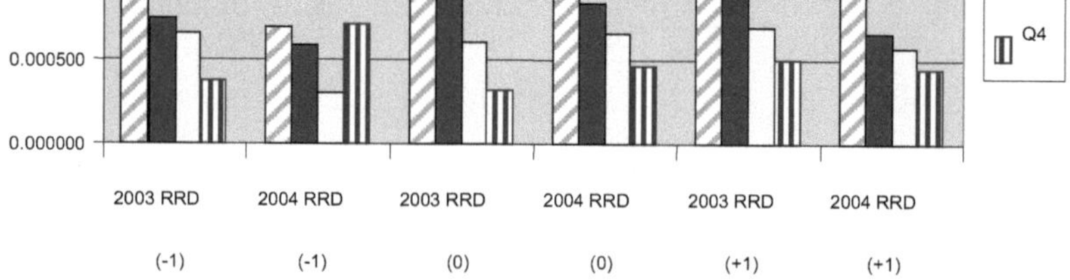


Exhibit 22. Average Relative Return Dispersion Estimates for Size-based Quartiles

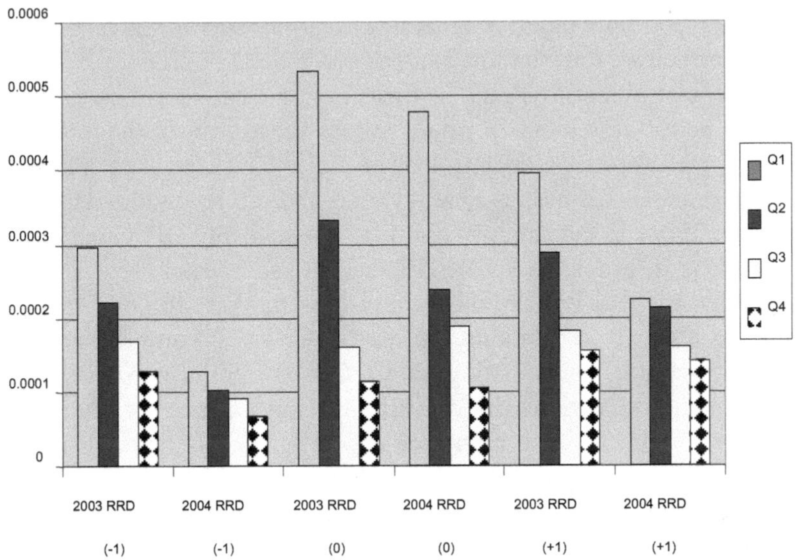


Exhibit 23. Median Relative Return Dispersion Estimates for Size-based Quartiles

## CONCLUSION

Closing Cross's raison d'être lies in the price dislocations that are known to have occurred in the past at NASDAQ closings. NASDAQ is not the only market to have faced the problem of achieving reasonable price discovery at the close. In the latter part of the 1990s, a widespread demand of participants for better closing prices led to the introduction of a closing call in Paris and, for the same reason, closing calls have now been instituted throughout all of the major market centers in Europe. Our study of the Paris market (Pagano and Schwartz, [2003]) suggests that these innovations were successful and, based on three call auction features of Closing Cross, we anticipate a similar result in the NASDAQ market. First, Closing Cross pools orders together for simultaneous execution in a single batched trade at a single price, thereby amassing liquidity and systematically sharpening price determination. Second, as the book builds for the closing auction, order imbalances are displayed to the market. Third, NASDAQ's new facility gives participants time to exploit the imbalances and, in the process, to mitigate them by entering imbalance orders (the IOs).

We have conducted an early assessment of Closing Cross by examining the quality of closing price determination in the NASDAQ market on the days at and around the Russell rebalancings in 2003 and 2004. With approximately 1,700 NASDAQ stocks in it and less than three months of experience, the 2004 Russell rebalancing was indeed a tough test of Closing Cross. Nevertheless, the examination has yielded encouraging results.

Our key test statistic (RRD, a measure of relative return dispersion), indicates a better alignment of prices across the stocks in the Russell 2000 universe at the 2004 rebalancing than at the 2003 event. The improvement was most notable for issues that generally experience the largest price dislocations, those in the smallest quartile of stocks ranked by market cap.

A caveat is in order, however. Because of the myriad factors that affect stock returns, it is never easy to detect a new market structure's impact on prices. The Russell rebalancing in particular is a complex event, with different participants participating with different trading needs and different trading strategies at various times during the day of the rebalancing and on the surrounding days. Is the improvement in our test statistic attributable to the market structure change? Is it the chance result of participants, for their own reasons, interacting differently at the 2004 rebalancing than at the 2003 rebalancing? Are our findings, in part, attributable to both?

In light of Europe's experience with closing auctions, given our previous analysis of the Paris market and our current findings for the NASDAQ stocks in the Russell rebalancing (especially the improved performance of the smallest cap stocks which are most subject to pricing dislocations), and based on what one might expect from the architectural design of the facility itself, our conclusion at this time is that Closing Cross marks a positive step forward in market structure. We anticipate that further benefits will be realized in the future as participants learn better how to use NASDAQ's new facility better.

## REFERENCES

Amihud, Y., H. Mendelson, and, B. Lauterbach. "Market Microstructure and Securities Values: Evidence from the Tel Aviv Stock Exchange." *Journal of Financial Economics*, Volume 45 (1997), pp. 365-390.

Blume, M. E. and R.M. Edelen. "S&P 500 Indexers: Tracking Error and Liquidity." *Journal of Portfolio Management,* Volume 30 (2004), pp. 37-47.

Cohen, K. J., G.A. Hawawini, S.F. Maier, R.A. Schwartz, and D.K. Whitcomb. "Friction in the Trading Process and the Estimation of Systematic Risk." *Journal of Financial Economics*, Volume 12 (1983a), pp, 264-278.

Cohen, K. J., G.A. Hawawini, S.F. Maier, R.A. Schwartz, and D.K. Whitcomb. "Estimating and Adjusting for the Intervailing-effect Bias in Beta." *Management Science* Volume 29 (1983b), pp. 135-148.

Economides, N. and R.A. Schwartz. "Electronic Call Market Trading." *Journal of Portfolio Management*, (Spring 1995), pp. 10 - 18.

Fisher, L. "Some New Stock-market Indexes." *Journal of Business*, Volume 16 (1966), pp. 191-225.

Pagano, M.S., and R.A. Schwartz. "A Closing Call's Impact on Market Quality at Euronext Paris." *Journal of Financial Economics*, Volume 68 (2003), pp. 439-484.

Schwartz, R.A., and R. Francioni. *Equity Markets in Action: The Fundamentals of Liquidity, Market Structure & Trading*. New York: John Wiley & Sons, 2004.

Sofianos, G., and S. Su. "At Long Last: A Nasdaq Single-price Closing Cross." *Street Smart: Trading & Market Structure Analysis*, Volume 8, New York: Goldman Sachs, (2004a).

Sofianos, G., and S. Su. "Stress-testing the Nasdaq Closing Cross: June 25, 2004." *Street Smart: Trading & Market Structure Analysis* Volume 14, New York: Goldman Sachs, (2004b).

# Participant Biographies

**Paul Arlman** is a founding Board Member of the European Corporate Governance Institute (ECGI) and from 2001-2003, served as Chairman of the Industry Advisory Committee to the European Parliamentary Financial Services Forum (EPFSF). He worked in the International Affairs Department of the Dutch Finance Ministry, as Financial Attaché at the Netherlands Embassy in Washington and as Deputy Director for International Affairs at the Ministry of Finance. From 1981-1986, he was a full Member of the Board of the European Investment Bank in Luxembourg where he chaired the Policy Committee. In 1986, he was elected Executive Director of the World Bank Group and from 1988 also Executive Director at the Multilateral Agency for Investment Guarantees. From 1990-1997 he was the Secretary General of the Amsterdam Stock Exchange Association. He chaired its Equity Trading Committee. He initiated and was Member of the Dutch Peters' Committee on Corporate Governance.

**Kim Bang** joined Bloomberg Tradebook LLC as a founding member in April 1996. He assumed the title of President in December 1999 and then CEO in April 2004. Prior to joining Bloomberg Tradebook, Mr. Bang was President of Futech Capital Management, a hedge fund managing quantitative derivative strategies for institutional clients. Before joining Futech in 1993, he developed a European foreign exchange cross trading business for American International Group Trading Corp. From 1988-90, he created and developed a fixed income derivatives trading desk for Commerzbank in Luxembourg. His prior sales trading experience includes positions at BankAmerica Futures and Drexel Burnham Lambert.

**Andy Brooks** is a Vice President and Head of Equity Trading for T. Rowe Price Associates. Joining the firm in 1980, Andy serves as a Vice

President of the T. Rowe Price Equity Income, Value, Capital Appreciation and High Yield Funds. Andy earned a B.A. from Union College in Schenectady, New York. He is a past President of the Baltimore Security Traders Association and a past Governor of the Security Traders Association. He also has served on both the New York Stock Exchange's Institutional Traders Advisory Committee and Market Performance Committee, as well as NASDAQ's Trading Committee. Andy currently serves as a member of the Investment Company Institute's Equity Markets Task Force and is on the board of NOIP.

**Jeffrey Brown**, with over 22 years of industry experience, is a specialist in securities market structure and regulation, broker-dealer compliance and operations, clearance and settlement and securities transfer regulation, and foreign capital market development. He heads Charles Schwab's Office of Legislative and Regulatory Affairs in Washington, D.C., where he is responsible for managing the company's response to public policy initiatives and advocating for the development of government policies that help individual investors better achieve their financial goals. Mr. Brown joined Schwab in 2003 as Senior Vice President and General Counsel of Schwab Capital Markets, L.P., where he provided oversight of legal and compliance matters impacting Schwab's affiliated broker-dealers. In 1981, Mr. Brown began his career in the securities markets as an option trader on the floor of the Philadelphia Stock Exchange. After establishing his own proprietary option trading firm in 1988 and serving as a member of the Board of Governors of the Philadelphia Stock Exchange, Mr. Brown moved to the regulatory side of the industry by joining the U.S. Securities and Exchange Commission in 1992, where he served as Senior Counsel in the Division of Market Regulation. Upon leaving the Commission in 1995, Mr. Brown became Project Manager and Senior Legal Advisor to a U.S. project to assist the Government of Romania in creating their emerging securities market, which entailed adopting rules and regulations over brokers-dealers, collective investment vehicles, clearing agencies and depositories, and self-regulatory organizations. Returning to the United States in late 1996, Mr. Brown joined the law firm of Smith, Lodge, and Schneider, which merged into the law firm of Hopkins & Sutter in 1998. Mr. Brown's private practice included representation of broker-dealers, day-trading firms, investment advisers, futures commission merchants, transfer agents, self-regulatory organizations, and governmental agencies on regulatory, market structure, and commercial transaction matters. In early 1999, Jeffrey Brown assumed the duties of Vice President for Regulation and General Counsel at the Cincinnati Stock Exchange, which is now the National Stock Exchange. The role of exchange legal and regulatory officer placed Mr. Brown in a position to work on a daily basis with broker-dealers and securities regulators on matters confronting the markets, particularly those matters regarding market structure, competition among markets and self-regulation.

By studying the operations of the major financial markets in the mid-1990s, **Bill Christie**, along with Professor Paul Schultz, concluded that NASDAQ market makers were implicitly colluding to maintain artificially high trading profits at the expense of investors. His research subsequently resulted in a sweeping reform of the NASDAQ market and the introduction of the SEC Order Handling Rules. Professor Christie served as Dean of the Owen Graduate School of Management from 2000-2004, and stepped down in June 2004 to return to teaching and research as the Frances Hampton Curry Professor of Finance. Professor Christie joined the Owen faculty in 1989 after completing his Ph.D. at the University of Chicago. He received the Vanderbilt Chair of Teaching Excellence from 1996 to 1999, and the James A. Webb, Jr., award for excellence in teaching on three occasions between 1994 and 1998. Professor Christie is a five-time recipient of the EMBA Teaching award and was ranked either first or second among star faculty in each Business Week ranking from 1992 through 2000. He has served on the Business Accreditation Committee of the Association to Advance Collegiate Schools of Business; the Board of Directors of the Graduate Management Admissions Council; an Academic Director of the Financial Management Association, and served a three year term on NASDAQ's Economic Advisory Board. Professor Christie was co-editor of the Journal of Financial Intermediation from 1999 through June 2005. He assumes the role of Executive Editor of Financial Management on August 1, 2005. Professors Christie and Schultz won First Prize in the 1995 Smith Breeden competition for outstanding papers published in the Journal of Finance. In 2002, the same journal published his article, "NASDAQ Trading Halts: The Impact of Market Mechanisms on Prices, Trading Activity, and Execution Costs" (with Shane Corwin and Jeffrey Harris).

**Christopher R. Concannon** is Executive Vice President, Transaction Services for The NASDAQ Stock Market. In this role, he is responsible for the management and operation of NASDAQ's transaction services business. Mr. Concannon joined The NASDAQ Stock Market in May 2003 as Executive Vice President. As head of Transaction Services, Mr. Concannon has played a critical role in advising NASDAQ's CEO, Bob Greifeld on NASDAQ's core trading platform and in obtaining regulatory approvals on significant business issues. He is responsible for numerous trading enhancements to our trading platform and for the introduction of the NASDAQ Market Center, a technologically advanced, high performance system for trading NASDAQ, NYSE and AMEX securities all on one platform. During his time, NASDAQ has also launched the NASDAQ Closing Cross, Opening Cross, and more recently announced the upcoming launch of the Intraday Cross. Mr. Concannon also helped lead the Brut ECN acquisition, integration and NASDAQ's competitive positioning of the Brut ECN asset. More recently, Chris was a leading member of the acquisition of the INET platform and is currently overseeing the integration process of the newly acquired entity. Prior to joining NASDAQ, Mr. Concannon was President of Instinet Clearing Services, Inc., where he managed the clearing and execution services business offered by Instinet Clearing to numerous broker-dealer clients. During his career with Instinet, Mr. Concannon also served as Special Counsel and Senior Vice President of Business Development, where he coordinated and advised senior management on the integration of Instinet and Island ECN. Before the merger of Instinet and Island, Mr. Concannon was Special Counsel and Vice President of Business Development for Island. While at Island, he worked closely with the firm's strategic partners and investors, identified potential partners and managed Island's Business Development Department. Prior to joining Island, he was an associate at Morgan, Lewis & Bockius LLP in their New York and Washington offices. From 1994-1997 he was an attorney with the U.S. Securities and Exchange Commission in the Division of Market Regulation where he specialized in the review and approval of the rules of the various self-regulatory organizations, the regulation of securities underwriting and the regulation of the clearance and settlement of securities transactions. He began his career with the American Stock Exchange, where he served as a Legislative Analyst from 1992-1995, lobbying Congress and the Administration on a variety of securities related issues. Mr. Concannon received a B.A. from the Catholic University of America in 1989, an M.B.A. from St. John's University in 1991, and a J.D. from the Columbus School of Law, the Catholic University of America in 1994. He is a member of the New York Bar, New Jersey Bar and the District of Columbia Bar. Mr. Concannon serves as an advisory board member for The Journal of Trading, a newly launched *Institutional Investor Journal*, aimed at educating portfolio managers and traders on their execution options with strategic advice from industry experts.

**Paul Davis** recently retired from TIAA-CREF Investment Management LLC. He joined TIAA-CREF in 1983 after working at Prudential-Bache Securities in New York. Before his career on Wall Street, he taught mathematics and did mathematical research. He has an undergraduate degree from West Virginia University and a doctorate in mathematics from Carnegie Mellon University.

**Robert Felvinci** is a Senior Vice-President and Co-Head of U.S. Equity Trading for Alliance Capital Management. Robert has been with Alliance for 15 years and is responsible for the trading of all U.S. equity products including equities, convertible bonds, program trading and derivatives as well as being responsible for budgeting and many of the administrative jobs involved in managing a trading desk. Robert serves on the Institutional Traders Advisory Committee to the New York Stock Exchange and The Advisory Committee for Institutional Investors' TraderForum. Robert is a Co-Chair of The Wall Street Committee for St. Jude Children's Research Hospital and a committee member for the Eden Foundation.

**Reto Francioni** has been Chief Executive Officer of Deutsche Börse AG since 1 November 2005. Since April 2002 Reto Francioni has been member of the Board of Eurex. From April 2002 to October 2005 Reto Francioni was Chairman and President of the SWX Swiss Exchange. Prior to assuming this post, he was co-CEO of Consors Discount Broker AG, Nuremberg. Earlier in his career, he was named in 1993 to the board of Deutsche Börse AG, where he was responsible for its entire cash market division and, as of 1999, became Deputy CEO. Reto Francioni studied law in Zurich where he also earned his PhD in law. He held different management positions in the securities exchange and banking sectors of Switzerland and the USA, as well as in the directorate the corporate finance division of Hofmann LaRoche AG, Basel. He is adjunct professor of economics and finance in the Zicklin School of Business, Baruch College, City University of New York and member of the International Advisory Board of Instituto de Empresa, Madrid, Spain.

**Roger Freeman**, CFA, covers the brokers, asset managers, and exchanges. He has been covering the exchange sector since August 2004 and recently added brokers and asset managers to his area of concentration. In addition, Roger covered transaction processors from November 2003–February 2006. Previously, Roger covered the automotive supplier sector as an associate on the automotive research team at Lehman Brothers from 1999-2003 and at Merrill Lynch from 1997-1999. Prior to equity research, Roger worked in investment banking in the industrials corporate finance group at Salomon Brothers Inc from 1995-1997. Roger holds a Bachelor of Science in international economics from Georgetown University.

**Adena Friedman** is Executive Vice President of Corporate Strategy and Data Products for the NASDAQ Stock Market, Inc. Friedman's responsibilities include identifying and developing strategic opportunities for the world's largest electronic stock market. They also include maintaining the integrity of all market data disseminated to the public and working with NASDAQ Technology Services to create new data products to serve the industry's information needs. Additionally, Friedman serves as the senior administrator for NASDAQ in its capacity as the Exclusive Securities Information Processor for NASDAQ-listed securities. Friedman joined NASDAQ in 1993. She served for one year as a Senior Vice President of NASDAQ Data Products. In addition, she served for three years as a

Director, and subsequently, Vice President, of NASDAQ Trading and Market Services, the division of NASDAQ that supported Market Makers and other market participants. She was responsible for the strategy and successful operation of the OTC Bulletin Board®, a quotation facility for unlisted stocks; the Mutual Fund Quotation Service, a net asset value reporting tool for money-management firms; and NASDAQTrader.com, the central NASDAQ Web site for member firms and buy-side traders. Prior to that position, Friedman served as Marketing Manager in NASDAQ Trading and Market Services. Additionally, she developed the department's annual budget and financial plan and participated in ongoing strategic planning initiatives. Friedman earned an M.B.A., with honors, from Owen Graduate School of Management, Vanderbilt University, in Nashville, TN. She holds a B.A. in Political Science from Williams College in Massachusetts.

**Robert Greifeld** is President and Chief Executive Officer of The NASDAQ Stock Market, Inc. (NASDAQ: NDAQ), the largest U.S. electronic stock market. Since joining NASDAQ in May 2003, Greifeld has focused the NASDAQ mission on providing the most efficient, transparent trading platform for investors by leveraging advanced trading technology, capturing the majority of U.S. IPOs, and attracting listings and trading from competitive exchanges. Tapping his 20-year industry experience and leadership with electronic trading systems, Greifeld has led a significant enhancement of NASDAQ's trading offerings. In April 2005 NASDAQ announced its purchase of the INET ECN, a trading platform which provides NASDAQ with superior trading technology and cost efficiency. In the prior year, NASDAQ acquired Brut ECN, which provided NASDAQ with enhanced capabilities including order routing to the New York Stock Exchange. Today, Brut is a top provider of liquidity to the floor of the NYSE. In February 2005, Greifeld led NASDAQ in completing a secondary stock offering and listing NASDAQ on its own market, Global Select (formerly the National Market). Since that time, NASDAQ has completed two additional stock offerings and purchased a significant strategic stake in the London Stock Exchange. Greifeld spearheaded NASDAQ's innovative "dual listing" program, which for the first time allowed NYSE-listed companies to list on NASDAQ. This innovative initiative made worldwide news. Greifeld has been a vocal advocate for modernizing market structure and increasing public company CEO and board attention on the performance and quality of stock markets for the benefit of shareholders and all investors. Greifeld is an active speaker on financial market structure and regulatory issues. He has been vocal in Washington regarding enhancements to Sarbanes-Oxley for small companies and the use of stock options as a tool for business and economic growth. Greifeld has addressed organizations including The Investment Company Institute, the National Press Club, Los Angeles Town Hall, and the World Economic Forum. Prior to joining NASDAQ, Greifeld was an Executive Vice President with SunGard Data Systems Inc., where he was responsible for all of SunGard's sell-side businesses and its buy-side transaction routing businesses. While serving as President Chief Operating Officer of Automated Securities Clearance, Inc. (ASC) from 1991-1999, Mr. Greifeld led the team that created BRASS and made it the industry standard trade order management system for NASDAQ stocks. Greifeld holds a Masters in Business from New York University, Stern School of Business and a B.A. in English from Iona College. His graduate school thesis was on the operation of The NASDAQ Stock Market. Greifeld is an avid runner and has completed four marathons. He is Chairman of the USA Track & Field Foundation and serves as a Vice Chairman on the Kennedy Center Corporate Fund Board. In addition he is a board member of the Partnership for New York City, an organization devoted to enhancing the local economy.

**Allan Grody** is a 40 year veteran of the financial industry. He has been an advisor to many exchanges here and around the world. He advised members of the first NMS Advisory Board in the early 1970's, represented many options, futures and stock exchanges before the SEC in the 1980's, conducted the first global survey of electronic markets in the early 1990's, and was involved in some of the recent landmark patent infringement cases dealing with electronic exchange trading systems. He has advised the Netherlands, Italian, Vietnamese and Kuwait financial community on developing capital and risk mitigation markets.

**Frank M. Hatheway** is Chief Economist of the NASDAQ Stock Market Inc., and is responsible for a variety of projects and initiatives to support the NASDAQ market and improve its market structure. Prior to joining NASDAQ, Dr. Hatheway was a finance professor at Penn State University and a researcher in market microstructure. He has authored academic articles in the *Journal of Finance, Journal of Financial Intermediation* and other leading finance journals. Dr. Hatheway has served as an Economic Fellow and Senior Research Scholar with the U.S. Security and Exchange Commission. Dr. Hatheway received his Ph.D. in Economics from Princeton University.

**Robert Hegarty** is managing director of TowerGroup Securities & Investments Group, the umbrella for three practice areas: Securities & Capital Markets, Investment Management and Brokerage & Wealth. Rob's group focuses on technology trends and strategies in the brokerage, capital markets, investing, and asset management industries. Rob has over 20 years of experience in the financial services technology industry. Before joining TowerGroup, in 1999, he was vice president of trading systems at Putnam

Investments in Boston. Prior to Putnam, he was with Fidelity Investments in Boston for eight years. As vice president of technology of the institutional broker-dealer arm of Fidelity Investments, Fidelity Capital Markets, he had overall responsibility for technology for this $300 million company. His responsibilities included strategic technology planning, business analysis, project management, trading floor support, market data, and telecommunications. He also had overall technology responsibility for building FCM's 230-position trading floor as well as managing the technology integration for acquisitions FCM was undertaking. Earlier he held positions in product development for electronic trading and in technology consulting to the many internal companies at Fidelity. Previously, he was division vice president at Drexel Burnham Lambert in New York and was with the IT management consulting division of Coopers & Lybrand's Boston office. In 2002, Rob was elected to membership of the Advisory Board of Institutional Investor's US Institute, a group composed of CEOs and leaders of more than 50 major asset management firms. He was a member of the Financial Information Exchange (FIX) Executive Committee from 1994 until 1999, first on the sell-side representing Fidelity Capital Markets and then on the buy-side representing Putnam Investments. He has also served on many other industry and vendor boards. Quoted frequently by publications such as The Wall Street Journal, Barron's, Business Week, Forbes, Institutional Investor, Securities Industry News, Global Investment Technology, and Wall Street & Technology, Rob has been a featured speaker at dozens of industry conferences and has appeared on CNBC-TV, ABC-TV and syndicated radio. Rob holds an MBA with a finance/marketing concentration from Babson College and a BS in computer science from North Adams State College. He is also NASD Series 7 and 63 registered.

**Peter Jenkins** was named senior vice president, Institutional Client Group, of the New York Stock Exchange. Mr. Jenkins reports to NYSE President and Co-COO Catherine Kinney. Mr. Jenkins is responsible for overseeing the NYSE's relationship with the buy-side community and key individual buy-side stakeholders, including mutual funds, public and corporate pension funds, non-profit organization, and hedge funds. Prior to joining the NYSE, Mr. Jenkins was managing director and head of North America Active Equity Trading for Deutsche Bank Asset Management. Before that, Mr. Jenkins served as head of Global Equity Trading for 16 years. Prior to that, Mr. Jenkins spent three years as a senior trader at Cigna Investment Management. He began his career as a trader at Scudder Stevens and Clark Investments in 1980. Mr. Jenkins graduated from the University of Connecticut in 1980.

**Andrew Kagan** heads up Lava's Sell-side Product Management group, where he is responsible for Lava's intelligent order routing and market data products. With over 20 years of experience delivering leading-edge technology to the equity markets, Andrew has an in-depth understanding of US equity market structure, exchange and OTC trading. Prior to joining Lava, Andrew was Vice President of Customer Relationship Management at Vie Financial Group, Inc., an early provider of algorithmic trading. Previously, he was Vice President of Business Requirements and Quality Assurance at OptiMark, and a Consulting Segment Manager at IBM® focusing primarily on the securities industry. Andrew received his B.S. in Computer Applications and Information Systems from New York University and earned his MBA from New York University's Stern School of Business. He is a member of the SIA Trading Committee, the Financial Information Forum (FIF), and the FIF Regulation NMS Working Group.

**David Krell** is a founder and President & CEO of ISE. From 1997 to 1998, he was Chairman and co-founder of K-Squared Research, LLC, a financial services consulting firm. From 1984 to 1997, Mr. Krell was Vice President, Options and Index Products, of the New York Stock Exchange where he managed marketing, systems and new product introductions for the division. From 1981 to 1984, Mr. Krell was First Vice President at the Chicago Board Options Exchange, responsible for the management and operation of the Marketing and Sales Division. Mr. Krell was also a Vice President of Merrill Lynch from 1978 to 1981 and founded its Managed Options Service. Mr. Krell is active in numerous industry groups. He was a Director on the Board of the International Federation of Technical Analysts, a president of the Market Technicians Association and a Director on the Board of The Options Clearing Corporation. Mr. Krell formerly was an Adjunct Professor at Rutgers University Graduate School of Management and at the Graduate School of Baruch College. He has taught, coordinated and directed numerous seminars and workshops at the New York Institute of Finance.

**Matthew Lavicka** is a Managing Director in the Equities Division at Goldman Sachs. He is responsible for US Shares Electronic Trading/Routing and Market Structure.

**Mark Madoff** graduated from the University of Michigan in 1986 with a degree in Economics. After graduating, Mark joined his family business, Bernard L. Madoff Investment Securities LLC. Mark has had a wide range of responsibilities at the firm, including overseeing the trading of NYSE Listed stocks, statistical arbitrage, convertible bonds, options and equity derivatives. He is currently the Director of Listed Trading, and helps manage the firm's technology and principal trading initiatives. Mark is very active within the securities industry and is currently Chairman of

NASDAQ's Intermarket Trading Committee, a member of the NASD's Membership Committee, Co-Chair of the STA's Trading Committee, a member of the SIA's Institutional Brokerage Committee and member of the NASD's Mutual Find Task Force. In addition, Mark is the past chairman of the NASD's District 10 Committee as well as a member of the National Adjudicatory Council.

**Michael Murphy** is President and Founder of Piney Run Capital LLC, a financial service firm located in Baltimore, Maryland. Previously he was head of Equity Training at Wachovia Securities. Prior to joining Wachovia, Mr. Murphy was a founding partner of Kern Capital Management, where he was director of Trading. He has also been Director of Trading at Morgan Grenfell Capital Management and Partner at Alex Brown & Sons where he headed up Sales Trading. Mr. Murphy has served on a variety of industry committees including the Upstairs Traders Advisory Committee at the NYSE, the Institutional Trader's Advisory Committee at the NYSE, the NASD'S Institutional Committee and the Investment Company Institutes Institutional Trading Committee. He is also a member of NOIP. Mr. Murphy is viewed as an expert on market structure issues and is a frequent speaker at industry conferences. He was educated at West Virginia University and resides in Baltimore.

**Michael S. Pagano** is an Associate Professor of Finance at Villanova University. Professor Pagano has conducted several empirical analyses related to various issues in market microstructure, financial institution management, risk management, cost of capital estimation, and interest rate determination. He has published in numerous finance journals such as the *Journal of Financial Economics, Journal of Banking and Finance, Journal of Portfolio Management*, and the *Financial Analysts Journal.* In addition to serving on the editorial boards of two academic journals, Professor Pagano has been a Fulbright Scholar at the University of Costa Rica and has received awards for both teaching and academic scholarship. Prior to earning his doctorate and joining the Villanova University faculty, Professor Pagano spent over 10 years in the financial services industry. He holds the Chartered Financial Analyst (CFA®) designation and has experience both in commercial lending activities at Citibank and in investment valuation analysis at a financial consulting firm, International Capital Markets Corp., as well as Reuters PLC. In addition to his duties at Villanova University, Professor Pagano has been a consultant to several companies including Citibank, PaineWebber, Fidelity Investments, GTE Investments, Philadelphia Suburban Corp., Aqua America, and Bank Julius Baer.

**Gerald Putnam** is president and co-chief operating officer of NYSE Group, Inc. In this role, Mr. Putnam, 46, is responsible for the Group's market operations, technology initiatives, new products, and information business. Prior to joining NYSE Group, Inc., Mr. Putnam founded and served as chairman and chief executive officer of Archipelago Holdings, Inc., an all-electronic exchange based in Chicago. While at Archipelago, Mr. Putnam attracted major investors from the institutional and retail sectors and was a leader in industry consolidation and transformed Archipelago into a public company. He gained a detailed understanding of the securities industry through various positions held at several financial firms including, Jefferies & Company, Paine Webber, Prudential Walsh Greenwood and Geldermann Securities, Inc. In 1994, Mr. Putnam founded Terra Nova, an on-line broker-dealer where he served as president until January 1999. He currently serves on the board of directors for Terra Nova. Mr. Putnam received a B.S. in Economics with a major in accounting from the Wharton School of the University of Pennsylvania in 1981. In January 2000, Mr. Putnam was inducted into the Entrepreneurship Hall of Fame sponsored by the University of Illinois at Chicago. In October 2000, he was named one of Time Magazine's Outstanding Innovators.

**Brett Redfearn** is a Senior Managing Director at Bear Stearns in the Institutional Equities division focusing on market structure strategy. In that role, Brett examines how new technologies, regulations and business trends are changing the equity trading business. His responsibilities include: (1) helping Bear Stearns develop external public policy positions on market structure issues, (2) addressing market structure related implications and business responses related to a Bear Stearns' equity trading operations; and, (3) authoring Commentaries and analyses on changes and developments in market structure for internal and external consumption. Much of his current focus relates to Regulation NMS and the NYSE's Hybrid market proposal. Prior to Bear Stearns, Brett was at the American Stock Exchange, where he was Senior Vice President of Business Strategy & Equity Order Flow. Brett's department ran the Amex's equity transactions business and, as such, oversaw the Amex's efforts in relationship management (with buy and sell-side trading desks), competitive research, and strategic initiatives. Brett's latest focus at the Amex was in trying to help the Amex revamp its technology platform and business offering to better compete in an electronic trading environment. Brett is a regular speaker at industry events and a member of the Security Traders Association. He received his M.A. from the New School for Social Research in New York and his B.A. from The Evergreen State College in Olympia Washington.

**Rich Repetto** is a Principal of Sandler O'Neill & Partners, L.P. His research coverage includes the eBrokerage, Execution Venues, and eSpecialty Finance Sectors. Mr. Repetto has received numerous accolades for his equity research. The Wall Street Journal (WSJ) and Thompson Financial recognized him in their "Best on the Street" Analysts Surveys for

2003, 2002, and 2000. In 2003, the WSJ ranked Rich #1 in stock picking for the Securities Brokerage industry. In 2002, he was one of six analysts cited by the WSJ for stock picking in two industry categories, Securities Brokerage and Internet. In 2003, Forbes.com/StarMine ranked Rich the #10 overall stock picker among 3,200 research analysts, and Rich was the only analyst to be ranked in the top ten for two consecutive years (he ranked #2 overall stock picker in 2002). Forbes.com/StarMine also ranked Rich the #1 stock picker for the Capital Markets industry in 2003. Prior to joining Sandler O'Neill, Mr. Repetto was a Managing Director and analyst responsible for eFinance and eBrokerage at Putnam Lovell NBF. This position followed his work at Lehman Brothers, where Rich established the firm's research coverage of the Internet Financial Services Sector in May 1999 and was part of the top-ranked Institutional Investor specialty finance team. Prior to his work at Lehman Brothers, Rich had a 10-year career at Mobil Oil Corporation in sales and marketing. Mr. Repetto holds a B.S. in General Engineering from the United States Military Academy and an MBA in Finance from the Wharton School of the University of Pennsylvania. He is a Chartered Financial Analyst (CFA) Charter Holder and a member of the New York Society of Security Analysts (NYSSA) and the CFA Institute (formerly the Association for Investment Management and Research, or AIMR).

**C. Thomas Richardson** has 10+ yrs of experience in Institutional Trading and has spent his entire trading career at Citigroup Global Markets, Inc ("CGMI"). Tom is currently a Managing Director in US Equities with responsibilities that are more strategic in nature. Tom is currently responsible for elevating and expanding the breadth of CGMI's trading platform, and making the traders more efficient. Additionally, Tom is actively involved in current market structure issues and is considered CGMI's outwardly facing "go to" market structure point person. Tom began his career at CGMI in Feb 1994, when he joined the Smith Barney Sales and Trading Associate Program. His first job out of the program was to become an assistant NASDAQ trader. He began trading his own list in 1997 and was elevated to Telecom Sector Captain in 2000 which encompassed managing a group of senior traders in addition to trading his own pad. Tom was promoted to Head Trader, NASDAQ in 2001 and the following year became the Deputy Head of Cash Trading, with the responsibility of managing the desks' risk book. Tom's educational experience culminated in his graduating from the University of Richmond (May, 1985) with a Bachelor of Science degree in Business Administration. From 1986-1994, Tom worked in the Financial Services business for EAB and Key Bank. Currently, Tom is Chairman of CGMI's Best Execution Committee. Tom is also Chairman of the NASDAQ Quality of Markets Committee, a member of the NYSE

Market Performance Committee, a member of the Securities Industry Association Trading Committee and a member of the Board of Directors of STANY.

**Howard Ross** is a Professor of Economics and Finance at Baruch College whose latest research is on productivity, employment and off-shoring and the impact of concentration in product markets on investment and returns. A Columbia PhD he believes that investors, the public and the economy will benefit from the standards of accountability and transparency that were ignored before Sarbanes-Oxley.

Since 2001, **Dan Royal** has been Co-Head of Equity Trading for the Janus Capital Group, where he has focused on Domestic Equity and Foreign Exchange trading for the firm. Prior to joining Janus, Dan worked as a Senior Global Trader for the CTA (commodity trading adviser) firms of J.W. Henry and Co. in Boca Raton, Florida and SJO Asset Management in Chicago. He also spent 11 years with Cargill Investor Services where he served as both a Trading and Floor Manager on the Chicago Mercantile Exchange. Dan has more than 20 years of industry experience and is a graduate of the University of Wisconsin - Madison.

After graduating Baruch College with a BS in Finance in 1972, **Stephen Sax** started with the NASD. He rose through the ranks in five years initially as an examiner, then senior examiner and finally to investigator which is the highest field enforcement level. From there he joined R.W. Pressprich, a NYSE member firm, as its compliance officer and corporate secretary. From 1982 through 1987, Stephen was involved in both marketing and compliance for a NASD member in tax-advantaged private placements. In 1995, he joined Floor Broker Network Inc., a NYSE floor broker, to head their marketing and sales efforts. For the last three years, Stephen has had the added responsibility of being the firm's chief compliance officer. Stephen holds securities licenses: Series 7,63,24,87,14,55.

**Justin Schack** is a Senior Editor at *Institutional Investor* magazine. Schack oversees and regularly contributes to the magazine's coverage of Wall Street and corporate finance. He has authored more than 20 cover stories for the magazine since joining the staff in 1999. Previously he ran the weekly publications *Wall Street Letter* and *Corporate Financing Week* for II's newsletter group, after a stint as a public-affairs reporter for the *Jersey Journal*, a daily newspaper in Jersey City, NJ. His work as been recognized with awards from the National Press Club, the Society of Professional Journalists, the American Society of Business Publication Editors and the North Jersey Press Club. He holds a bachelor's degree in history from Seton Hall University and a Master's degree in history from the University of Connecticut.

**Jamie Selway** is responsible for research, finance, and administration at White Cap. Previously, he was Chief Economist at Archipelago, where he served a variety of functions, including strategy, quantitative research, regulatory and governmental liaison, and new business development. One of the architects of the Archipelago Exchange, he was integral in the technical implementation of its market structure, and led the effort to educate clients before and after its launch. Jamie has written articles published in both the industry press and academic journals, and has been quoted in the *Wall Street Journal*, *Securities Industry News*, *Traders Magazine*, *Institutional Investor Magazine* and the *Financial Times*. He currently serves on the Users Subcommittee of the Intermarket Trading System. Jamie's other past professional experiences include the Equity Derivatives Research group of Goldman Sachs and three years in Economic Research at the National Association of Securities Dealers. He holds Series 7, 63, 55, 24, 4, and 27 registrations and received a M.S. in Financial Mathematics from the University of Chicago and a B.A. in Mathematics and European History from Washington & Lee University, *Phi Beta Kappa*.

**Benn Steil** is Senior Fellow and Director of International Economics at the Council on Foreign Relations in New York. He is also the Editor of *International Finance* (Blackwell Publishers); a co-founder and director of Efficient Frontiers LLC, a markets consultancy; a nonexecutive director of the virt-x stock exchange in London; and a member of the European Shadow Financial Regulatory Committee. Prior to his joining the Council in December 1998, he was Director of the International Economics Programme at the Royal Institute of International Affairs in London. He came to the Institute in 1992 from a Lloyd's of London Tercentenary Research Fellowship at Nuffield College, Oxford, where he received his PhD in Economics. Dr. Steil has written and spoken widely on international finance, securities trading, and market regulation. His research and market commentary are regularly covered in publications such as the *Wall Street Journal, Financial Times, New York Times, International Herald Tribune, USA Today, The Economist, Barrons, Business Week, Crain's New York Business, Forbes, Fortune, Newsweek, Time, Securities Industry News,* and Reuters and Bloomberg outlets. His latest book is *Financial Statecraft: The Role of Financial Markets in American Foreign Policy*, published by Yale University Press in January 2006. Among his earlier books are a critically acclaimed analysis of *The European Equity Markets*; a major text on *Institutional Investors*; a widely reviewed policy study on *Building a Transatlantic Securities Market*, which has been the topic of numerous conferences in North America and Europe; and edited volumes on cross-border antitrust (*Antitrust Goes Global*) and the economics of innovation (*Technological Innovation and Economic Performance*).

**Bruce C. Turner** is a Managing Director at CIBC World Markets, a full service Institutional Brokerage firm. He has been at CIBC for two and a half years. Prior to joining CIBC, Bruce was an Executive Vice President of the NASDAQ Stock Market's Transaction Services group. Prior to NASDAQ Bruce spent nine and a half years on the NASDAQ trading desk of Solomon Smith Barney. Mr. Turner graduated from Connecticut College in 1987 with a BA in Economics.

**Lisa Utasi** is a Director and Senior Equity Trader at Citigroup Asset Management (a division of Citigroup Global Markets Inc.) CAM with $180 billion in equity assets under management is a multi style manager. The firm's client base is comprised of mutual fund, institutional and high net worth investors. Lisa joined CAM through its predecessor in 1986. Lisa is the 2005 Past President of the Security Traders Association of New York. STANY is a professional trade organization serving individual traders in the New York metropolitan area. STANY works to improve the ethics, business standards, and working environment for its members, who are engaged in the purchase, sale, and trading of securities. STANY represents the shared interests of its approximately 1,700 members from over 300 firms and is the largest affiliate of The Security Traders Association (STA). Lisa has been a Governor of the STANY'S parent organization the STA since 2000 and is currently serving as an Executive Director and STA's Treasurer. She is the Chairperson of the STA Affiliate Liaison Committee and a Member of the Institutional Committee and Trading Issues Committees. Lisa serves on the NASDAQ Quality of Markets Committee. She is a Past Chairperson of the NASDAQ Institutional Traders Advisory Committee. Lisa is a member of the NYSE Institutional Traders Advisory Committee. She also participates in Inst. Investor's Trader's Forum and the Investment Company Institute's Equity Markets Committee. Lisa holds a B.A. in Political Science and a B.B.A. in Finance from Southern Methodist University. Lisa is extremely active in the NYC charity community. She currently serves as Co Chairperson of the MDA Wings over Wall Street Fund Raising Committee. Lisa has also worked on the MDA Muscle Team fundraising committee. She is a member of the Eden Institute and St. Christopher–Ottilie Charity Golf Committees. Lisa has completed eight Full Running Marathons including two of which she dedicated to fundraising for the Leukemia and Lymphoma Society's Team in Training. Lisa is an avid marathon runner, tennis player and golfer.

**Wayne Wagner** is a Consultant at ITG, Inc., and Former Chairman and co-founder of Plexus Group, a Los Angeles based firm that provides implementation evaluation and advisory services to U.S. and Global money managers, brokerage firms and pension plan sponsors. Mr. Wagner and Plexus Group were chosen as the 1999 Consultant of the Year by Plan

Sponsor Magazine. Investment News named him one of the 'Power Elite 25' for 2001. Plexus Group is an independent subsidiary of JPMorgan Investor Services Company, a division of JPMorgan Chase. Mr. Wagner is author and editor of The Complete Guide to Securities Transactions: Improving Perform-ance and Reducing Costs, John Wiley & Sons, 1989. His most recent publishing effort is a popular investment book written with friend Al Winnikoff entitled MILLIONAIRE: the simplest explanation of how an index fund can turn your lunch money into a fortune; Renaissance Books, 2001. He has written and spoken frequently on many trading and investment subjects. He has received two Graham and Dodd Awards from the Financial Analysts Journal for excellence in financial writing. Mr. Wagner served as a Regent of the Financial Analysts Seminar and served on the AIMR Blue Ribbon Task Force on Soft Dollars and the AIMR Best Execution Task Force. Mr. Wagner was a founding partner of Wilshire Associates and served as Chief Investment Officer of Wilshire Asset Management. Earlier, Mr. Wagner participated in the design and operation of the first index funds at Wells Fargo Bank. In an earlier century Mr. Wagner earned a MS in Statistics from Stanford University and a BBA in Management Science/Finance from the University of Wisconsin.

**Henry Yegerman**, Director of Research Product Management for ITG Inc., is responsible for the management and development of pre and post trade transaction analytic products. He joined ITG in 1999 from Reuters, where he was Director of Marketing for Asset Management products. Prior to that, Henry was responsible for new product development for Morgan Stanley Capital International. He has an M.B.A. in Finance from New York University.

**Ken Zimmer**, CFA, is the senior trader at Boston based Frontier Capital Management, a $5 billion investment manager owned by its 30 employees and Affiliated Managers group. He oversees a three-person trading desk. Ken has been at Frontier since 2000. Prior to joining the firm, he spent two years as a sell-side sales trader at Hoenig & Co, and four years as a sales trader at Merrill Lynch. Before entering the financial industry, he was an officer in the U.S. Army. Mr Zimmer is a Chartered Financial Analyst (CFA). He received a BA in economics from the College of the Holy Cross and an MBA from Yale University. He is a member of the Boston Security Analyst Society, Market Technician's Association and the Boston Security Trader's Association.

# INDEX

FSC
www.fsc.org
MIX
Papier | Fördert gute Waldnutzung
FSC® C083411

Kolibri 360 GmbH
Ferdinand-Jühlke-Straße 7
99095 Erfurt, Deutschland
produktsicherheit@kolibri360.de